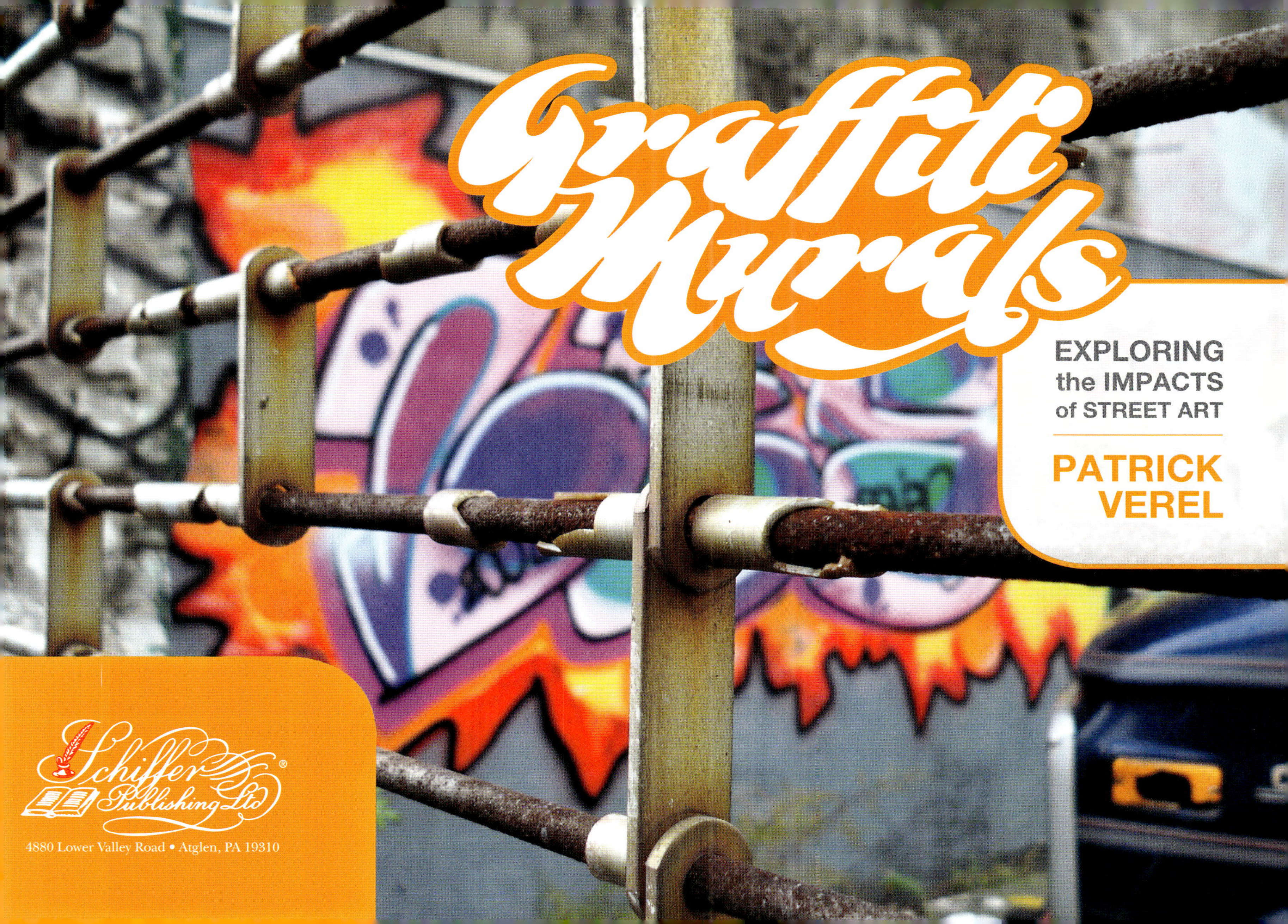

Graffiti Murals

EXPLORING the IMPACTS of STREET ART

PATRICK VEREL

Schiffer Publishing Ltd
4880 Lower Valley Road • Atglen, PA 19310

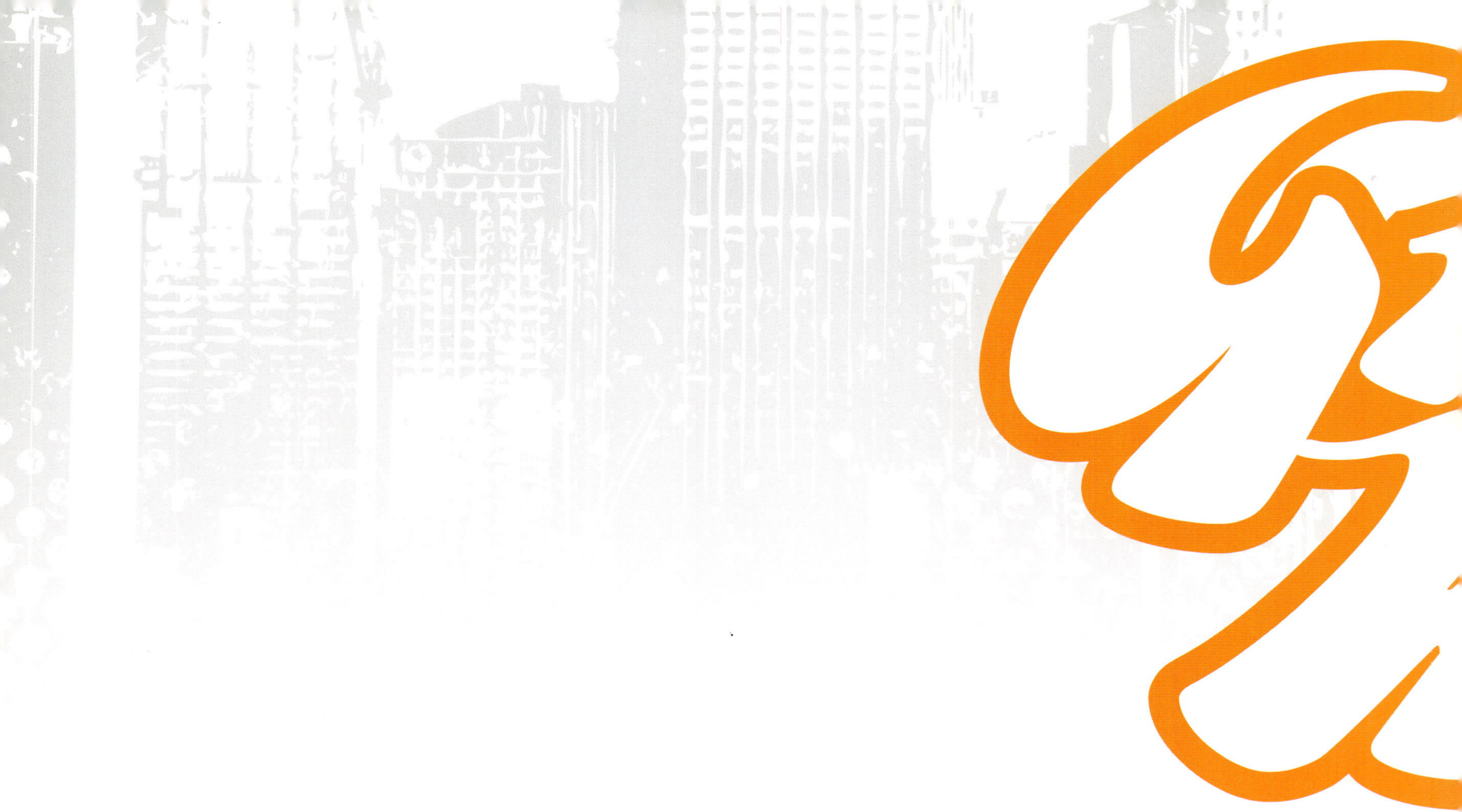

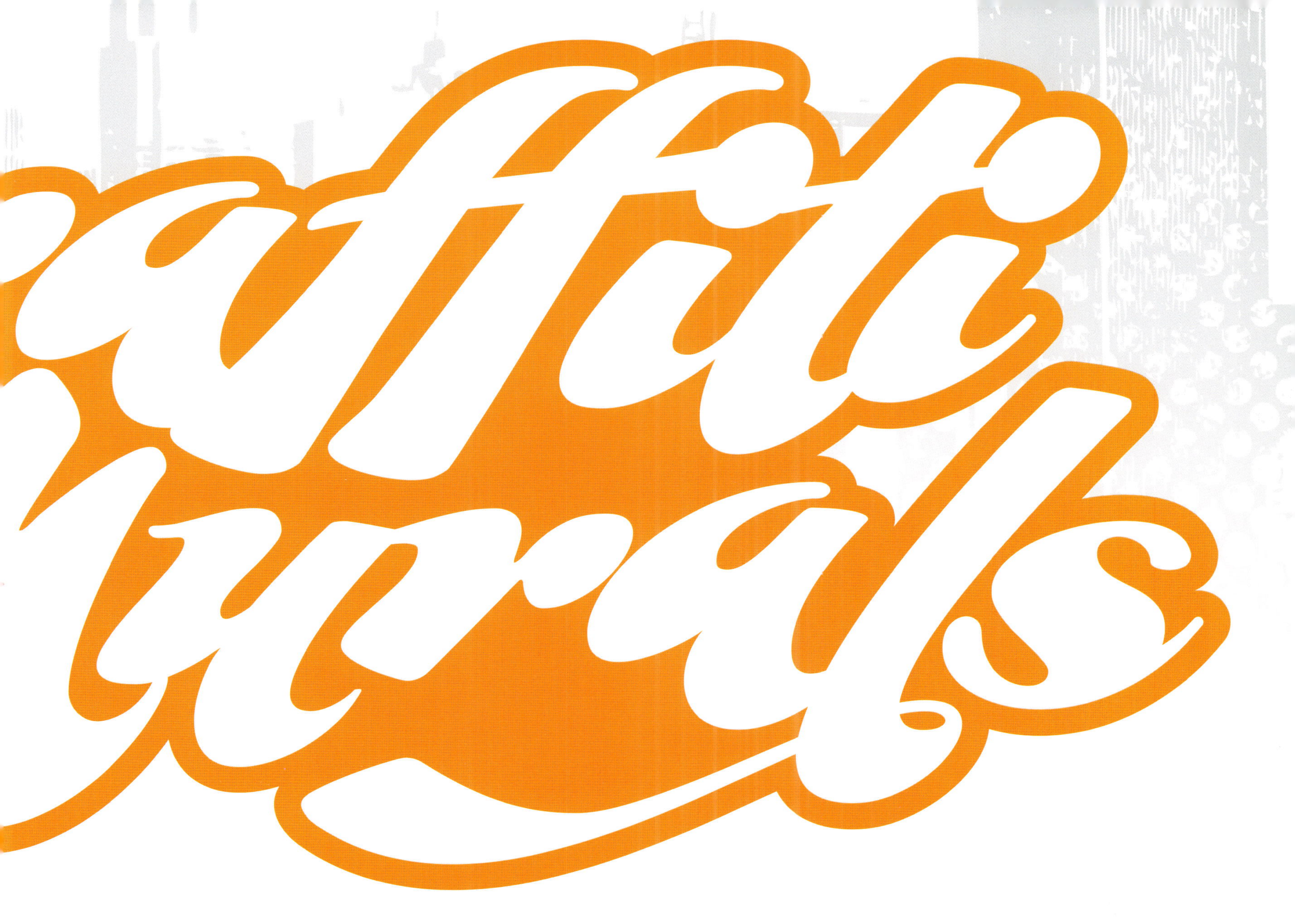

Library of Congress Control Number: 2015938720

Designed by Justin Watkinson
Type set in Whomp/Univers LT Std/Minion Pro

EAN: 978-0-7643-4899-0
Printed in China

Published by Schiffer Publishing, Ltd.
4880 Lower Valley Road
Atglen, PA 19310
Phone: (610) 593-1777; Fax: (610) 593-2002
E-mail: Info@schifferbooks.com

Title page image: Gowanus, Brooklyn graffiti mural, circa October 2009. Photo by Patrick Verel

Contents

Preface

Legal graffiti murals, far from being the nuisance that is often associated with traditional graffiti, are beneficial to the neighborhoods they inhabit. When authorities in cities such as New York overly concern themselves with the elimination of graffiti in all its forms, their zero-tolerance policies run the risk of squelching a vibrant art scene that has evolved beyond old stereotypes. In fact, when artists collaborate with building owners, graffiti murals can be just as effective at deterring vandalism as the city's current buffing efforts.

My hope is to show that graffiti murals that have been done by artists with a connection to the neighborhood are a cost effective way both to keep surfaces free from vandalism and to create visual cues to residents that the place they call home is desirable. This is in direct contrast with blank walls, which may be seen as a sign of order within a chaotic urban environment, but offer no respite from otherwise drab surroundings.

Acknowledgments

This book started as a research paper for *Introduction to Urban Studies* in the fall of 2009 as part of the urban studies master's degree at Fordham University. While I may have been the one pecking away at the keyboard over the years, this book has the fingerprints of many on it, and I'd like to extend my thanks to them.

Dr. Rosemary Wakeman welcomed me into the urban studies program in 2009 and has advised me ever since. She has been a constant source of feedback during that time, and her critiques of my research pushed me to rethink, update, and improve the theory I ultimately used to frame the case studies that are the heart of the book.

Visual arts professor Abby Goldstein challenged me to embrace the New York City Department of Transportation and Groundswell for their contributions to public art. She also helped me think more critically about the darker aspects of unchecked graffiti and to make serious distinctions between vandalism and graffiti murals.

Sections of the text were also formulated in classes at Fordham, where Drs. Ronald Nerio and Chris Rhomberg offered encouragement and valuable feedback on the process of formulating my argument. My classmate David Goodwin was an amazing soundboard for my ideas. Katherine Lorimer, aka "Luna Park," also made my life immeasurably better with her patient responses to my queries regarding her encyclopedic knowledge of graffiti. And of course, there are the writers whose work is featured—they're like the light of a million stars illuminating the dark corners of my ignorant mind; all praise to them.

My parents, John and Mary Verel, likewise deserve a veritable dump truck bursting with my gratefulness, as they have been the loudest and most consistent cheerleaders of my journalism career. They were with me when I flunked algebra and chemistry in college and decided to give writing a shot instead, and I wouldn't have gotten half this far without them.

My wife, Kelly, has been my bedrock, listening patiently as I describe a recent trek to some distant corner of New York, taking time out of a New Orleans vacation to find a Banksy mural near an abandoned hospital, and lending an editor's eye to more versions of this than she probably cares to admit. As fascinating as this subject is to me, it is only this way because I get to share it with her.

Finally, our daughter Eliza was born midway through my studies, but still managed to point out awesome graffiti to me before she learned to count to ten. This one's for you, babe!

Introduction

When you walk down a street in New York City, there are sights, sounds, and smells that you can always rely on to help you find your place. A street sign overhead tells you where you are on the map. The drifting smells of a food cart inform you that lunch is not far away. Even with your eyes closed, snippets of overheard conversation can tell you whether you're in Corona, Queens, or the Upper East Side.

What does graffiti tell you? Well, it depends…

In New York City, there exists a disconnect between those whose job it is to erase graffiti regarded as vandalism and those who promote the beautification of the city through murals created with the same tools as graffiti.

If a citizen wishes to have illegally created graffiti removed, he or she can file a complaint with the city's 311 hotline. A sophisticated system will log the request, and depending on how the owner of the property with the graffiti on it responds, the city may dispatch a cleaning crew to "buff" the space clean. Meanwhile, groups such as Groundswell and the Department of Transportation commission murals on private and public property, respectfully. The two groups—the graffiti removal teams and the mural promoters—are pursuing the same goal: making the city a more visually appealing place. But they are using opposing methods.

But there is another aspect of neighborhood beautification occupying a middle ground between graffiti eradication and mural making: Graffiti murals. These murals are being commissioned and created outside of the system, in many cases by an older generation of graffiti writers who have sworn off the illegal pastime of their youth in favor of the artistic challenge that comes from working together with private property owners. Using the tools (aerosol spray cans) of a phenomenon that has negative connotations to create murals that directly reference the styles of graffiti, these writers are simultaneously paying homage to an art form that was born in New York City and doing more to improve public space than any blank, buffed wall ever could.

I explored the effects of graffiti murals through six case studies in the New York City metropolitan region and Trenton, New Jersey. I chose these particular cases because in each one, those responsible for the murals approached private property owners and convinced them to lend their space for the artwork. In many instances, the property owners allowed the artists to paint the property because the owners understood that the murals serve as a deterrent to the sort of graffiti they consider vandalism.

What constitutes "vandalism" and what does not when it comes to graffiti is an important distinction. For the purposes of this book, I rely upon these definitions:

Tag (n.) A writer's name and signature. (v.) To execute a signature.

Throw-up (n.) A quickly-executed illustration, consisting of an outline with or without a thick layer of spray paint for fill-in.

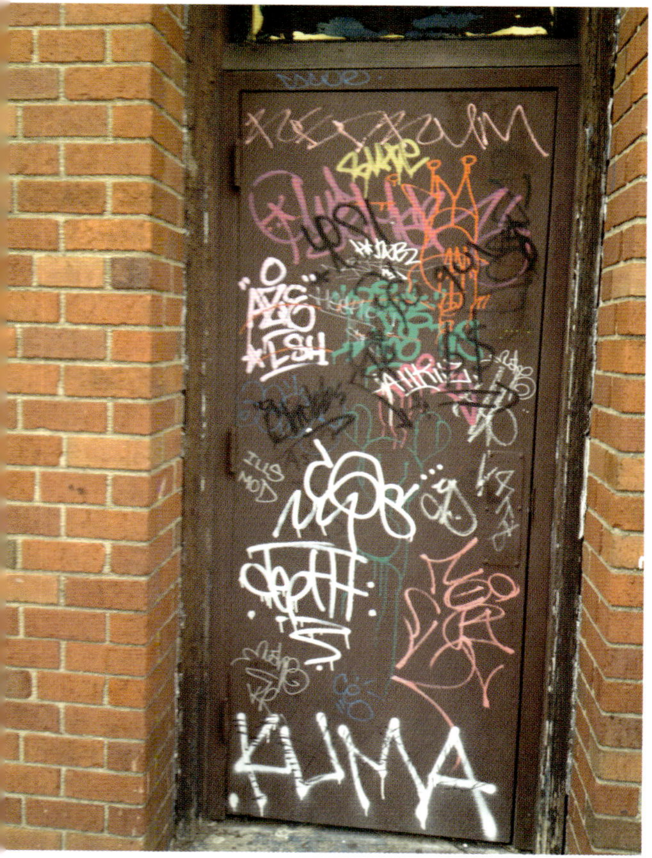

Multiple tags on a door in Park Slope, Brooklyn, circa August 2013. Photo by Patrick Verel

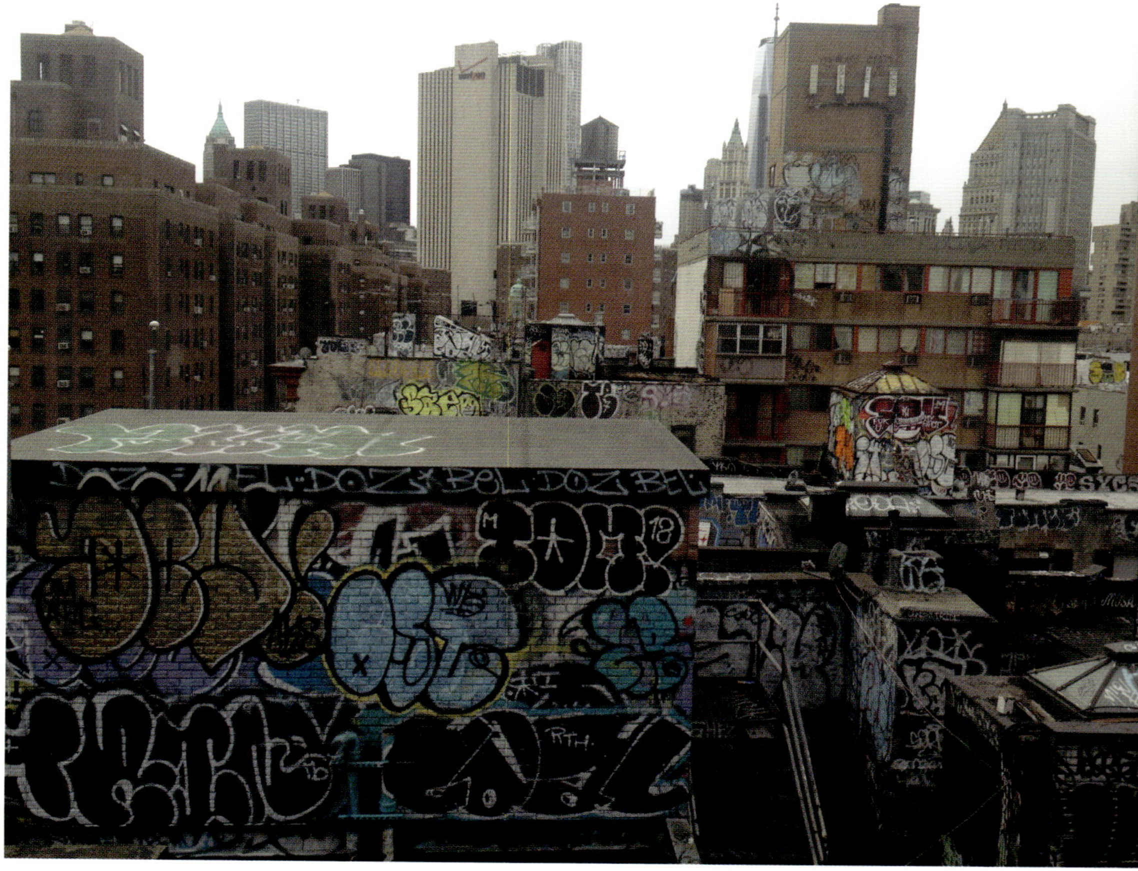

Countless throw-ups and tags, with five throw-ups to the left in the foreground, as seen from the south side of the Manhattan Bridge, circa March 2014. Photo by Patrick Verel

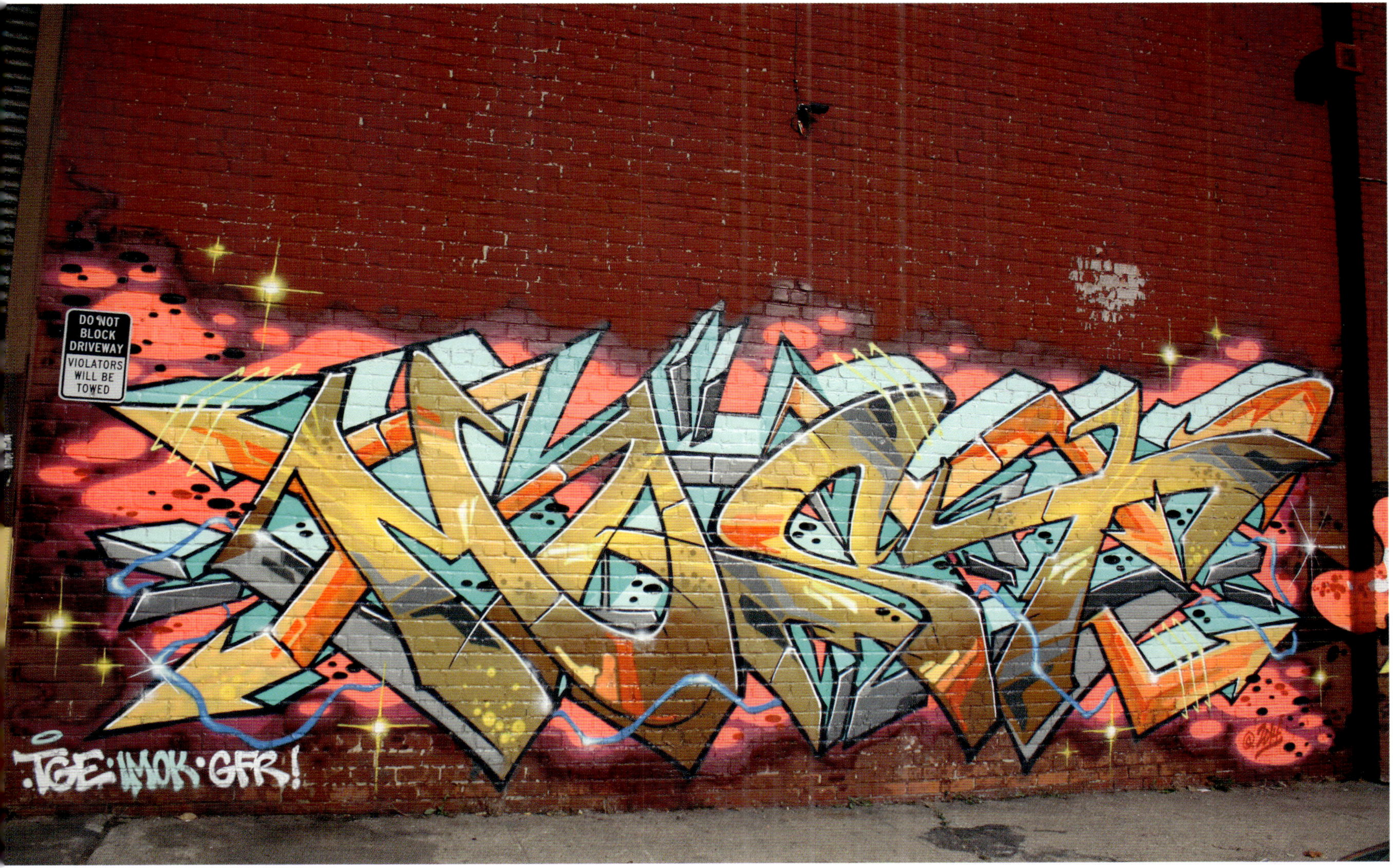

A piece by MAST in Gowanus, Brooklyn, circa July 2014. Photo by Patrick Verel

La Lucha Sigue, a production by Chup, Cor, Perscka, and Sorick at Welling Court, Queens, circa June 2011. Photo by Patrick Verel

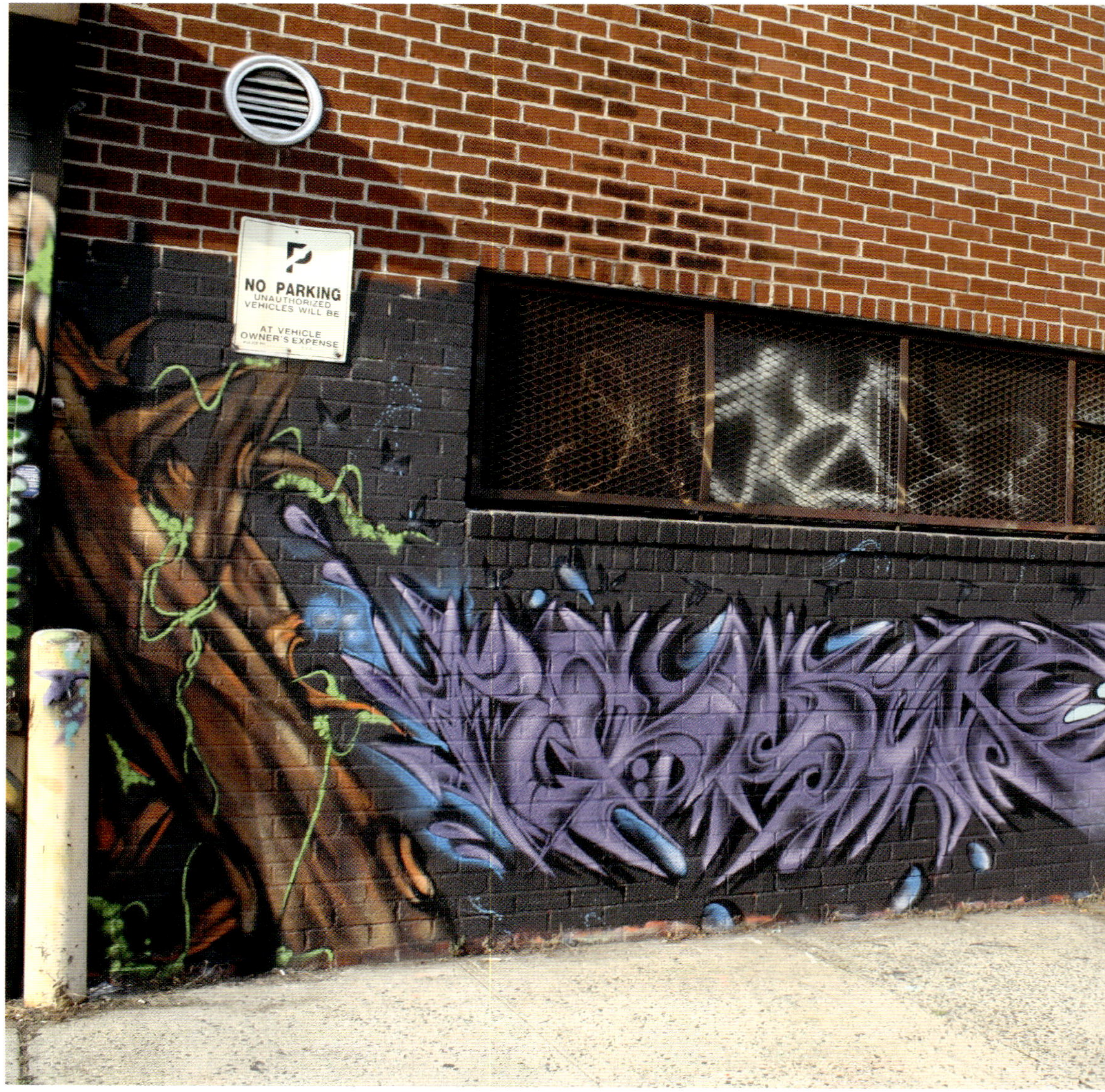

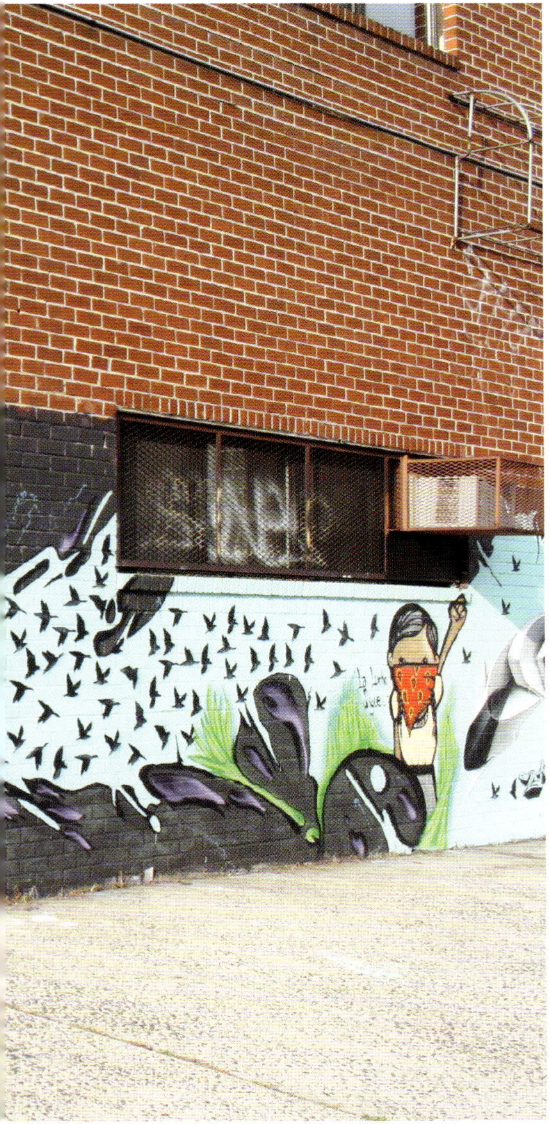

Piece (n.) Short for "Masterpiece," an artistic and complex form of writing featuring stylized letters, color, depth, and a variety of designs. (v.) To execute a piece.

Production (n.) A large-scale mural with detailed pieces and illustrations.[1]

Buff (v.) To remove writing or artwork.

Graffiti Mural (n.) For the purposes of this book, I will be using the term "graffiti mural" in this paper to describe both pieces and productions, as they share many characteristics.

Although there are still debates about whether tags and throw-ups constitute vandalism, I treat them as such in this book. I base this judgment not so much on my own perspective, as I have observed both in forms that I consider quite beautiful, but rather based on a consensus gathered from interviews conducted for the book. Two important aspects separate the throw-up and the tag from the piece and the production: time and space. The former require little of either, the latter cannot be executed without them. It is for this reason that tags and throw-ups are favored by those who write illegally, and it is for this reason that they are the prime targets for buffing.

My aim is not to suggest that tagging should be completely decriminalized; to do so would ignore thirty years of evolving laws, as well as widespread public opinion about the acceptability of unauthorized marking of property. Rather, I hope to show how spaces in a variety of settings throughout New York City, when adorned by pieces and productions, are aesthetically superior to both spaces that have been tagged and those that have been buffed. Visuals play an important role in this argument, as do interviews with those affected on a daily basis by the murals.

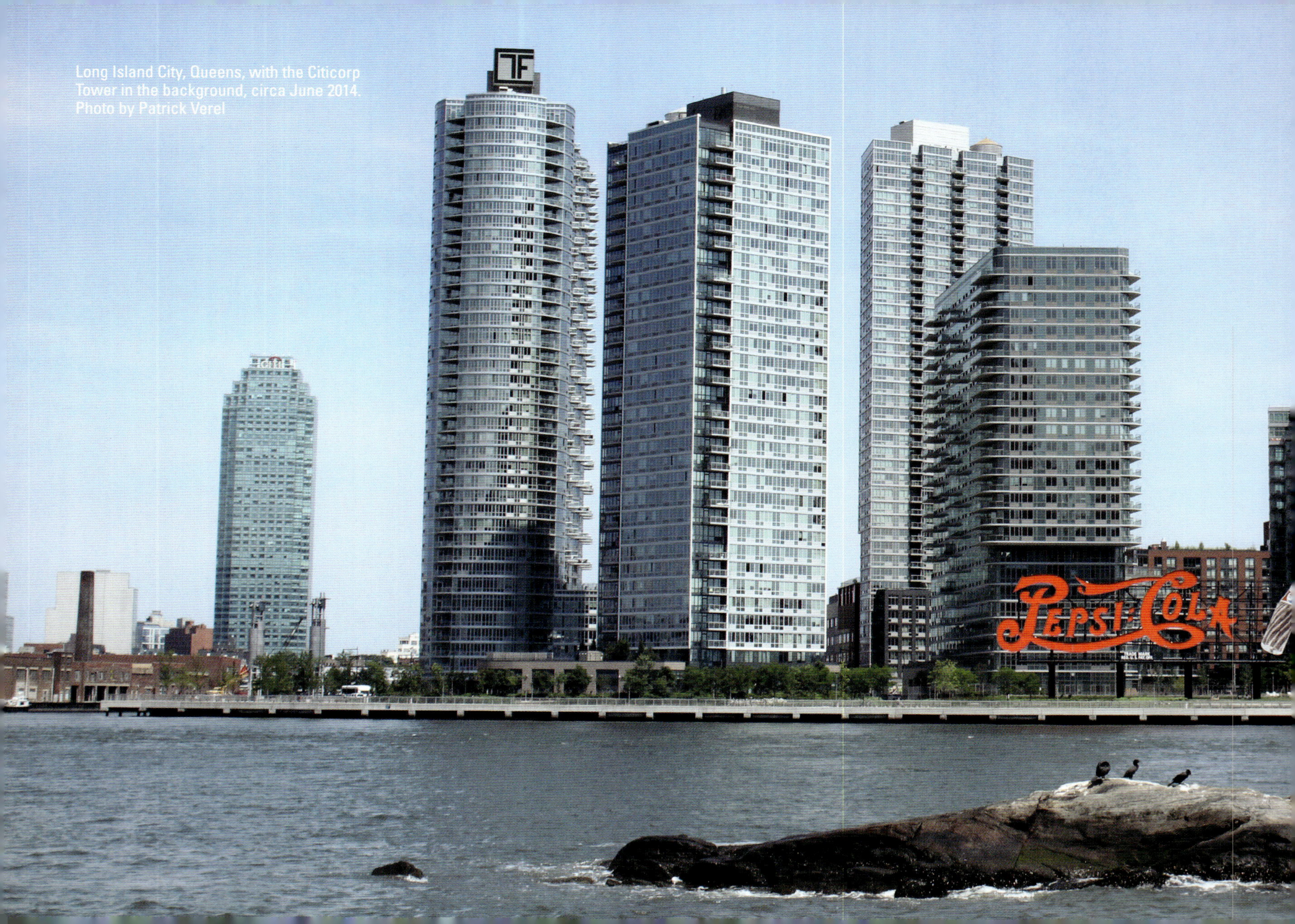

Long Island City, Queens, with the Citicorp Tower in the background, circa June 2014. Photo by Patrick Verel

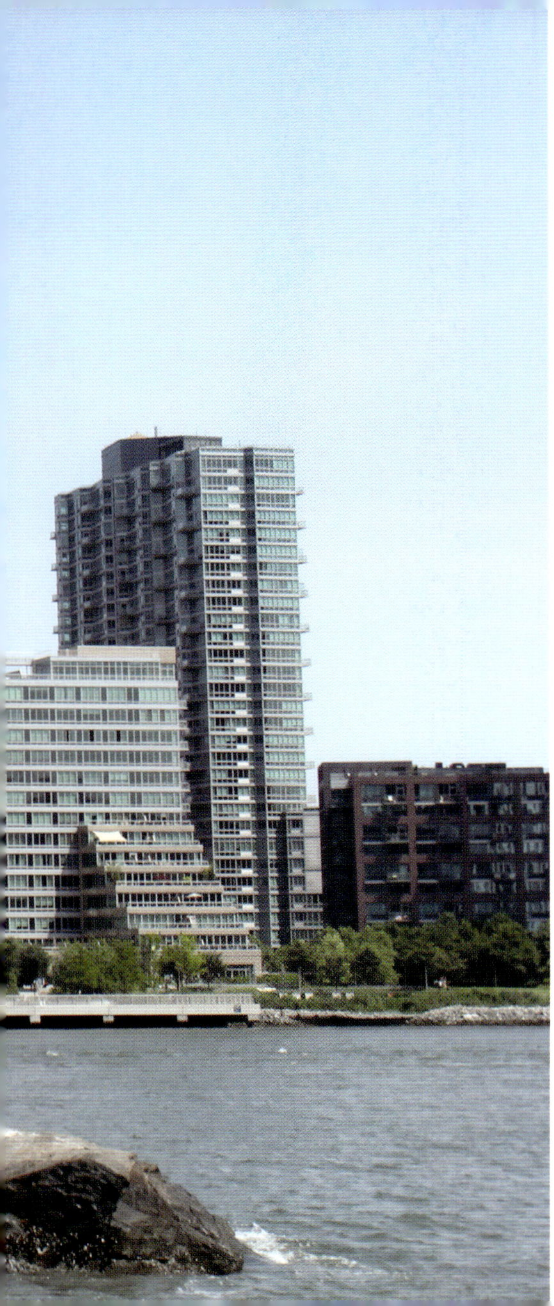

Culture vs. Capital

Public Art's Place in a Global Real Estate Hub

There is an inherent tension that exists between building owners and graffiti artists. Some of the resistance owners exhibit when they are asked to lend their space to graffiti artists stems from negative attitudes toward aerosol art that have been ingrained since the 1970s, when the emergence of graffiti coincided very closely with the bankruptcy of the city of New York.

I'm painting with broad strokes here, of course, as not every property owner is hostile to graffiti. But it's fair to say that most in New York City are, and it's foolish to merely dismiss out of hand the connections made between graffiti and vandalism. In fact, there are larger forces at work, and to understand the actions of private property owners and a government that acts on their behalf, I turn to cultural Marxism. Join me, won't you?

In his *Rebel Cities* (Verso, 2012), Marxist scholar David Harvey writes that capitalism as practiced in the United States is predicated on the notion that as profits are earned, they must constantly be reinvested in opportunities elsewhere, before a competitor invests in that next opportunity first. To wit:

> Capitalism rests, as Marx tells us, upon the perpetual search for surplus value, (profit). But to produce surplus value, capitalists have to produce a surplus product. This means that capitalism is perpetually producing the surplus product that urbanization requires.[2]

In New York City, this surplus value is manifested most intensely in the real estate market. The effects of the surplus are seen most obviously in Manhattan, where the 1811 street grid laid down that produced 2,028 blocks was proposed by Simeon deWitt, Gouverneur Morris, and John Rutherford as a way to "facilitate the buying, selling, and improving of real estate."[3] But the rest of the city has been affected, too, in particular in neighborhoods such as Williamsburg, Brooklyn, and Long Island City, Queens. In the post–World War II years, the city was the scene of countless projects initiated by the government (bridges, beaches, parks, public housing), but in the twenty-first century, the business of building is, with few exceptions, the purview of the private sector.

Whereas Robert Moses in the 1950s carved up the San Juan Hill neighborhood in Manhattan to make way for the sixteen-acre city-owned Lincoln Center for the Performing Arts, today a similarly ambitious redevelopment taking place two miles south is by and large a private affair. Hudson Yards—a $4.5 billion, twenty-six-acre, mixed-use development centered around a platform above the train yards between West 30th and 34th streets and 10th and 12th avenues—is being spearheaded by Related Companies, a privately held real estate firm known for building the Time Warner Center. Billed as the largest private real estate development in the history of the city, it is a prime example of how, more than ever, private interests now "create surplus product" in ways that reshape the city's physical footprint.

As Harvey explains, what has not changed is the inherent ugliness of the process.

> Surplus absorption through urban transformation has, however, an even darker aspect. It has entailed repeated bouts of urban restructuring through "creative destruction." This nearly always has a class dimension, since it is usually the poor, the underprivileged, and those marginalized from political power that suffer first and foremost from this process. Violence is required to achieve the new urban world on the wreckage of the old.[4]

Given all the changes it has undergone in its 350-year existence, "creative destruction" is an excellent unofficial motto of New York City. Although this has been the case for centuries, when it comes to real estate, it has accelerated in recent decades as the city has joined London and Tokyo in becoming—to use sociologist Saskia Sassen's term—a "global city."[5]

The most obvious example of "creative destruction" is that age-old, double-edged sword, gentrification. I say double-edged because gentrification has the potential both to promote art when new, artistically inclined residents move in (and thus invest capital in the neighborhood) and to threaten it when rents rise so high (because the amount of capital invested is so high) that the only residents who can afford it end up at odds with the freedom and unpredictability inherent in artistic expression. When wealthy families moved into a new condominium in Chelsea in 2012, for instance, they were aghast to learn that their new abode overlooked an annual, raunchy, gay block party.[6]

If you ask Harvey, he'll tell you that the final frontier for a space that is gentrifying (and thus absorbing excess capital) is the blessing of corporations, and he cites Times Square as an example. The process of cleaning up the area that former mayor Rudy Giuliani started in the mid-1990s succeeded in evicting all but a few token red-light businesses, and at the same time, the term "Disneyfied" was coined to describe an area that had been scrubbed clean of any trace of local culture. Today, the area is an economic success, but it caters less to New York City residents than to outsiders.[7]

This take-over by corporate entities, or "Disneyfication," is a real threat. Harvey suggests that Barcelona, Spain, which over the years has gradually amassed symbolic capital and accumulated "marks of distinction," is a cautionary tale. The city's architecture, history, and art, combined with infrastructure upgrades from the 1992 Olympic games, make it unique. But while that uniqueness has helped rejuvenate the city, it has also drawn the attention of developers with big pockets and the city is now threatened by bland waterfront developments, gentrification, and displacement of local merchants by multinational stores. Again, I'll let Harvey explain:

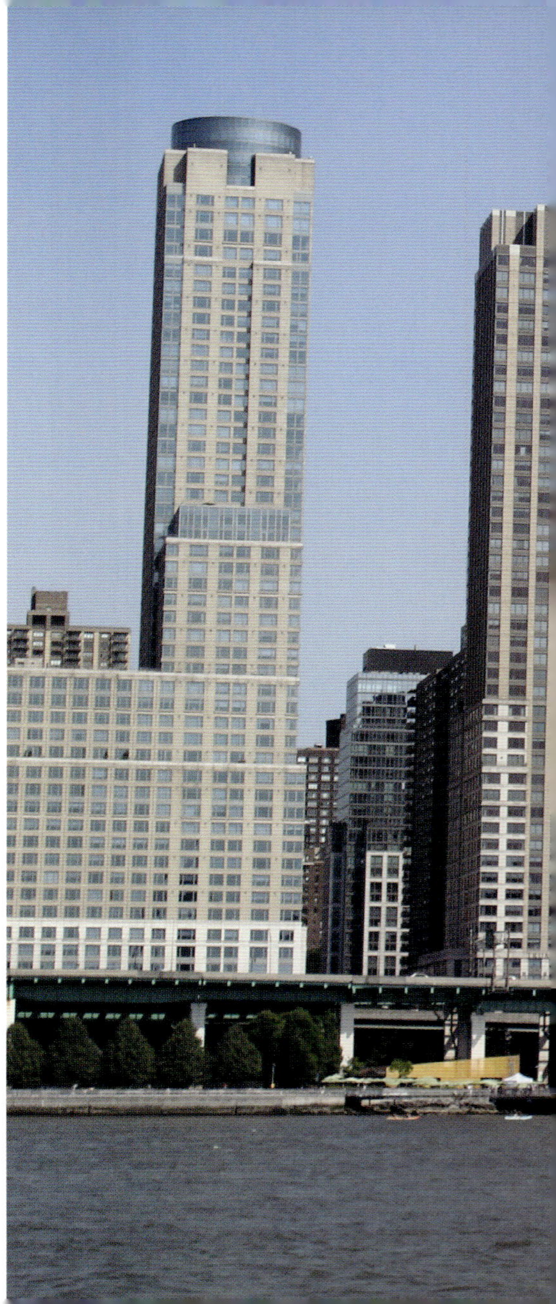

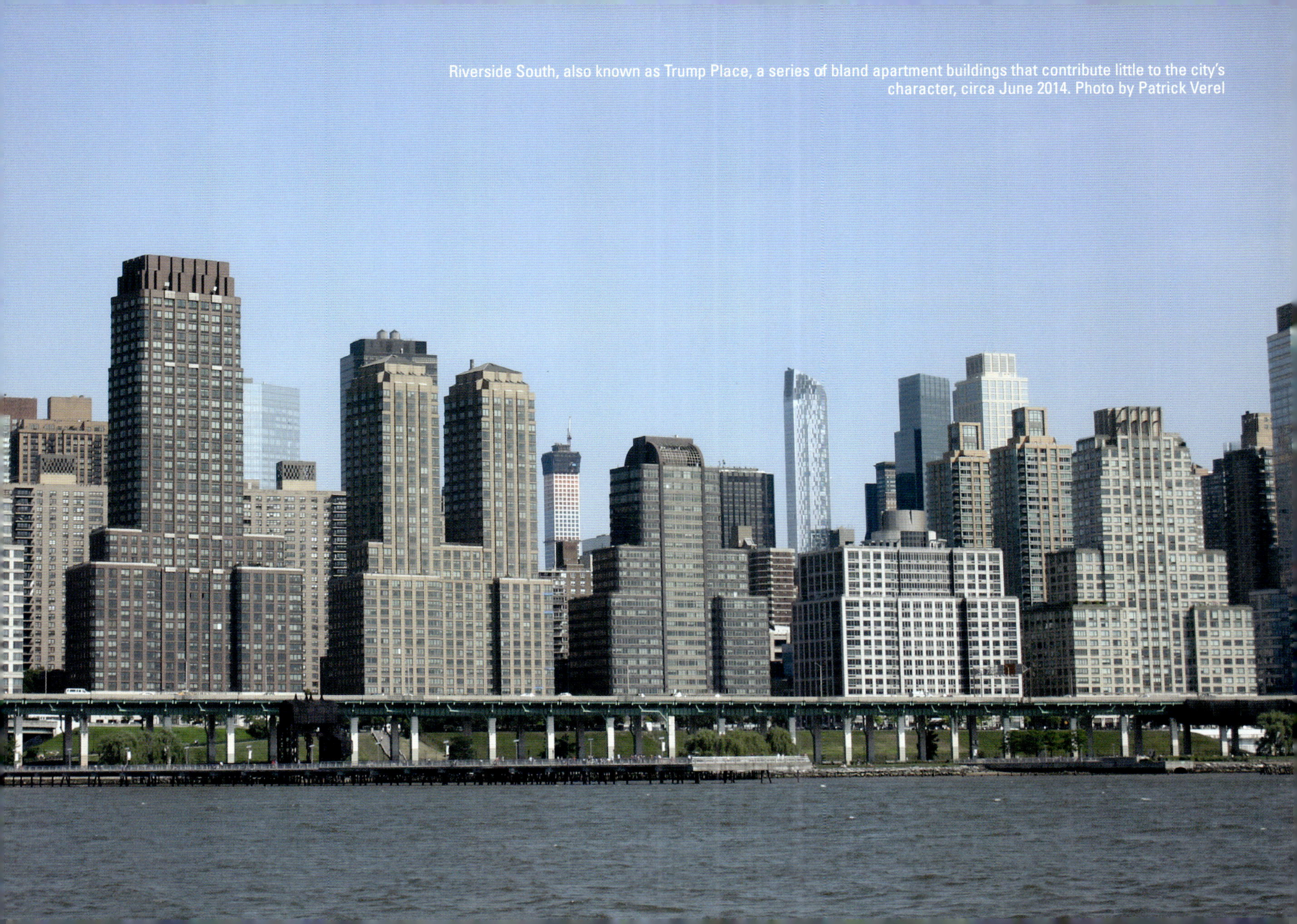

Riverside South, also known as Trump Place, a series of bland apartment buildings that contribute little to the city's character, circa June 2014. Photo by Patrick Verel

> The collective symbolic capital that Barcelona has accumulated depends on values of authenticity, uniqueness, and particular non-replicable qualities. Such marks of local distinction are hard to accumulate without raising the issue of local empowerment, even of popular and oppositional movements. At that point, of course, the guardians of collective symbolic and cultural capital—the museums, the universities, the class of benefactors, and the state apparatus—typically close their doors and insist on keeping the riff-raff out.
>
> The stakes here are significant. It is a matter of determining which segments of the population are to benefit most from the collective symbolic capital to which everyone has, in their own distinctive ways, contributed now and in the past. Why let monopoly rent attached to that symbolic capital be captured only by the multinationals, or by a small, powerful segment of local bourgeoisie?[8]

It's not surprising that Harvey implicates museums, as they are often beholden to board members whose interests dovetail with private development. One need look no further than the Brooklyn Museum to see how graffiti is still anathema in official circles in New York. In 2011, the loss of sponsorships forced the museum to abruptly cancel planned participation in the *Art In The Streets* show after it finished its run at The Museum of Contemporary Art in Los Angeles.[9]

Which brings us to the relationships between artists, building owners, and residents that this book is all about. While some owners are using graffiti murals as a vehicle for capital accumulation, others are—due to either their geographic circumstances or personal agendas—less affected by the market demands for the greatest surplus value. And although Harvey's arguments in *Rebel Cities* concern explicit political power, it's worth noting that the very existence of graffiti murals in the public sphere signals that power is being wielded by those not traditionally associated with the top tier of society. One last time, in his own words:

> If capital is not to totally destroy the uniqueness that is the basis for the appropriation of monopoly rents (and there are many circumstances where it has done just that and been roundly condemned for so doing), then it must support a form of differentiation and allow divergent and to some degree uncontrollable local cultural development that can be antagonistic to its own smooth functioning. It can even support (though cautiously and often nervously) transgressive cultural practices precisely because this is one way to be original, creative, and authentic, as well as unique.[10]

Harvey's definition of "monopoly rent" is the power that social actors can use to realize an enhanced income stream over an extended time by virtue of their exclusive control over some directly or indirectly tradable item that is in some crucial respects unique or not replicable. Or, to put it another way, it's what you can do when you own a product that's unique (a fine bottle of wine) or occupies a central physical location.

In New York City, centrality of location is the main driver of monopoly rent, as demand for housing close to the city's center is exponentially higher than the available supply. The colloquial way of expressing this is that real estate is all about three things: location, location, and location. Over the years, the pressure to extract monopoly rents from residential developments has had a cascading effect on commercial and industrial areas, as real estate concerns agitate to have unproductive industrial areas rezoned for mixed-use redevelopment. The aforementioned Long Island City and Williamsburg were rezoned in 2001 and 2005, respectively.

This illuminates not only challenges that artists face, but also the rationale for my conclusion, which is that more should be done to partner artists with building owners. That's because in contrast to Philadelphia, the twin birthplace of graffiti, New York City hasn't come to grips with the idea that spray paint can be a force for good. This isn't to say there aren't city-sanctioned groups promoting murals—Groundswell and the NYC Department of Transportation for instance—but direct, unequivocal support is sorely lacking. Veng, a graffiti artist whose story I explore later, summarizes the conundrum nicely when he notes that when he paints outside with brushes,

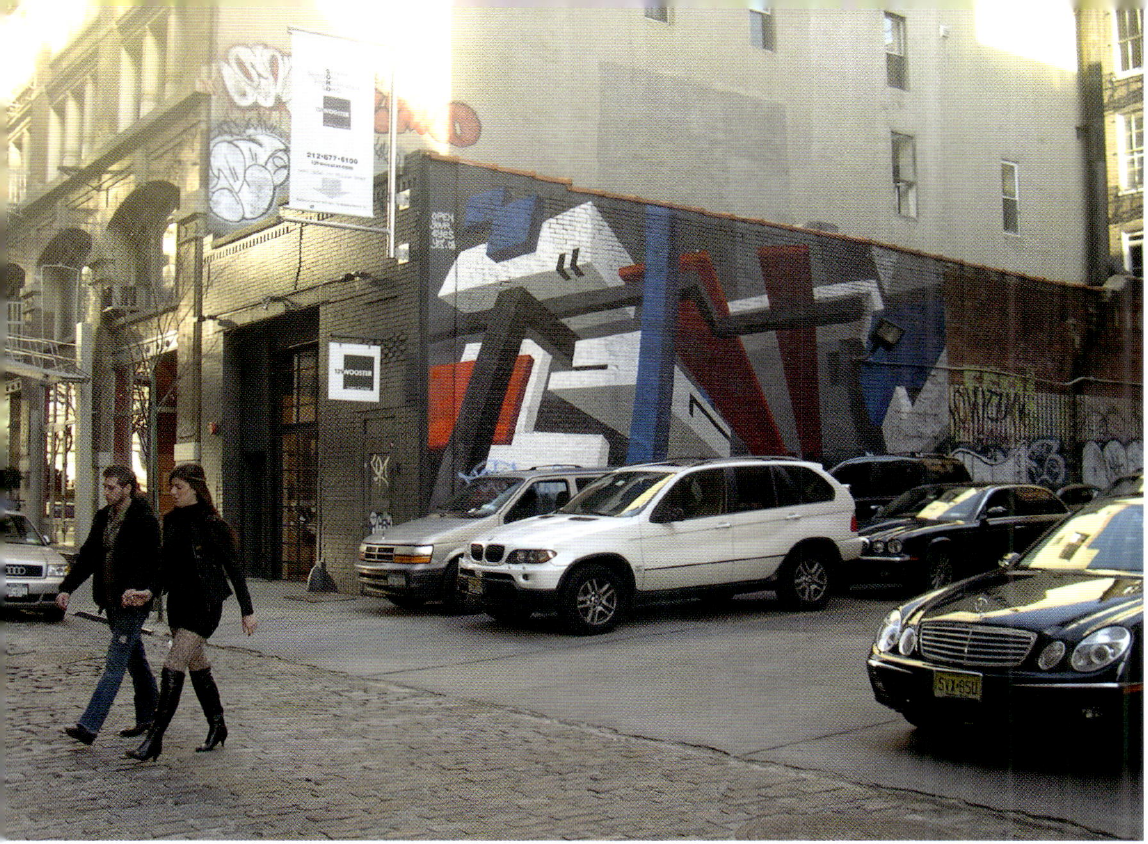

Wooster Street in SoHo, a neighborhood whose economic vitality manages not to be damaged by graffiti, circa January 2007. Photo by Patrick Verel

he is ignored. When he paints the same piece with an aerosol can, he is viewed with suspicion and questioned by the police.

Artists like Veng are walking a tightrope between the freedom to create and the freedom to pollute that are at the heart of what makes cities so much more exhilarating and unique than suburbs or the countryside. While there is certainly a place for officially sanctioned removal of unauthorized graffiti, there is no official counterweight that encourages the kind of art that Veng practices.

The fact that the city assists private property owners in their quest for monopoly rents via graffiti removal should be no surprise to anyone who observed the state of New York exercise eminent domain in 2009 to deliver privately owned property into the hands of the private developer of the Atlantic Yards arena, in exchange for a loosely defined public benefit.[11] While the city government is doing everything it can to help owners extract surplus value from their property, it fails to appreciate that preserving uniqueness is as important as investments that rejuvenate housing.

Graffiti is one source of uniqueness, even if it has been the source of a conflict in New York City since it first appeared in the 1970s. Part of the reason is there is such a visceral reaction to it is that even today, many graffiti writers only consider their work to be authentic if is done without permission. The entire enterprise is boiled down to a zero-sum game: either spaces are free of graffiti, and are therefore efficient uses of capital, or they are scarred, and are a drain on capital.

There are those who reject that notion of "authenticity" though, and embrace the tension that flows from working with the owners of their chosen canvas while still paying tribute to a home-grown artistic style. Although the city does not recognize it at the moment, a sizable number of graffiti writers who relentlessly tagged New York City in the 1970s have either grown up and evolved or given up.

Harvey also touches on the mentality of those in charge in his book *Spaces of Hope* (University of California Press, 2000) when he speaks of the "supreme rationality of the market versus the silly irrationality of anything else," and indeed, the phrase brings to mind a building owner in Gowanus, Brooklyn, I spoke to who rejected graffiti murals as childish and silly. It was not surprising. Research from the Philadelphia Mural Arts Program shows that murals of all sorts provide an economic benefit to the neighborhoods they inhabit, but that benefit is not as obvious as the raw forces of the real estate market that are present in New York.

Why might painting be "acceptable" with a brush but not with a spray can? Why might the same spray paint be off limits when it comes to tags but be fine for murals? The key is "symbolic interactionism," which is the theory that people interact with each other by interpreting or defining each other's actions instead of merely reacting to each other's actions. It is a theory born out of American pragmatism and advanced by George Herbert Mead, who argued that people's selves are social products, but that these selves are also purposive and creative. Back in 1937, Mead's former student Herbert Blumer coined the term, which he summarized as such:

1. People act toward things based on the meaning those things have for them.
2. These meanings are derived from social interaction and modified through interpretation.[12]

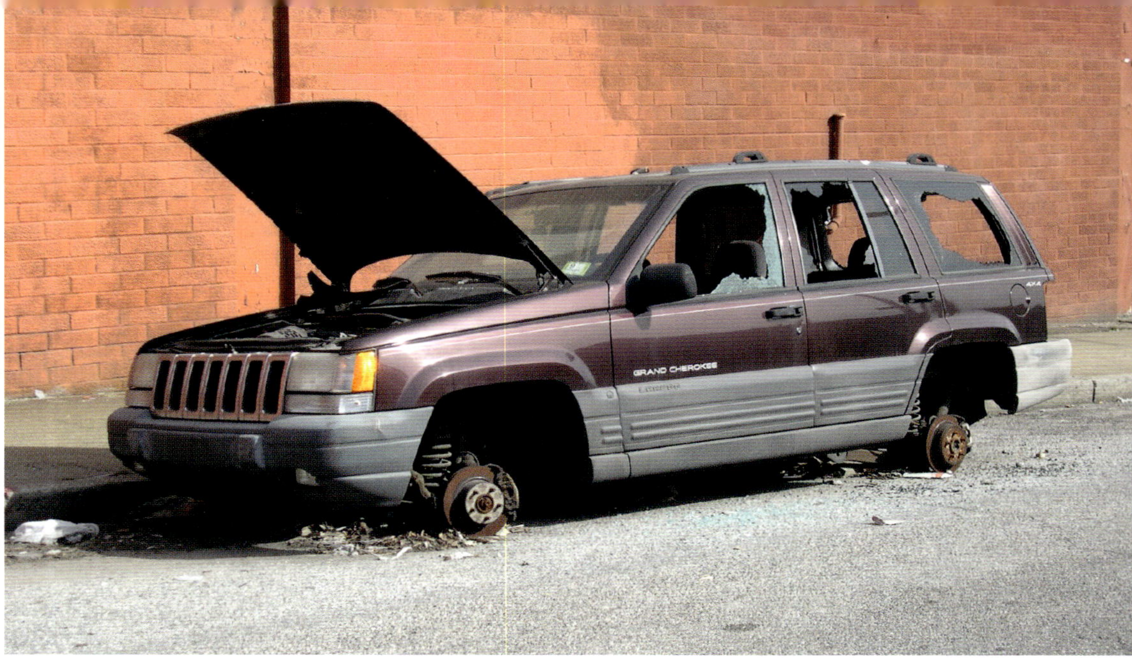

A Jeep Grand Cherokee in Gowanus, Brooklyn, that had seen better days. Was it a coincidence that it was ditched in a semi-barren part of the neighborhood? Circa February 2007. Photo by Patrick Verel

There is strong evidence that when it comes to graffiti murals, works composed with paintbrushes are interpreted by the general public as art, whereas identical pieces done with spray cans and markers are equated with vandalism, regardless of their legality. The meanings that the public ascribes to murals differ a great deal from the meanings it assigns to graffiti not affiliated with murals.

Research also suggests that cities are ripe environments when it comes to symbolism that affects peoples' behavior. For instance, in 1976, Philip G. Zimbardo, a professor of psychology at Stanford University, conducted a demonstration in which he "abandoned" two identical cars in the Bronx and in Palo Alto, California. Although both cars featured raised hoods and missing license plates that serve as so-called ethological "releaser cues" for potential vandals, they attracted very different reactions from local residents.

In California, the car was left alone, and in fact, a resident called the police when Zimbardo had it towed at the end of the study. In the Bronx, however, it took all of ten minutes after they'd set up observation equipment for someone to poke his or her head under the hood and steal something. Over a forty-eight-hour period,

Zimbardo's group observed twenty-three separate instances in which someone either stole something or damaged the vehicle. Most of the people who committed the vandalism were adults who acted in broad daylight, leading Zimbardo to conclude that because there was a missing sense of community, people in the Bronx interpreted their surroundings as making them anonymous.

In noting that vandalism and graffiti may be interpreted as an individual's attempt for public notoriety in a society that de-individuates him or her, he says:

> I now feel that any environmental or societal conditions that contribute to making some members of the community feel anonymous—that no one knows or cares who they are, that no one recognizes their individuality and thus their humanity—makes them potential assassins and vandals, a danger to my person and my property—and yours.[13]

By analyzing the ways in which artists, property owners and residents act upon the way they interpret the differences between traditional graffiti and graffiti murals, I hope to show that what people fear is not graffiti itself, but rather what it represents: a loss of control of the surplus capital that is the lifeblood of our capitalism-driven economy. This can be broken down as such: Lose control of the property's appearance, and one loses the capital it represents.

I aim to show that there is another way: Graffiti murals that retain the energy or "aura" of the art form, while providing the important symbolic control that property owners need. When successfully executed, the partnerships that bring these murals to life extend a degree of power to others, and most importantly, they preserve a uniqueness that is essential to New York City's identity.

Theories & Think Pieces

Going Deep on Graffiti's Effect on Society

Cultural Marxist criticism forms the backbone of my research, but I'm also interested in symbolic interactionism and the "broken windows" theory. The idea is to marry these theoretical observations to my own observations and interviews with the key players involved in graffiti murals.

Those players include graffiti writers who in most cases have made money selling their artwork. This is hardly surprising, as graffiti has been shown in galleries as far back as 1973.[14] It also helps explain why they're not always motivated to collaborate with building owners for purely aesthetic reasons, and in fact highlights a commonality they share with building owners who, above all, value the capital their buildings provide.

A little trip through the literature is useful for setting the table further.

A Social History of Graffiti Writing in New York City, 1990-2005 by Ronald Kramer is indispensable when it comes to the graffiti-style murals. He spent five years observing and interviewing twenty artists and conducting document analysis. He focused on two historical trends: the increase in legal, commercialized graffiti, and the official government reaction to graffiti, which has not deviated since the "broken windows" concept was first formulated.

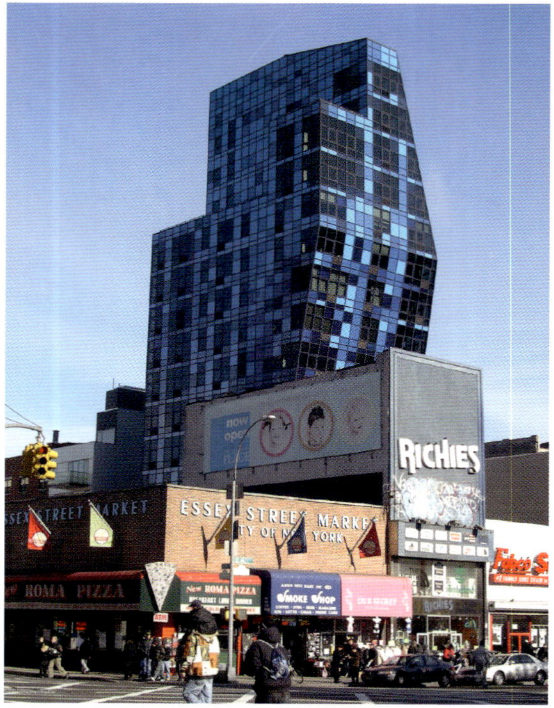

The Blue Tower, a sixteen-story condo that opened to great fanfare in 2007 on the Lower East Side of Manhattan, whose developers were unfazed by the prospect of neighboring buildings with graffiti. Circa November 2007. Photo by Patrick Verel

On its graffiti task force web site, the city of New York lays out that concept, which was originally unveiled by James Q. Wilson and George L. Kelling in a 1982 article in the *Atlantic Monthly*:

> The "broken windows" theory—that unaddressed disorder is a sign that no one cares and actually invites further disorder—has been a cornerstone of recent governing and crime fighting strategies in New York City. This theory was the basis for the July 11, 1995, Mayoral Executive Order No. 24, that formally established the Mayor's Anti-Graffiti Task Force as a vital part of the City's effort to improve the quality of life for all New Yorkers.[15]

Kramer further expands upon the theory to show how the city integrates it into its goals of increased quality of life for all New Yorkers:

> The presence or absence of graffiti determines the social, cultural and economic composition of the city. If the city allows graffiti, then surely "urban decay" will surely follow. If the city does not allow graffiti, then a condition of "urban vitality" will follow. That is, when the city fights graffiti, businesses will come to the city and tourism will boom. This will, in turn, create jobs and increase the tax base. All the residents of the city will benefit from such arrangements.[16]

Kramer's argument—that the disparity between the official reaction to graffiti and the contemporary realities of graffiti writing culture is driven by political and economic ends and not the search for any real truth — helps explain why a phenomenon that could ideally be viewed in shades of gray is instead treated by mainstream media outlets and government officials as an issue of distinct right (blank walls) and wrong (graffiti). He also notes that because the public nature of graffiti dictates that the work of amateurs be displayed alongside those of experienced writers, it makes it easier for those not familiar with the form to dismiss and fear all of it.

While one can make the case, as proponents of the "broken windows" theory do, that unregulated, undisturbed, and unchallenged tagging has a way of changing the atmosphere of an area for the worse, Kramer's research illustrates how graffiti culture has changed in subtle ways over the last several decades, while official reactions to it have stayed static.

The subtlety of this change is less surprising when one reads Mark Halsey and Alison Young's "Our Desires are Ungovernable: Writing Graffiti in Urban Space, (*Theoretical Criminology,* August 2006). Unlike Kramer, they didn't focus on writers who worked legally. Rather, they analyzed the language that writers of illegal graffiti use to describe what they do, to show how it separates their actions from those of someone who commits vandalism by breaking a window or smashing a sign.

Where they really shine is when they address buffing, which is both the traditional alternative to and threat to graffiti-inspired murals. They start from the premise that the desires that drive artists to write graffiti are unlikely to be deterred by harsh laws or the destruction of their work, and note that:

> The writer who repeatedly tags a wall that is consistently painted "clean" by the authorities knows that there is a better than even chance that a roller brush will eventually be used to bring the wall up to pristine condition. The same writer knows that he has helped turn a porous surface into a non-porous canvas. The latter is one this body can connect with in a more visually affective way.[17]

When I wander neighborhoods where the walls of buildings are dotted with a pastiche of blocky, mismatched swatches of paint that appear to have been hastily applied to cover up graffiti, I can't help but wonder how these splotches are aesthetically superior to what they replaced. And when fresh tags show up in exactly the same place, I also wonder if I'm witnessing a writer exacting revenge of sorts on the building owner for erasing his previous work, or if, as Halsey and Young posit, the new paint actually makes that spot a more attractive place to write again.

Of course, when one describes the desires of writers that are "ungovernable," it begs the question: desire for what? Greg Snyder, in *Graffiti Lives: Beyond the Tag in New York's Urban Underground* (New York University Press, 2009) makes the case that it's for recognition by ones' peers. In some of the more virulent critiques of graffiti, this is dismissively equivocated with dogs marking their territory and gang members staking out turf.[18] But recognition comes from a variety of feats: the sheer number of tags one posts around town, tags that are done in extremely hard to reach locations or, in the case of graffiti murals, the creative style and size of the piece or production. As Snyder says:

> Piecing with style requires more time and more supplies than tags and throw-ups, so piecing illegally often exposes writers to way too much risk from the police. Legal walls allow writers to showcase their talents and even enjoy creating art in the light of day. This process is also one of the few times that writers can socialize with each other.[19]

What is "piecing with style?" Well, before one can answer that, you need to go back to the beginning, to the lowly, hotly debated, tag. In *Street Art: The Graffiti Revolution*, Cedar Lewisohn (Belknap Press of Harvard University Press, 2009) argues that before one can understand how a complex, multilayered mural comes into existence, it is important to also see the talent inherent in a well-executed tag.

Just as musical notes come together to form songs, tags form the basis for everything in graffiti, from throw-ups to pieces to murals. But as a general rule, the public's revulsion at graffiti is reserved for the tag and the throw-up, which

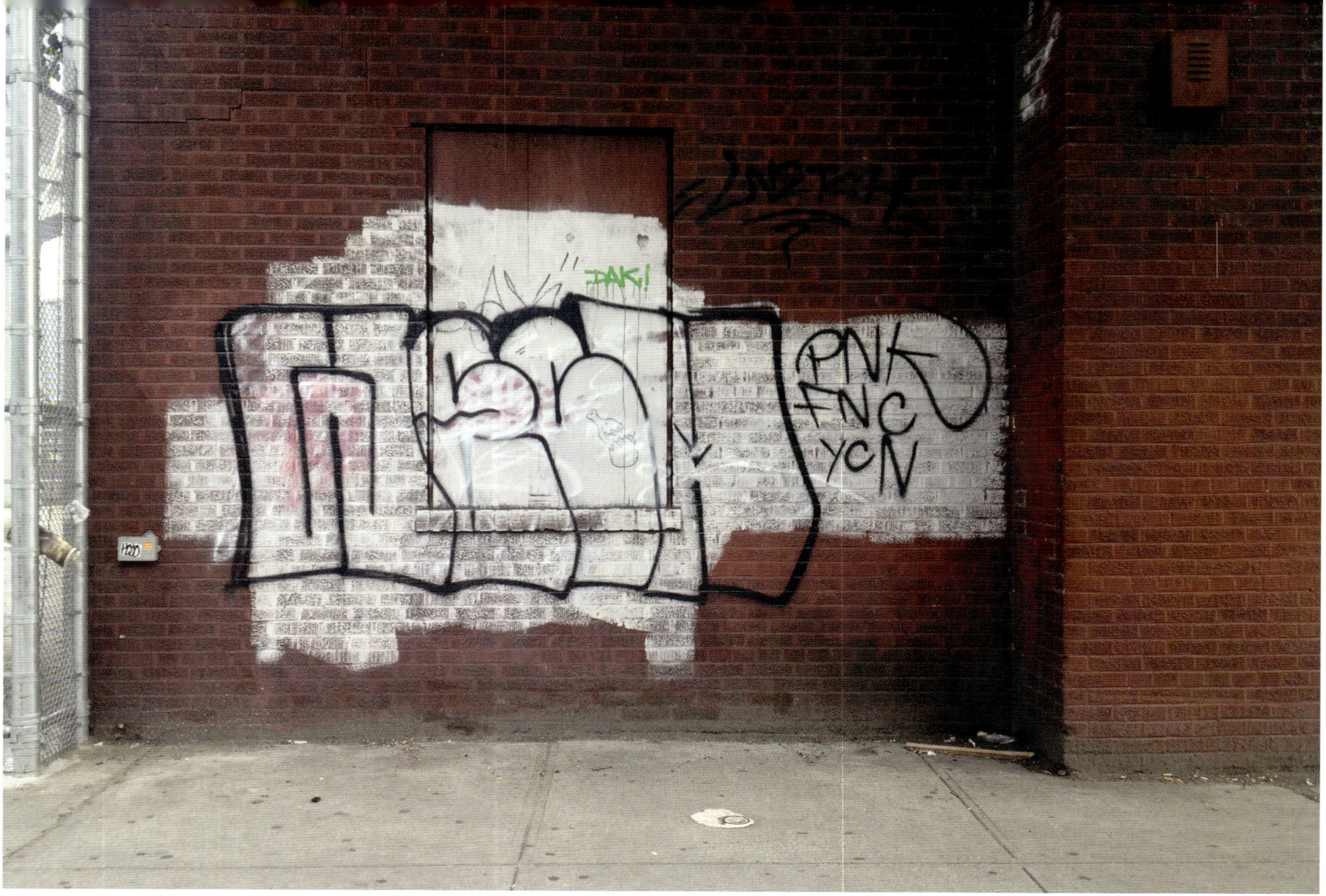

A building in Gowanus, Brooklyn, that has been buffed with white paint and subsequently tagged again by at least four different writers. Circa July 2014. Photo by Patrick Verel

are far and away done without permission. This makes possible the new relationship between writers who do pieces—which are generally done with permission—and property owners. This subtle distinction—that the "bad" tag can eventually lead to the "good" piece and mural in the public mind—is part of the conversation that is not happening at the higher levels of power. He notes:

> It's common to hear people say "I like the colourful graffiti; it's just those messy tags I can't stand." To the graffiti connoisseur, this is equivalent to saying "I like rock music; It's just those noisy guitars I can't stomach."[20]

Finally, *The Work of Art in the Age of its Technological Reproducibility* by Walter Benjamin (Abrams, 2008) is useful for addressing the issue of the space that is being competed for so fiercely. If it is true that graffiti has become an internationally recognized phenomenon, showcased in museums and galleries and utilized in marketing campaigns for Fortune 500 companies, and if it is also true that the Internet makes it possible to instantly share pictures of graffiti with like-minded people, why would anyone still go to the trouble to create murals that are outdoors, exposed to the elements and whims of the public?

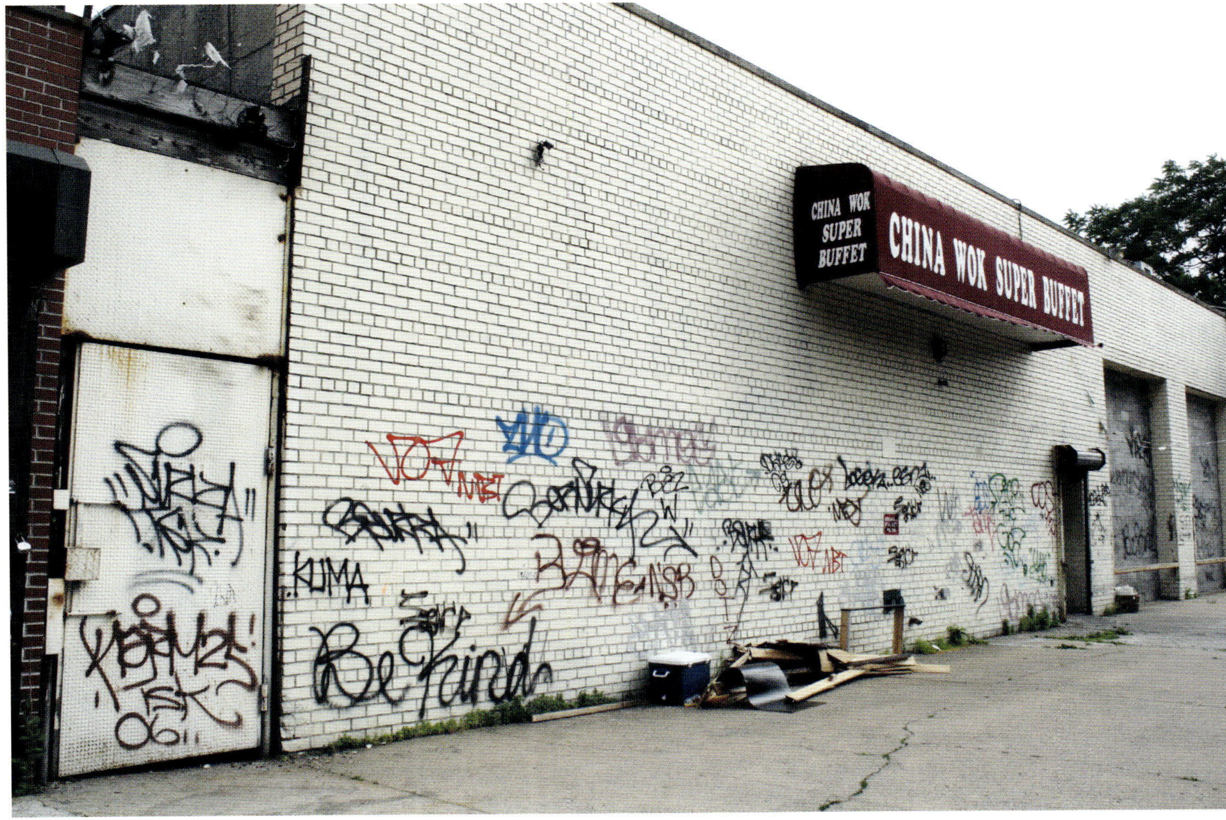

Who in the general public could explain which one of these tags in Bushwick is a "good" one? Circa June 2011. Photo by Patrick Verel

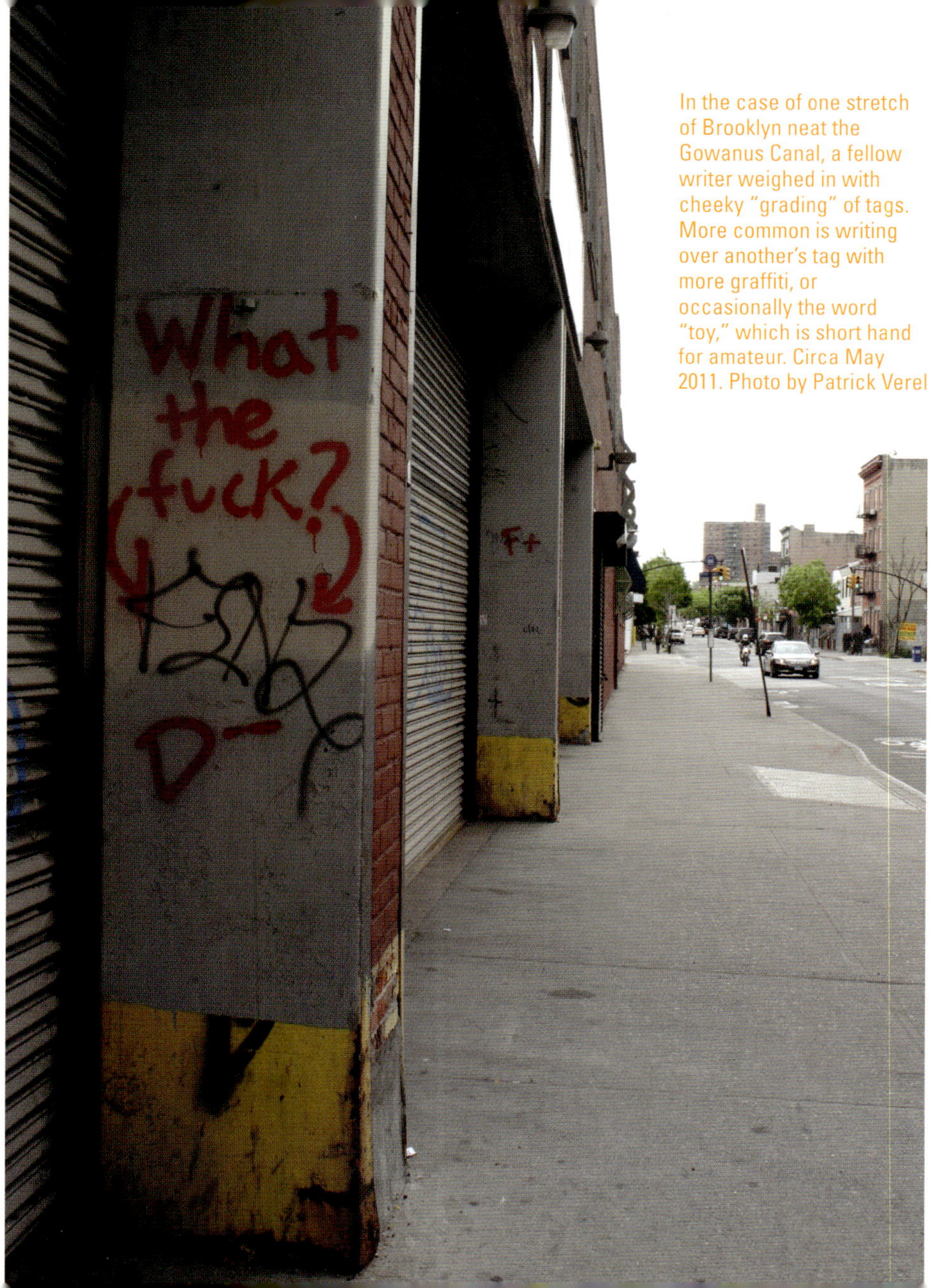

In the case of one stretch of Brooklyn neat the Gowanus Canal, a fellow writer weighed in with cheeky "grading" of tags. More common is writing over another's tag with more graffiti, or occasionally the word "toy," which is short hand for amateur. Circa May 2011. Photo by Patrick Verel

Benjamin wrote *The Work of Art* in 1939, well before the word graffiti was commonly used in the United States, but his argument—that a work of art can lose its power to shock, amaze, inspire, or impress if taken out of the environment distinct to it—is just as applicable now as it was then. He writes:

> The uniqueness of the work of art is identical to its embedded-ness in the context of tradition. This tradition itself is thoroughly alive and extremely changeable. What was equally evident to both was its uniqueness, its aura.[21]

In contemporary American life, the word "aura" is closely related to "authentic," and what could be more important to an artist than the authenticity of their work? The location of a graffiti muralists' work is every bit as important as the content of it, because its embedded nature on the streets keeps it firmly "in the context of its tradition." This is always appreciated, as evidenced by the aquisition of two pieces of street art by the artist Banksy from walls in Jerusalem by gallery owner Stephan Kezsler, who has since tried unsuccessfully to sell the freestanding concrete blocks for as much as $750,000. Kezsler has been the subject of blistering derision for his actions.[22] Graffiti was born in the public sphere forty years ago, and so its latter day reincarnation, the graffiti mural, belongs there too.

A Brief History

Graffiti's Dirty Past

Graffiti first started appearing in New York City on the subways in 1969 thanks to writers who went by the tags JULIO 204 and TAKI 183. TAKI in particular gained widespread fame thanks to an article in *The New York Times* in 1971.[23] TAKI earned that fame in part because his job as a courier put him in subways, and so he choose a canvas for his writing that rolled along roughly 842 miles of track in four boroughs. Both of them were unknowingly following in the footsteps of Daryl Alexander McCray, who had been writing CORNBREAD around Philadelphia since 1965.

A plethora of writers soon surfaced, and over the next twenty years, the subways became the primary venue for an ever-growing cornucopia of work, from simply sprayed and written tags, and throw-ups, to wild style pieces varying in depth, size, color, and style. All form the basis for the legal murals that one sees today in neighborhoods across the New York metropolitan area.

As the graffiti evolved over the years, so too did the efforts to suppress it, and after a prolonged battle waged by the Metropolitan Transit Authority (MTA), the last graffiti-covered train was pulled from the system, and in an April 1989 *Daily News* article announcing the event, TAKI expressed regret for his role in spawning the graffiti craze. "When you think back, and saw what eventually happened to the trains, you feel bad about it," he said. "I never thought it would be such a big thing. But the subways were so lousy anyway... they were pretty filthy. I thought that kind of justified it."[24]

Victory for the M.T.A. did not mean that graffiti was gone though. It simply meant that writers had to find new surfaces, and they did—on bridges, buildings, trucks, doors, tunnels, abandoned structures, highway abutments, and anywhere else that had a smooth, flat service. In response, New York City authorities steadily ratcheted up the penalties for graffiti. The current law covers everything from the act of defacing property owned by the city or a private entity to the possession of instruments of graffiti with intent to use them to the possession of said instruments by anyone under the age of eighteen. In fact, a merchant who carries spray paint or broad-tipped markers in New York is legally barred from displaying the actual product in their window, and must display an empty facsimile in its place.[25]

Pictures of the earliest graffiti illustrate how simple the form was in the 1970s and 1980s, and just as the style grew more sophisticated and complicated and characters started appearing along with words over time, its practitioners changed, too. Many of the writers in their teens who were writing on subway cars back then grew up, moved into their own homes, got jobs, started families and took on the kinds of responsibilities that would preclude them from engaging in risky activities such as tagging. Many gave up writing, just as they would give up pursuits like spitballs, prank calls, and shoplifting. Where the writers who did not put down their cans and markers ended up is where this story picks up.

Methodology

My Six Case Studies

I interviewed people in the New York City metropolitan area and Trenton, New Jersey. I compared the results of these interviews with documents and information from opposing factions: those that support murals (Philadelphia's Mural Arts Project and New York's Groundswell) and those that have antagonistic relationships with graffiti (New York City's Graffiti Free NYC and a building owner in Gowanus, Brooklyn).

I arranged my interviews and observations through contacts I made via websites and from my own personal experience. In Manhattan, past visits to the Inwood neighborhood alerted me of the presence of graffiti murals there. In Brooklyn and in the Bronx, I was referred to mural sites by "Luna Park," a photographer with deep roots in the graffiti world who displays her work on Flickr.com. For Jersey City, I reached out to the administrator of NJGraph.com and was put in touch with the SAGE Collective. The group hails from Trenton, a very different environment from Jersey City, so I also interviewed a different member of the group in Trenton. None of the artists I met in any of the aforementioned groups could recommend anyone in Staten Island, so I reached out to the Staten Island Arts Council, and they put me in touch with the nonprofit group NYC Arts Cypher. The president of Arts Cypher is not a graffiti artist, but routinely calls upon them for projects.

Finally, as part of a project that pre-dated this book, I visited 5 Pointz in Long Island City, Queens, because the site, a massive warehouse covered in graffiti, was impossible to miss while riding the number 7 subway. I revisited the site again in the fall of 2012. Although it was different in many respects from the other case studies, I include it because no book about legal graffiti in New York City would be complete without paying homage to the site. Alas, the timing would turn out to be fortuitous; the building was completely buffed in November 2013.

When it came to locations, I focused on either high-profile locations like 5 Pointz, or I let the artists pick the location they thought made the most sense. This worked because I knew that not only would the artist speak to me, but so would the owner of the property with the mural. This resulted in locations as varied as a downtown (Jersey City), industrial areas (Hunts Point in the Bronx, Trenton) a gentrifying area (Bushwick, Brooklyn) and a suburban locale (Staten Island).

The number of interviews I conducted was dictated by a desire to document as many corners of the Metropolitan New York area as possible in the time I had. Once I found artists who were willing to talk to me, I met them in person, usually close to the spaces where they had been working. I attempted to interview the owner of the space, as well as at least three people who had no connection to the project. These could be local residents, business owners, or random people nearby. In Hunts Point in the Bronx, for instance, this included truck drivers parked on the street next to the mural; in Jersey City, it was shoppers on their way to and from local stores. Repeat visits were often required to include what usually ended up being five to seven interviews for each site.

I also took note of the contrast of the murals with the surrounding areas, which without fail were shabby, desolate or some combination of the two. The contrast of the murals with tags in the area was also evident; unlike other surfaces, most of them were unscathed.

{1}

CASE STUDY

Manhattan

Back in Action under the Tracks

In northern Manhattan, a little more than a mile from the block where TAKI 183 first started writing his name in the 1960s, is a gritty block in the shadow of the elevated 215th street subway station. Visitors who descend the stairs from the 1 train to the north side of Tenth Avenue are confronted with a graffiti mural stretching the length of a squat, two-story building on the corner of 215th Street. From an architectural standpoint, it's an unremarkable building, home to Ming Moon Chinese Buffet on the Broadway side and Broadway Mechanic Services and 5060 Auto Services Inc., on the Tenth Avenue side. Graffiti pieces that comprise the mural stretch from one end on the side fronting Tenth Avenue, around the corner onto 215th Street, all the way to Broadway. All told, the twenty or so pieces take up half the building from the ground up to about ten feet.

The man responsible for making this graffiti mural a reality is Eddie Pabellon, who goes by the tag "Crane." Crane recently re-entered the graffiti world after a long hiatus (1979–2003), during which time he only painted on canvas. In addition to this graffiti mural, he overseas two others nearby, on a building that faces the 1 train near 203rd Street, and on the back of a BP gas station at Sherman Street and Isham Avenue. Crane stopped doing graffiti after he was arrested and subsequently got married. When I met him, he was driving to McDonald's with his two teenage daughters. He never stopped writing; rather, he swore off walls in favor of the canvas. But in May 2003, he ventured back out the street to paint again, this time with the blessing of property owners.

His proposal to the owner of the first wall he approached, on 203rd Street, was straightforward:

> The walls were all destroyed, so I told the guy, "Look, I got guys who can paint, and can actually do something that's better than what you've got there." He said all right, and from that point, he just gave us the wall.[26]

This pitch—that a space could be made "better" if it was surrendered to a writer who would take responsibility for it—was one that Crane repeated at the two other spaces. He was not shy about his motivation for taking over the space, which was a combination of self-promotion and street credibility.

> We're cleaning up to make it look better, so the public doesn't say, "Well, that's all the graffiti that they know how to do, is destroy." The older generation is not about going out and destroying stuff. It's really about trying to make a name for ourselves again.[27]

The man who gave Crane the go-ahead at 215th Street was Romeo, who has managed 5060 Auto Services Inc., since 1999. In 2007, he said Crane approached him with a proposal:

> **Q:** How did you first get in touch with Crane?
> **A:** He actually came to propose, because it

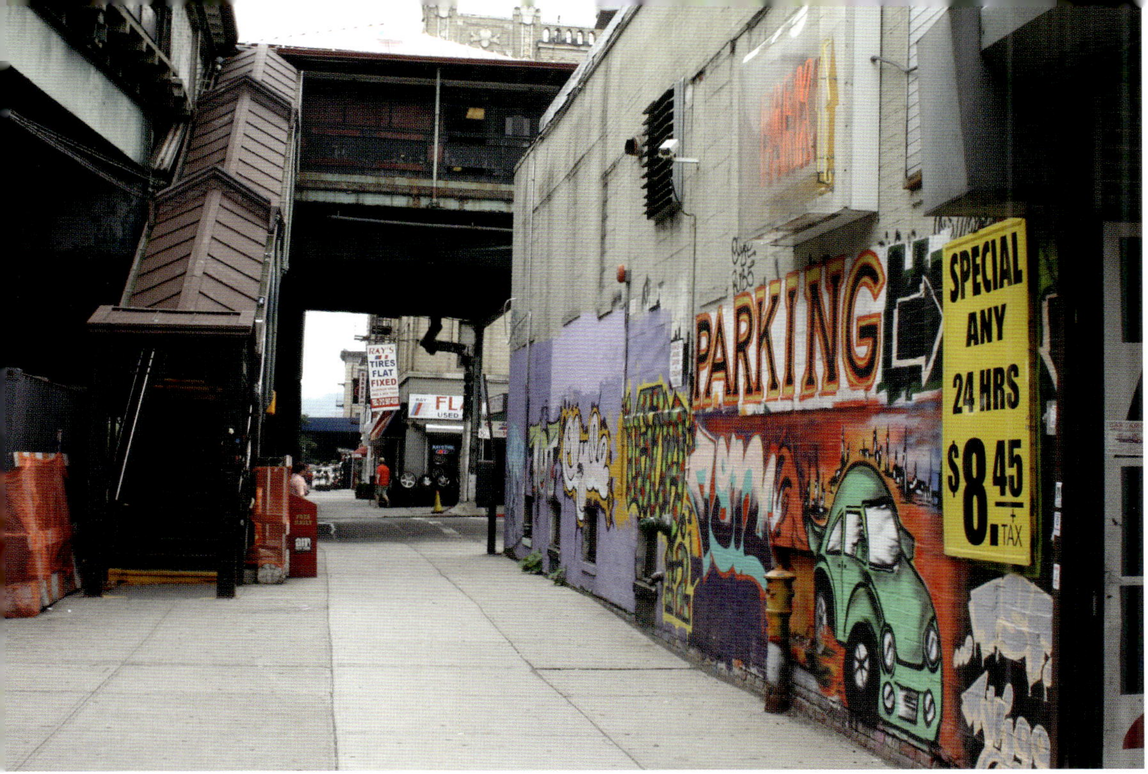

SDT56, Clyde, Lava and CEN by the 215th street entrance to the 1 train, circa July 2011. Photo by Patrick Verel

was very ugly. The building was very ugly, and he wanted to make it nicer. He said, "You don't want to do it?" I said, "It's not up to me." So I said. "Let me talk to the boss, the landlord, and if he accepts that, we'll do it." And you know, I have nothing against, you know, so I said, "Go ahead, do it."

Q: So you were sort of the go-between, between him and the landlord?

A: Exactly. I said (to the building owner), "Listen, it's ugly how it is before, so let's make it nicer." So they agreed with that.[28]

Romeo said it took Crane and his crew two Sundays to finish the first mural, and they've repainted it every spring and fall, at their own expense. The only things he saw before the work began were some pictures of Crane's past work, and he only asked that they paint something on the wall to advertise the garage. Once the owner of Ming Moon got wind of the project, Romeo said he asked for the same. Romeo's rationale for convincing the owner of the building to let him turn it over to writers is similar to Crane's, but with an important twist: He prefers clean walls to murals, but he hates tagging even more, and he believes that Crane's mural is a better deterrent to the tags than buffing. In fact, Romeo turned down a city graffiti cleanup crew who offered to buff the building for free.

Q: Now, you'd mentioned the last time we talked about how the city had offered to come by.

A: Yeah, they tried to…they sent somebody who said they were going to clean it, but I'm afraid after they clean, it's gonna be again, ugly.

Q: Was that before you started working with Crane?

A: Yes, it was. It was before, when it was ugly, and I asked the guy who came here from the city, 'What is your opinion? Ok, we agree to clean it. What do you think is going to happen after that? It's gonna be ugly again, because people, they just wait.' Because, as you can see, in the parking lots outdoors, they paint the trucks. And I can send you to 231st Street and Broadway, and you're gonna see that outdoor parking lot with graffiti on trucks.[29]

Some of what drives Crane is a desire to stay relevant in a scene that he adores. He spoke

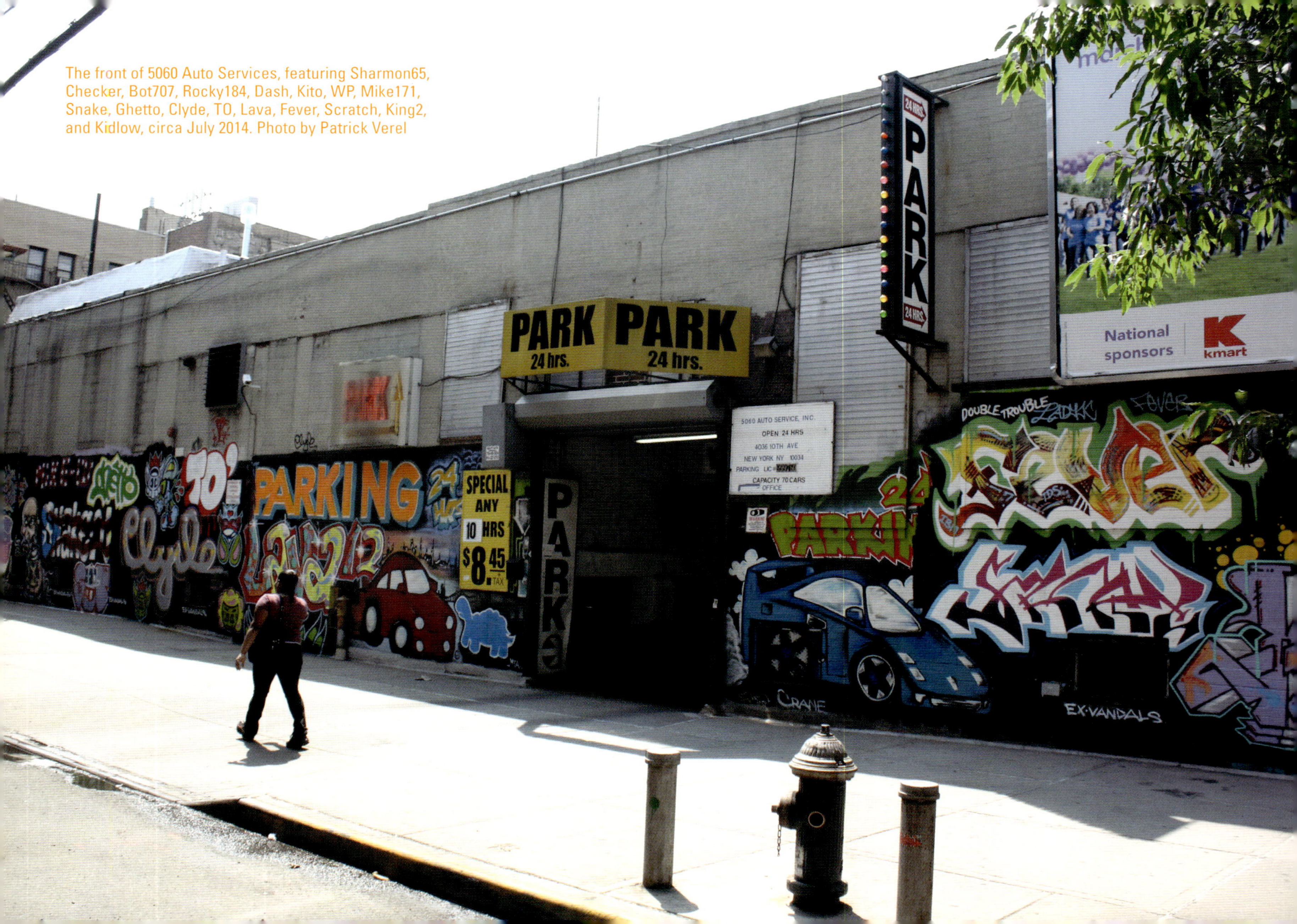

The front of 5060 Auto Services, featuring Sharmon65, Checker, Bot707, Rocky184, Dash, Kito, WP, Mike171, Snake, Ghetto, Clyde, TO, Lava, Fever, Scratch, King2, and Kidlow, circa July 2014. Photo by Patrick Verel

wistfully about being recruited as a teenager in the 1970s by Jack Pelsinger, the founder of Nation of Graffiti Artists, and selling a canvas for $1,000 when he was fifteen. A desire for a sense of community is a factor, too, as the wall now functions as a hub of sorts to other writers from around the world who want to paint in New York City. But while Crane is able to draw writers from as far away as Japan, the negotiations that he has to really put his energy into are local. Building owners might be interested in the style of the art that he is promoting, or they might simply view his murals as vandalism prevention. Either way, it's worth the negotiation to him.

> **Q:** When you approach a building owner about using their space, do you tell them that one of the reasons they should let you do this is it prevents other kinds of vandalism?
> **A:** I explain that, if any damages are done to the wall when we paint them, we will come back again and redo it again.
> **Q:** So if someone were to come along and tag it?
> **A:** Right, we will come back and redo a whole new mural. It might not be the same one; it would just be something maybe better than what they had. Sometimes they'll ask us to do something for the community, which we don't mind. Like I said, it's a give and take. So if you are the store owner or the building owner, and you say, "Eddie, I want a Puerto Rican flag and a Dominican flag incorporated in your mural," we have to give it to them. We can't say no. It's not, how can I say it? Beneficial to say no to them. They can always turn around and say, "OK, since you can't do this for us, brush it off."[30]

Romeo's concerns, and Crane's response to them, are very much in tune with symbolic interactionism, in that Romeo believes that a mural overseen by a local artist sends a signal of orderliness that a buffed wall does not. He believes this even though from a monetary standpoint, it doesn't matter what he does, as a buffed wall costs the same amount of money to him as a mural. Their relationship also validates Kramer's contention that graffiti culture has changed, as theirs is one of cooperation, not antagonism. That cooperation is the bedrock of the "urban vitality" that Kramer notes the city seeks to promote, and it is manifested physically in the mural itself.

The community is generally supportive of what they do, Crane said, once they explain what their intentions are and they don't get political. Mike, a black man in his 50s who has called Inwood home for the last eleven years, described the wall on Tenth avenue as part of the "spice" of the neighborhood that has "flavor," illustrates "expression," and is better than a "beat up, chipping brick wall." Of particular note was his answer to the question, "What is your general impression of graffiti?"

> Well, it used to be taboo back in the day, you know, when it was haphazard, and defacing stuff. But this is like, meant for this, you know? They get permission, they get contracted or whatever, and they do this. I think it's a good thing.[31]

Character, flavor, expression—these are not the kinds of words that one would use to describe a wall had it been buffed. Marisol, a Hispanic woman in her 40s who had come to 215th Street from her home in Harlem with her daughter to receive public assistance a few blocks away, was appreciative of the colorful addition to the block.

> **Q:** Do you think it makes the neighborhood a better place?
> **A:** Well yeah, it does sometimes.
> **Q:** Why?
> **A:** Because it gives it character, and it lightens up the neighborhood.
> **Q:** So you think it's better than say, like a blank wall?
> **A:** Yeah. For the simple reason is that life is beautiful. Why not? Draw something on a blank canvas and make it beautiful, and let other people see your artwork.[32]

Of course, this is still New York, where opinions can vary wildly about even the thinnest reed of a topic. Lillian, a black woman in her 20s who moved to the neighborhood in 2010 from 100th Street and Amsterdam Avenue in Harlem, had mixed feelings about the graffiti mural. She first called it nice and bright, but then "a little distracting." She deemed all graffiti art, and even noted that she has a friend

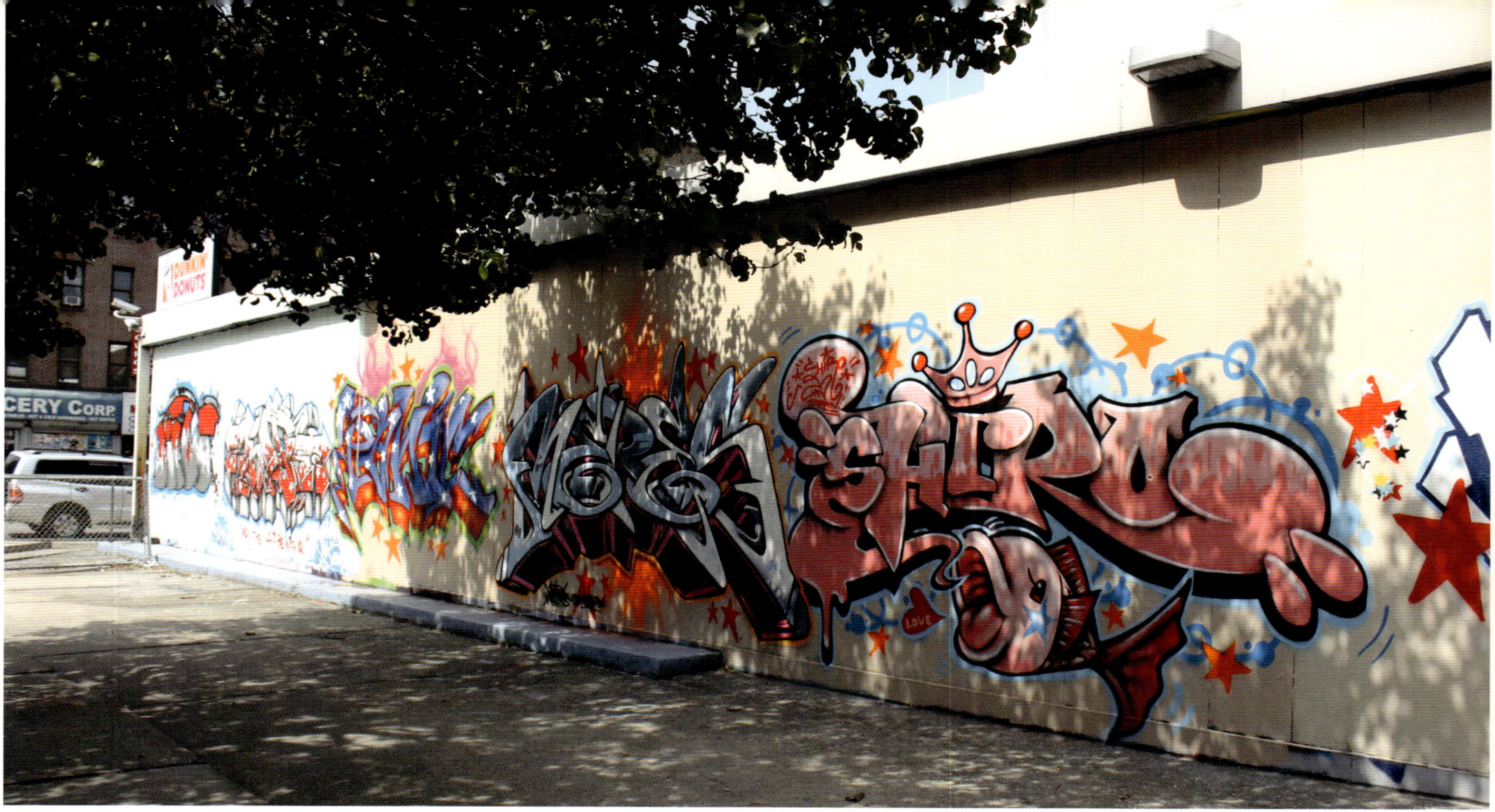

Kito, WP, Will Power, Panic, Meres, Shiro, Ree, and Clyde, on the back of Dunkin Donuts, circa July 2014. Photo by Patrick Verel

who is an "awesome" writer. But she seemed not to be enthralled by the murals, even as she allowed that others might be.

Q: Do you think it makes the neighborhood a better place?
A: Um, not really. But at the same time, if you're into art, it looks pretty.

Q: How do you think it compares to a blank wall, you know, like if they just painted it over and kept it…
A: Simple, plain. Less distracting. I mean, personally, I don't think they should be doing

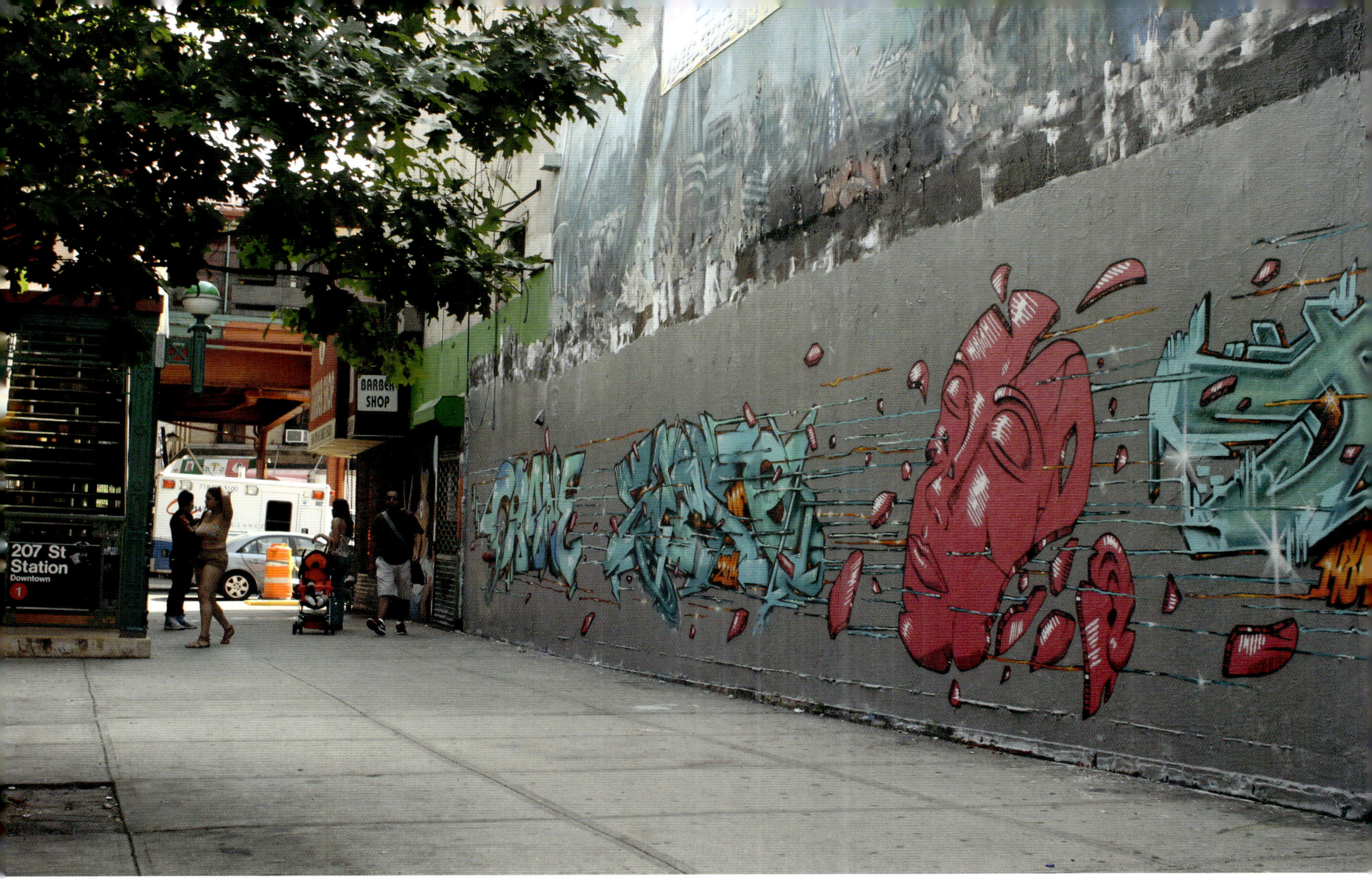

Crane, Vest, Import, and Just, by the 207th Street entrance, circa July 2014. Photo by Patrick Verel

> this to the wall, unless you're down at an art convention or something. That's different.[33]

Lillian's perspective puts her more in agreement with Romeo, who, without prompting, mentioned that he admired Philadelphia's murals. He cited the promotion they receive from authorities and the emphasis on appropriate sites as something that New York City could emulate.

> I spoke with my friends, and the mayor, they say, because they have graffiti everywhere, they call all of them and they say, "Guys, you want to do it somewhere, don't do it all over the whole city. You have these walls, do it here." And they paint the bridges, and they paint some walls, you know? And they do it over there. I took some pictures in Philadelphia. They have a huge building where there's a huge design in graffiti. So the city looks beautiful.[34]

His take on New York's support for murals is less positive.

> They don't want to see nothing like this on the wall anymore, they want everything blocked out. I believe that the city should open up spots for these kids to paint. That way you keep them away from the establishments. Just like Europe. When you go to Europe, you got walls that say permission walls.[35]

"Everything blocked out" versus "cleaning up to make it look better." One represents a property manager's impression of the city's graffiti cleanup effort; the other is the justification given by a writer who once played the part of the vandal but now negotiates within the realm of acceptable societal behavior to ply his craft. And while the goal of both sides of this conflict is to bring about a sense of community and order to the neighborhood, the interviews with Romeo and the three residents illustrate that it's not clear that buffing this space would be preferable or even effective, given its location.

{2}

CASE STUDY

Brooklyn

Robots Will Kill in Bushwick

In the industrial section of Bushwick, Brooklyn, 36 Gardner Street is not much to look at, nor are its neighbors. Among the major landmarks within easy walking distance is Newtown Creek, a 3.8 mile-long waterway that was recently declared a Superfund site by the Environmental Protection Agency. It is not, however, isolated, as it is one block away from Flushing Avenue, a major north/south artery for industrial traffic, and four blocks from the Jefferson Avenue L subway station. But what it lacks in charm, it makes up for in utility. For Veng, a writer from Staten Island, it (and several neighboring buildings) is the perfect canvas for his art. It's large, it's flat, and when he and other members of the collective Robots Will Kill show up on weekends to paint, the neighborhood is quiet, which allows for easier concentration.

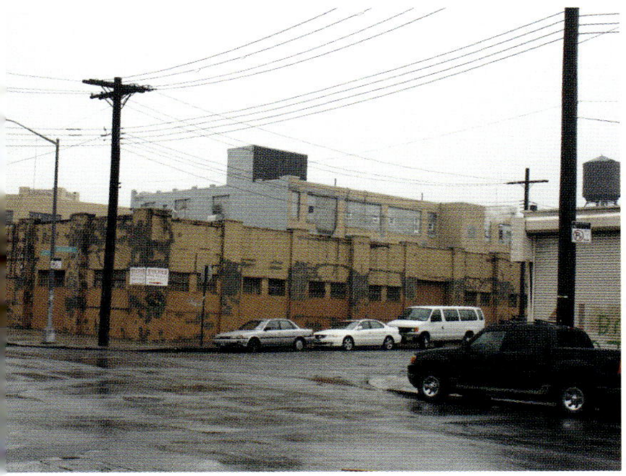

The view across the street from 36 Gardner Street. Photo by Patrick Verel

Veng found this spot through his art supplies connection. The building is the warehouse for SoHo Arts Supply in lower Manhattan, which is where Veng, whose real name is Herb, buys supplies for his canvas-based work. He started writing his name around Staten Island in 1994 and graduated to tagging with a spray can in 1996. It didn't take long for him to get caught and arrested two years later, and so in 1999, he stopped tagging and started doing legal graffiti murals. He recalls painting a tornado with books flying out of it on the front of a bookstore. He wasn't compensated for it, but at the time, money wasn't his motivation:

> I think they supplied the paint for it, if I remember correctly. I was a young kid back then, and I don't even think the idea of being paid was something I was worried about. I was just happy to be out in the street painting, and this whole new thing after being out painting in the streets illegally, to come out legally in the middle of the day, was kind of surreal at first. [36]

In addition to moving on from writing only his chosen tag, Veng has also added characters to his repertoire, and when I interviewed him outside 36 Gardner, the building was festooned with images of a frog, a panda bear, a bird and a man with a gorilla head for a hat, as well as two extremely complex productions. Visages of

36 Gardner Street, featuring Flying Fortress, Veng and Chris RWK, circa March 2010. Photo by Patrick Verel

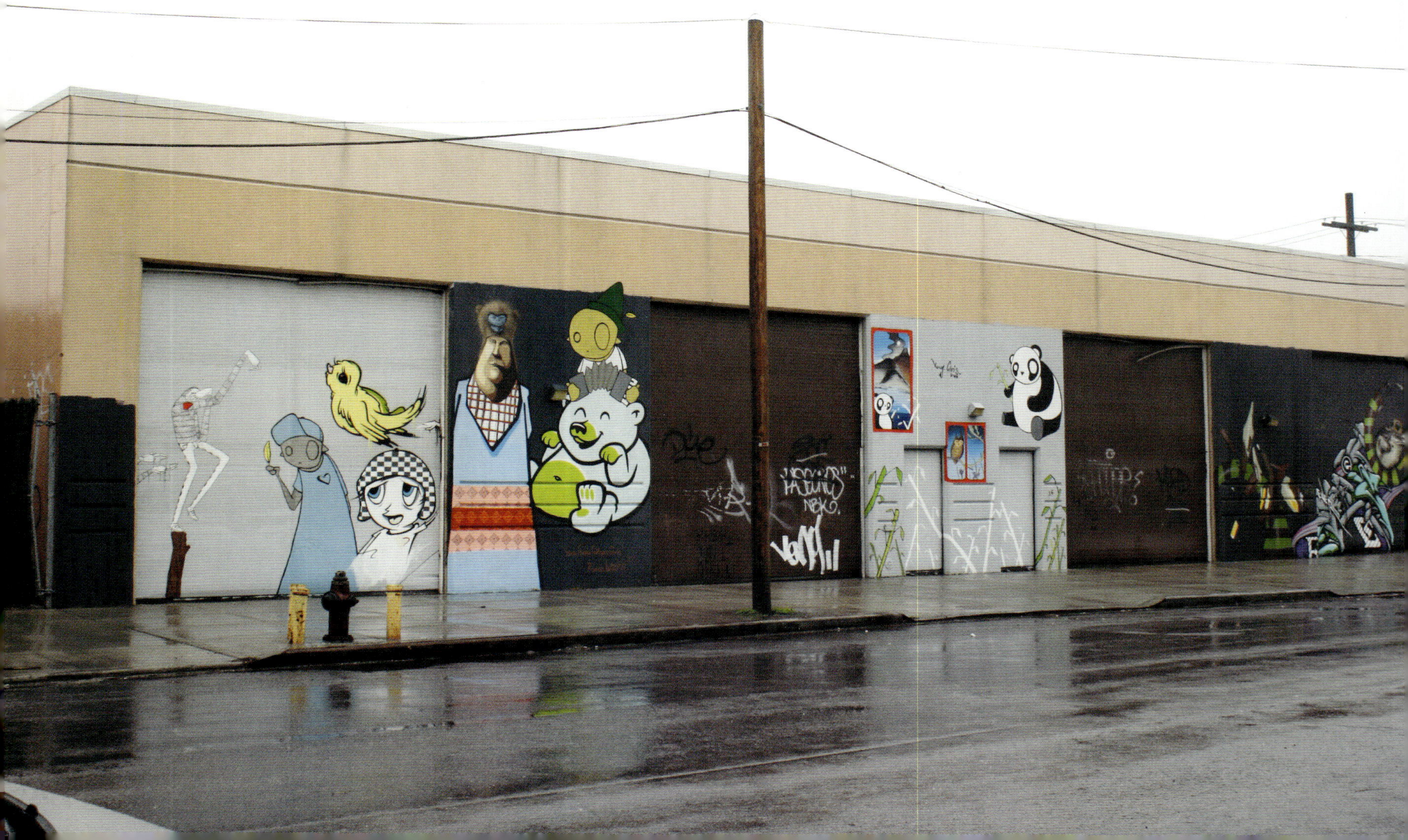

Jam Master Jay, from the rap group Run D.M.C., and Woody Allen were next door. Characters are actually Veng's preferred subject now and are the bulk of the canvases that he sells for a living. But he still loves to paint outdoors on walls, and Bushwick in general, and Gardner Street in particular, is the perfect location for it.

> It's much easier to paint out here in Bushwick, or Williamsburg, where it's a little more art friendly, and it's more of an art neighborhood, so you can get away with it a little more, as compared say, painting in Clinton Hill, where they might not mind it as much as long as it's pretty things. So, you try to stay closer to neighborhoods like Bushwick, Williamsburg—you know, industrial neighborhoods are great because they're not populated by families. They're filled with young people, and young people usually are into arts or at least appreciate it, so that makes it easier. During the week, its all workers and stuff, and on the weekends, these neighborhoods are semi-desolate.[37]

The connection was a fairly straightforward one, because the owner of the building, being in the business of art supplies, was already predisposed toward art. Having already painted, by his estimate, upwards of 500 murals, Veng had a pitch down pat anyway.

> I've always had a portfolio, which I've shown to them of previous work I've done, and say, "This helps in the removal of graffiti, it does keep the other graffiti writers away because they understand it's the same guys going out trying to paint a wall." Not always, but generally. You know, it looks a lot better than a peach building, some tan building with nothing on it. I can do nice landscapes, animals, and that brings attention to the business as well.[38]

Jonny Seigel, who along with his father Marv owns SoHo Arts Supply and has been at this location since 2007, has a similar recollection. The warehouse's previous location didn't have the kinds of walls amenable to murals.

> **Q:** Why did you say yes?
> **A:** Why not? I thought it would look nice and enhance the building. It gives it some character; it's not so drab.
> **Q:** What did it look like before? Was there anything at all?
> **A:** No, basically you can see if you look at the top, it was just painted one solid color. You can still see along the top of the building.
> **Q:** Was there any other graffiti?
> **A:** There were some tags originally, but once these guys do a mural on it, the guys don't tag. They respect each other, so they won't go over someone else's work.
> **Q:** Was that part of your thinking?
> **A:** Nah, I just thought it'd be cool to have it. Number one, it helps Herb out because it gives exposure to him, and it helps me out in that it makes it a little nicer.[39]

It's not surprising that Seigel would be loyal to a customer who lends an air of coolness to his establishment. SoHo is in the business of selling supplies to the very people who are most likely to gravitate toward the graffiti murals that Robots Will Kill create. Though it is an industrial area, the foot traffic on the block does warrant a small retail storefront for SoHo.Seigel admits as such in conversation, and also exhibits open-mindedness to art that makes the Bushwick/East Williamsburg area an attractive destination for his customers. He said he has a "gentleman's agreement" with Veng and his partner Chris, who come and go and update as they feel necessary; Seigel's only criteria is that whatever they do, it has to "expand the mind," even if it's political in nature. He's not worried about what neighbors might think either.

> **Q:** Have you ever heard from anyone from the city, say the NYPD?
> **A:** Not over here. I mean, we really don't see many cops around here; you don't see much going on.
> **Q:** Do you think that's because you're so isolated over here?

> **A:** I think it's accepted. Number one, it's tasteful, so it only enhances the area. So if it enhances the area, for any property owner, it only gives value to the area. The area itself is a lot of artists around here, so you're not going to have too many people fighting against it. And number two, it's not gang affiliated, where most tagging originally started. There's no bad thing about it. It's almost like opening a garden in an alley. I mean, you're giving beauty to something where there was nothing, so it's a good quality to have.[40]

"It's almost like opening a garden in an alley." I want to highlight this sentiment. Later in our conversation, Seigel contrasted what he was doing on his block to an abandoned building covered in tags that is giving off a distinct message of urban decay. Rather than embrace "where there was nothing," which is an obvious reference to the solid coloring of the building before the murals, he equates the block with the most life-affirming language of a garden. Whether he considers himself as a gardener and the writers of Robots Will Kill as plants is not clear, but clearly the end goal is beautification.

Like Romeo in Inwood, Seigel has shunned the notion promoted by the city that the "social, cultural, and economic composition of the city," in Kramer's words, will benefit by the absence of graffiti. He acknowledges the validity of arguments against allowing buildings to be abandoned and tagged, but embraces a positive use for the technique and motivation behind that tagging.

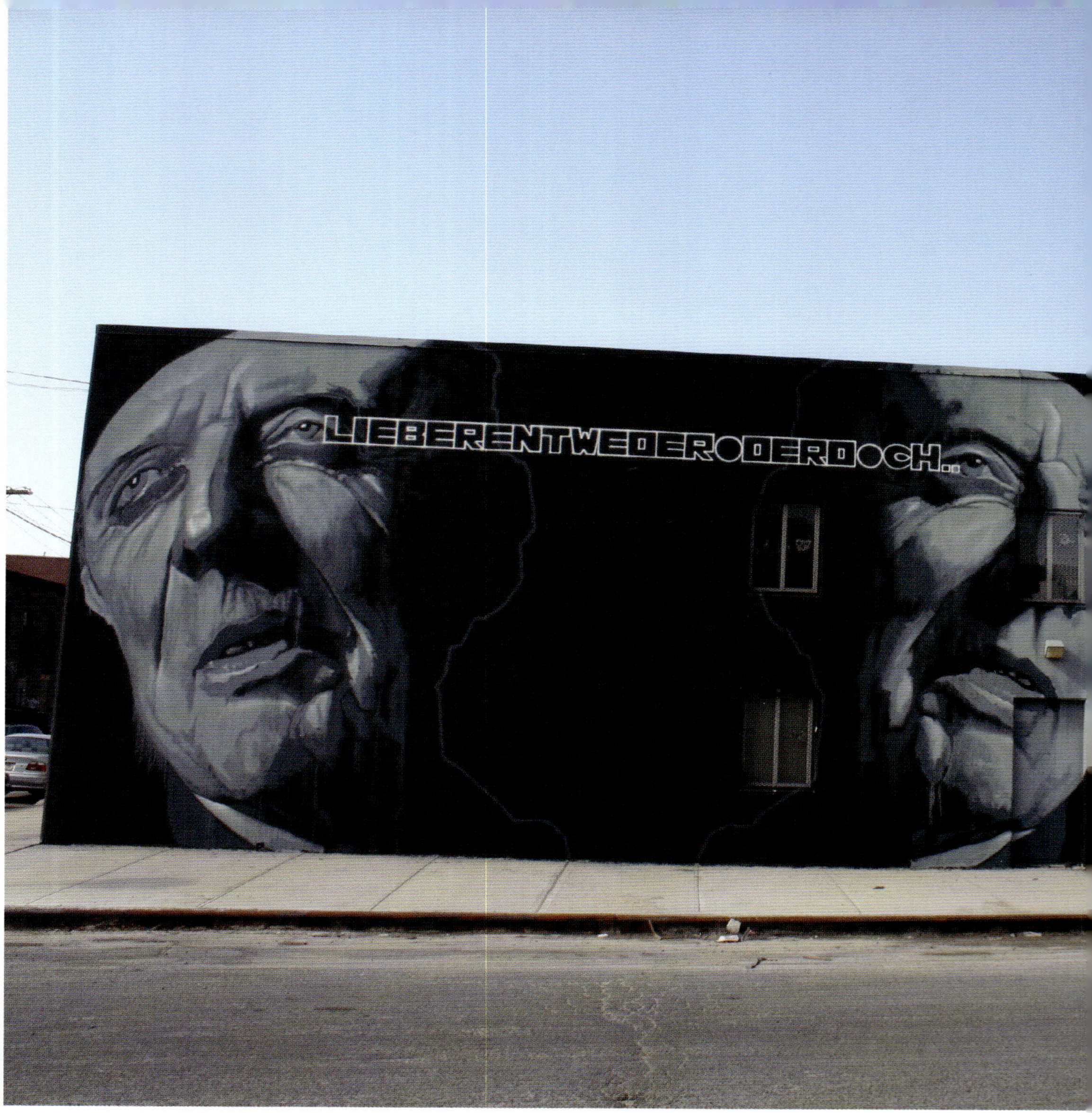

36 Gardner Street, as seen from Ingraham Street, featuring ECB, circa April 2010. Photo by Patrick Verel

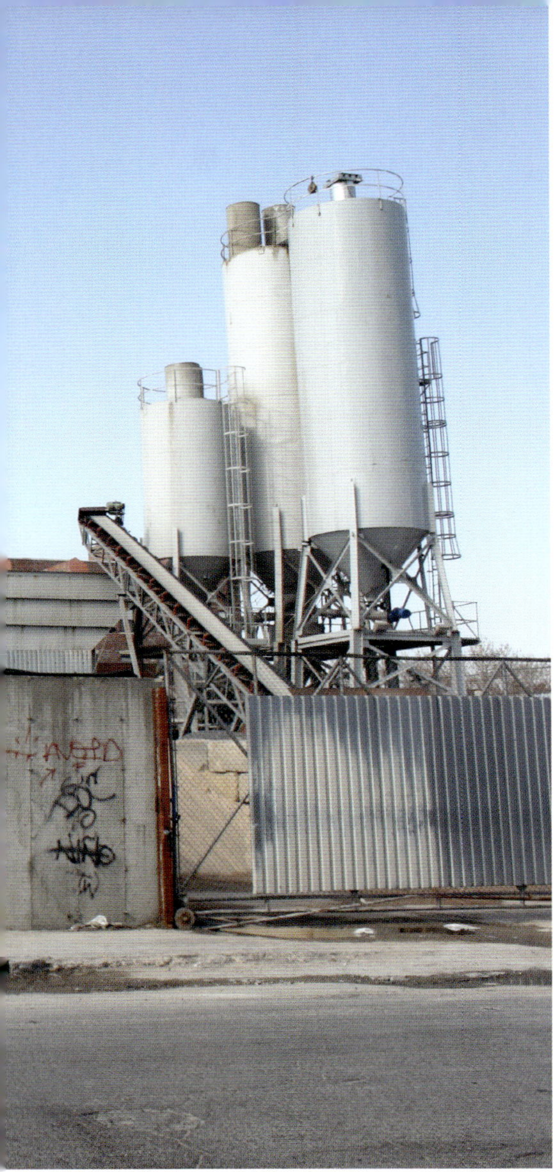

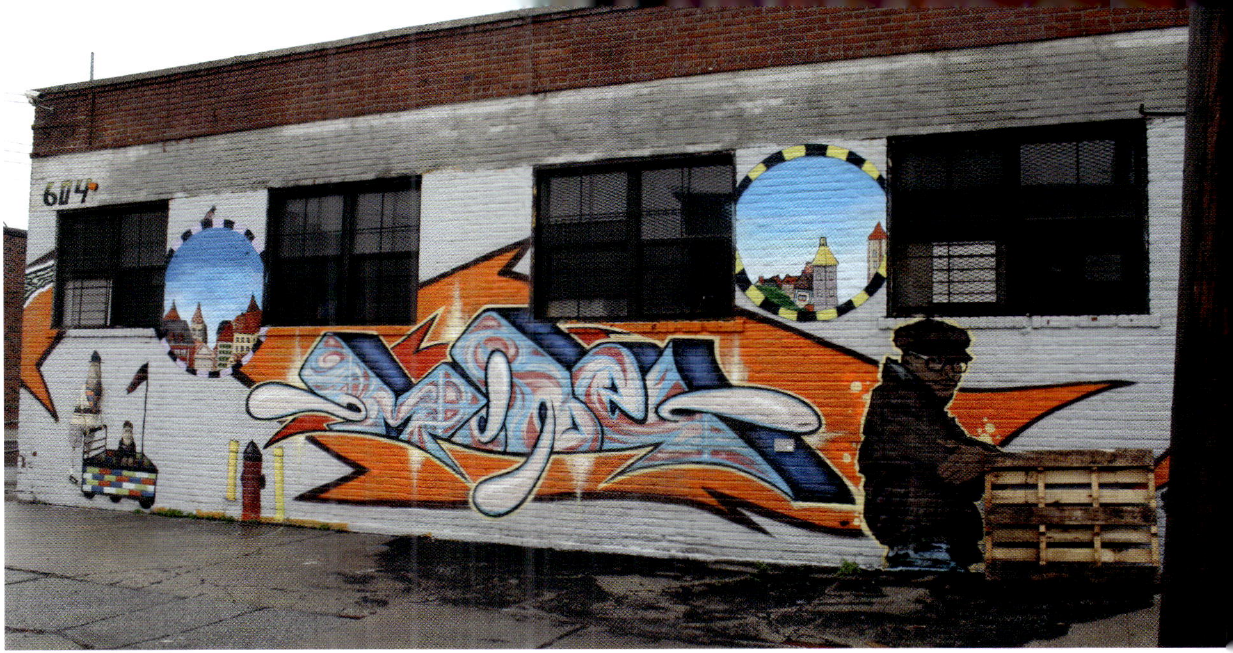

The front of Manhattan Molds and Casts, featuring Veng, Billy Mode and Chris Stain, circa March 2010. Photo by Patrick Verel

Max Brennan, the owner of Manhattan Molds and Casts, has less to gain from having murals on the outside of his shop, which is next door to SoHo Arts. Unlike Seigel's, his business, which revolves around the restoration of ornamental stonework, has no obvious link to Robots Will Kill's creations or the collective's fans. But he too agreed to let them take over his walls around the same time as Seigel. This is also the first time Brennan has owned a building of this kind, and also the first time he'd given permission for a mural. He called it an "over-glorified garage," and noted that Veng would have had a harder time convincing him to grant permission had it been a more attractive building. That permission brings Veng and various friends from the graffiti and street art scene to the building four times a year, and Brennan said he was so impressed, he referred Veng to a real estate agent around the corner on Johnson Street.

> It keeps the building from being tagged. They actually do respect the murals. We used to get a lot of bad graffiti on this building. You can see they'll still graffiti the doors. They'll try to work around it. But there seems

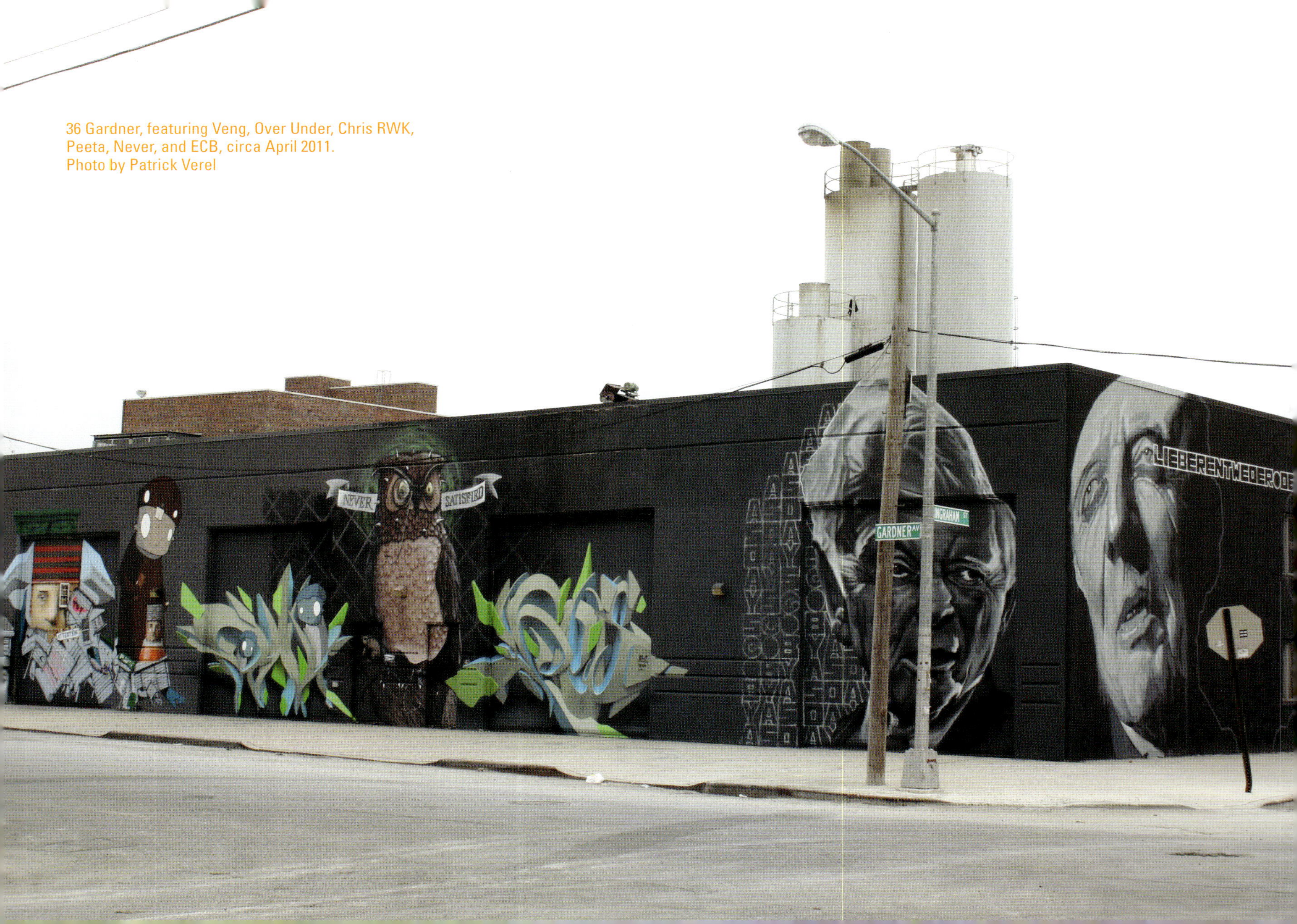

36 Gardner, featuring Veng, Over Under, Chris RWK, Peeta, Never, and ECB, circa April 2011.
Photo by Patrick Verel

to be a bit of honor among thieves. I'm not a big fan of defacing property, particularly. And these guys also have a very creative mindset. They change it often as well. I don't know a whole lot about their modus operandi. I know they've got a tie in with some German guys; I guess they take pictures of it and it gets syndicated somehow, but I've never asked Herb how he makes a living doing this, or if he makes a living doing it. But it's a pretty creative crew that shows up every now and then.[41]

Although his line of work is in the creation of castings for architectural restoration, Brennan clearly understands the phenomenon of graffiti, and of all the property owners I talked with, he perhaps best articulated the rationale for encouraging mural-making as a tool for fighting vandalism: Evolution. At one point in our conversation, I asked him: With so many high-caliber productions in one place, does he worry that other graffiti writers might travel to the area to see them, and then leave their own mark on other buildings in the area? He laughed the notion off, declaring that there are already so many random taggers running around New York City, they don't need any encouragement. No, what he hopes is that the productions visually goad them to "enlarge their vision, and move beyond pedestrian scrawls."

> It's one thing to have your tag, and that's another thing to generate kind of a whole allegorical, weird universe, which is what these guys create. Which is kind of interesting. The tags, you know, some of them are ok, but most of them are calligraphic scrawls that don't do a whole lot for me. I know it's a whole sub culture, and it has a lot to do with, as I understand it, the ubiquitousness of your tag and how dangerous the location is gives you a certain ranking in the sub culture. But how far can you go with that? Like everything else, there are good artists, and there are not so good artists, and in the graffiti world, these guys really have their shit together.[42]

Brennan is also very cognizant of the role that graffiti murals like these play in changing the character of the neighborhood. Like tattoos, cafes, and illegally converted loft apartments, the graffiti murals are tangible signs of the arrival of a new "tribe," as he calls them, of young residents who are gentrifying the area.

> It's certainly attracting enough hipsters that they want to hang out here and do it. I mean I know [murals are] in the Bronx. I've read articles about these wastelands where they've done murals, but it's a big blank canvas, and why not? But here, it's two blocks from the L train, the umbilical cord into Manhattan, so it's convenient, and it makes sense in that respect.[43]

The question of whether murals contribute to the gentrification of a neighborhood is a legitimate one, as one man's progress might be construed as another man's threat to his ability to afford his home. The possibility that murals might be a warning flare of sorts that artists, who are the vanguard of gentrification, have settled in, is not without merit. In fact, when Veng speaks admiringly about how friendly industrial neighborhoods like Bushwick and Williamsburg are, it's also worth noting what was left out. Like those two places, Sunset Park, to give an example, is a large industrial neighborhood in Brooklyn that is also accessible via the subway. There are, so far as I can tell, no major graffiti murals underway there; coincidentally there is little that is "hip" there either—such as bars, galleries, or restaurants catering to an upwardly mobile, artistically inclined population.

Of course, the primary reason gentrification stirs up emotions is that gentrification is by definition "the reinvestment of capital in the urban centre, which is designed to produce space for a more affluent class of people than currently occupies that space."[44] What complicates a potential "local resident versus newcomer" dynamic in Bushwick is the fact that, in a globalized city like New York, local building ownership is far from guaranteed. Veng's experience is instructive.

> Trying to find new spots, I could spend weeks trying to track down an owner. Sometimes you get the owner there, but

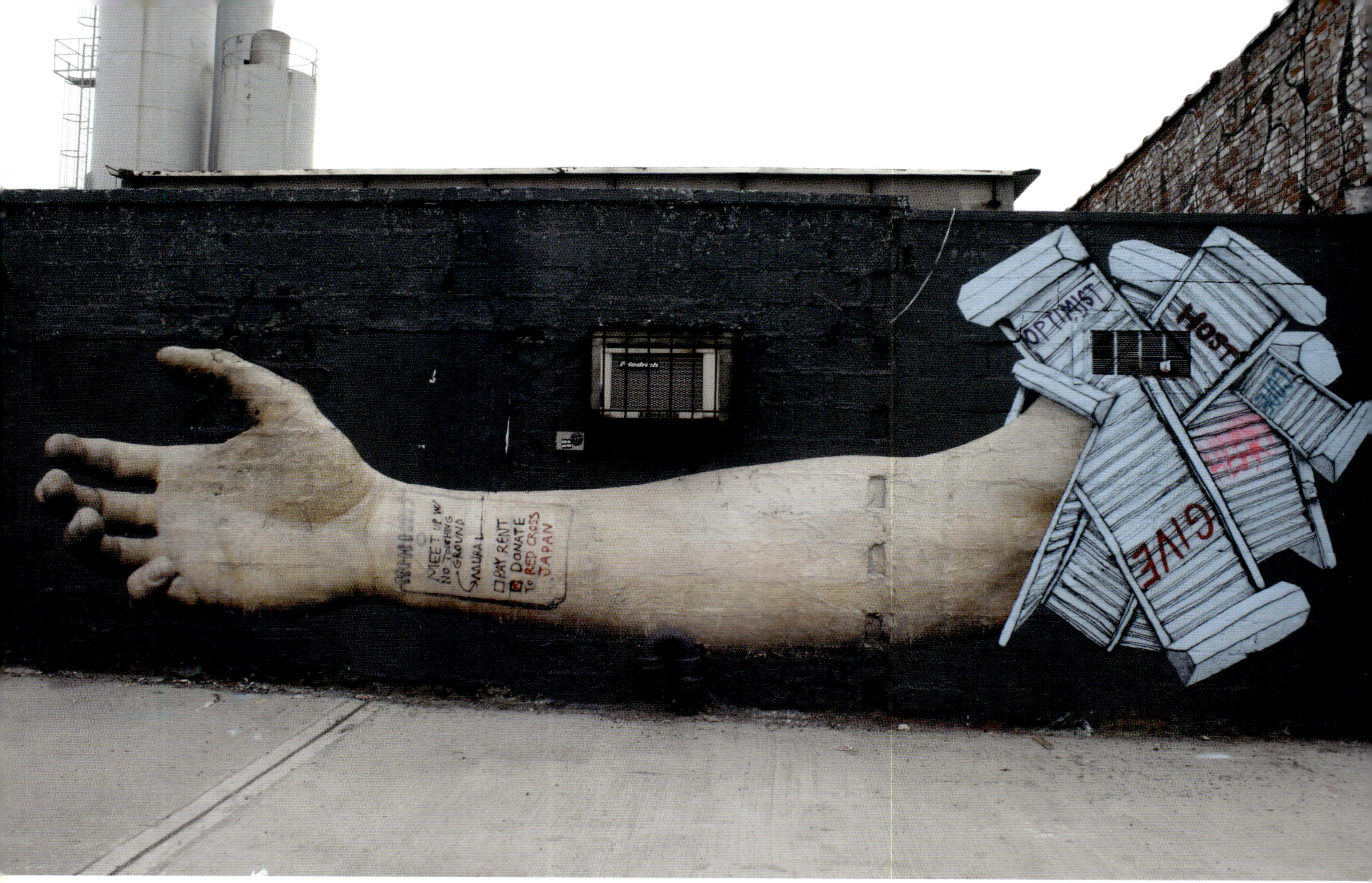

Just behind Manhattan Molds and Casts on Johnson Ave., featuring Over Under, circa April 2011. Photo by Patrick Verel

then you have to get the landlord's permission, and that's a nightmare in itself half the time. The worst case scenarios are where you've been given permission by an owner, the landlord lives in Colorado, and decides to come back for whatever reason, sees all this stuff on his building, throws a fit, and you've lost a spot. It's happened to some guys who don't even live here, but they don't want it.

A lot of buildings are owned by people who are out of state. It's crazy. You can go in and ask and the guy who will be like 'Yeah, it's ok, but the landlord lives in Oregon.' How am I supposed to persuade someone in Oregon to let me paint his building in Bushwick? It's crazy sometimes. [45]

As Jonny Seigel and Max Brennan make clear, this is not the case everywhere, and in fact this gets to an important point: The local nature of many of these collaborations roots them firmly, as Benjamin would say, "within the tradition from which they sprang," namely New York City, circa 1970. Given the fact that Bushwick is currently in the throes of gentrification, it should be interesting to see if Seigel and Brennan are able to look at the trends in the real estate market and see the possibility to extract, in Harvey's words, "monopoly rent" by selling to a new owner, thus endangering a relationship that lends uniqueness to the city.

After all, if there is criticism of the work, Veng says it's rarely for the content of the pieces. Rather, he feels a stigmatism revolves around the spray can, which is automatically linked to vandalism.

> If I'd been out there doing it with a brush, which I do use a brush for some stuff, you can probably do it in the middle of the day without even worrying about it. But the minute you whip out spray cans, in certain neighborhoods, everyone takes a different view of it sometimes. They still think its New York, circa 1980.[46]

As an example of symbolic interactionism, this is almost too perfect. People act toward things—in this case spray cans—based on the meaning those things have for them, which is vandalism and crime. This meaning is derived through social interaction—seeing the mural created—and modified through interpretation, in this case past experience with crime.

So what do folks who aren't connected to the property or the art world think? Jamar, a black man in his 50s who has lived and worked nearby for thirty-eight years, was effusive in praise for the work, even as he disparaged regular graffiti.

> **Q:** Have you seen this mural before?
> **A:** Yeah, I've seen it before. I seen when they was making it, doing it, and you know, it's nice to me.
> **Q:** So you're a fan?
> **A:** Half and half. Sometimes it don't look good on everybody's buildings. Especially my father; my father's got so much graffiti on his building. It's crazy.
> **Q:** I assume it's not like this.
> **A:** Nah, not like that. I wish it were like that.[47]

Jamar doesn't dismiss tags and throw-ups as merely vandalism, and even if he doesn't count himself as a fan, he says it's art. So it's perhaps unsurprising that when given the option of a 36 Gardner Street scrubbed clean or graced with a mural, he chooses the latter.

> It's better than a blank wall because when you walk by, you don't see nothing. You see graffiti; you can tell this person's sad. Now you can look at something and go, "Oh, that's a nice job." You see a blank wall, you'll be like, "Shit, it's just a blank wall." There's nothing to think about. [48]

There's *nothing* to think about. If there is a more perfect phrase that sums up the state of a freshly buffed industrial building, I have yet to find it. In fact, it could be said that that sentiment is what unites Deirdre, a white woman in her 30s, with Jamar. Although she lives in Clinton Hill, Deirdre rents studio space nearby, where she works on what she jokingly calls "boring, abstract paintings" that are nothing like the work that Veng and his cohorts embrace. She would not hang Robots Will Kill works in her apartment, she said, but said it's nice to see works outside institutions and people dedicated to making them over a long period of time. In this way, she echoed Jamar's assertion that it provides something to think about, as well as Veng's selling point that it makes the building look "better."

Deirdre does draw some distinctions between the places where murals should and shouldn't be located. When asked if she agreed that a mural is better than a blank wall, she demurred.

> Let's put it that way. So I'm not going to say it's better. It breaks up the monotony. The city planning around here is so haphazard, that it's like another part of the collage. But yeah, I wouldn't want it like, it would be a little bit overwhelming. I mean, you hear about cities…I feel like in Brazil I heard about there just being so much graffiti, it's overwhelming. Here it's like…there could be more, and I wouldn't be upset, but I wouldn't want like this entire block to be like this. Well, maybe this block, but the back and forth is nice.[49]

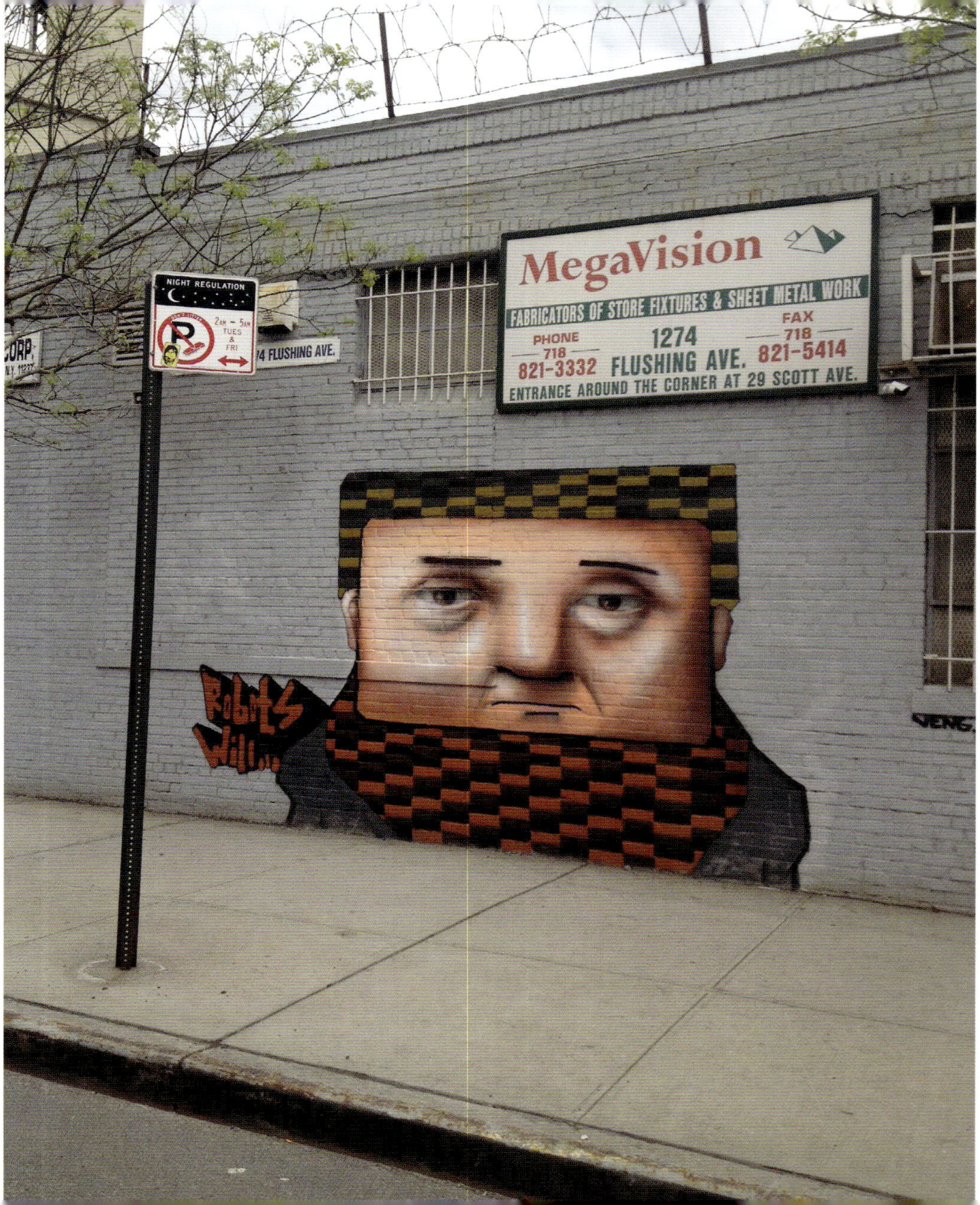

Veng, a block away on a wall shared by artists from the Bushwick Collective, circa May 2014. Photo by Patrick Verel

This could be construed as a criticism of Robots Will Kill taking over almost half a city block, but I don't think it is. Rather, it's an acknowledgement that space matters—murals here, but not necessarily everywhere. The key to understanding why that might be is Deirdre's reference to the city's planning as "haphazard." This is borne out by not only casual observations such as these but also the fact that the city has never in its history actually completed a central plan. Deirdre's musing about graffiti murals taking over the area has actually come to fruition, but not strictly because of Robots Will Kill's efforts. In 2012, Bushwick native Joseph Ficalora started the Bushwick Collective just three blocks west of 36 Gardner; it has grown at a furious rate, and now encompasses more than half a dozen blocks. Tellingly, Ficalora got the idea to invite street artists to paint his own building when he got fed up with buffing tags from them.[50]

Finally, there's Jaquay, an eighteen-year-old black man who moved to the area in 2009 from Pennsylvania. His perspective is important because it is teenagers who have traditionally been drawn to tagging. He is attracted to it, but he's well aware of the penalties that await him. "I could get locked up for that," he says. "I'm staying away from that. That's a first degree, so I'm staying away from that. I'm drawing in books." Murals like the one on Gardner Street, on the other hand, are the kind of thing he aspires to do some day. In the meantime, he also appreciates that there is something, rather than nothing.

> It's better than blank wall because a blank wall is plain. You want something to look at when you're walking. If you don't have no phone or nothing to do, there's murals all around to look at. And then the next one, you can try to be like, "Yo, I can be like that sometimes."[51]

{3}

CASE STUDY

The Bronx

The Most Amazing Art You'll Never See

Hunts Point, a predominantly industrial neighborhood in the South Bronx, is full of extreme juxtapositions. On the one hand, its location situates its 46,000 residents squarely in New York's 16th Congressional District, which is the poorest congressional district in the country.[52] Furthermore, it sits on a peninsula that juts into the Long Island Sound; water surrounds it on three sides; the elevated Bruckner Expressway is the fourth border. Finally, the two subway stations that serve the neighborhood, at Hunts Point Avenue and Longwood Avenue, are on the other side of the Bruckner, a large, dirty, forbidding structure whose main thoroughfares, access roads, and entrance ramps are often choked with cars and trucks.

But while Hunts Point residents may be resource poor, they are street art rich, in part thanks to men like Hector "Nicer" Nazario. The lifelong Bronx resident is a founding member of the TATS (Top Artistic Talent) Cru, along with Wilfredo "Bio" Feliciano. In one of the grimiest parts of New York City, they have turned their love of graffiti murals into a successful business venture, parlaying credibility built up from years of tagging and mural making into what they refer to as "guerrilla outdoor media advertising." On the website tatscru.net, they advertise custom murals, live painting and demos, outdoor media and promotional campaigns, custom vinyl banners, custom canvases, and workshops.

On the corner of Spofford Avenue and Drake Street, group members have taken the outdoor media aspect of the business and let their creativity blossom. Borax Paper Products occupies the better part of the block bordered by Spofford,

The front entrance to Borax Paper, circa October 2010. Photo by Patrick Verel

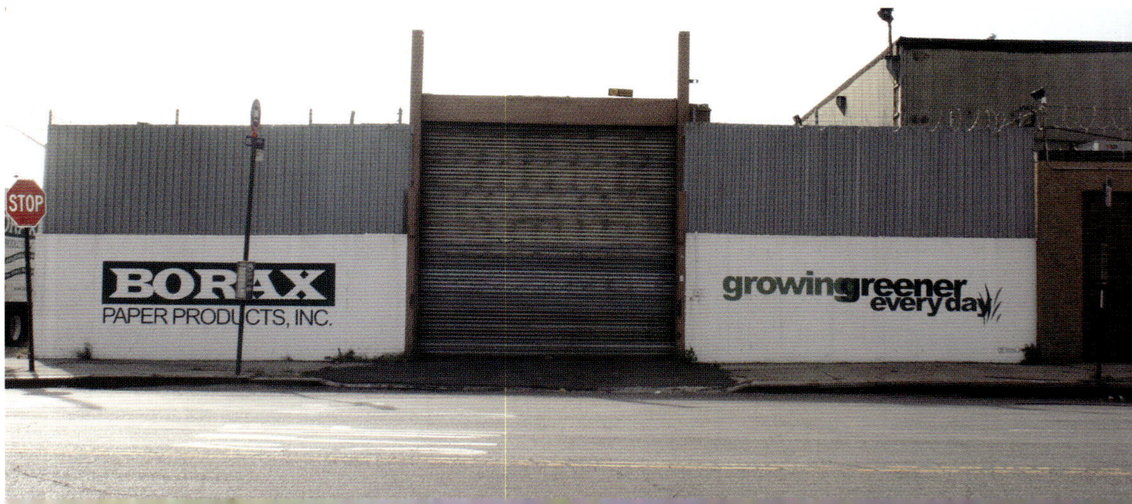

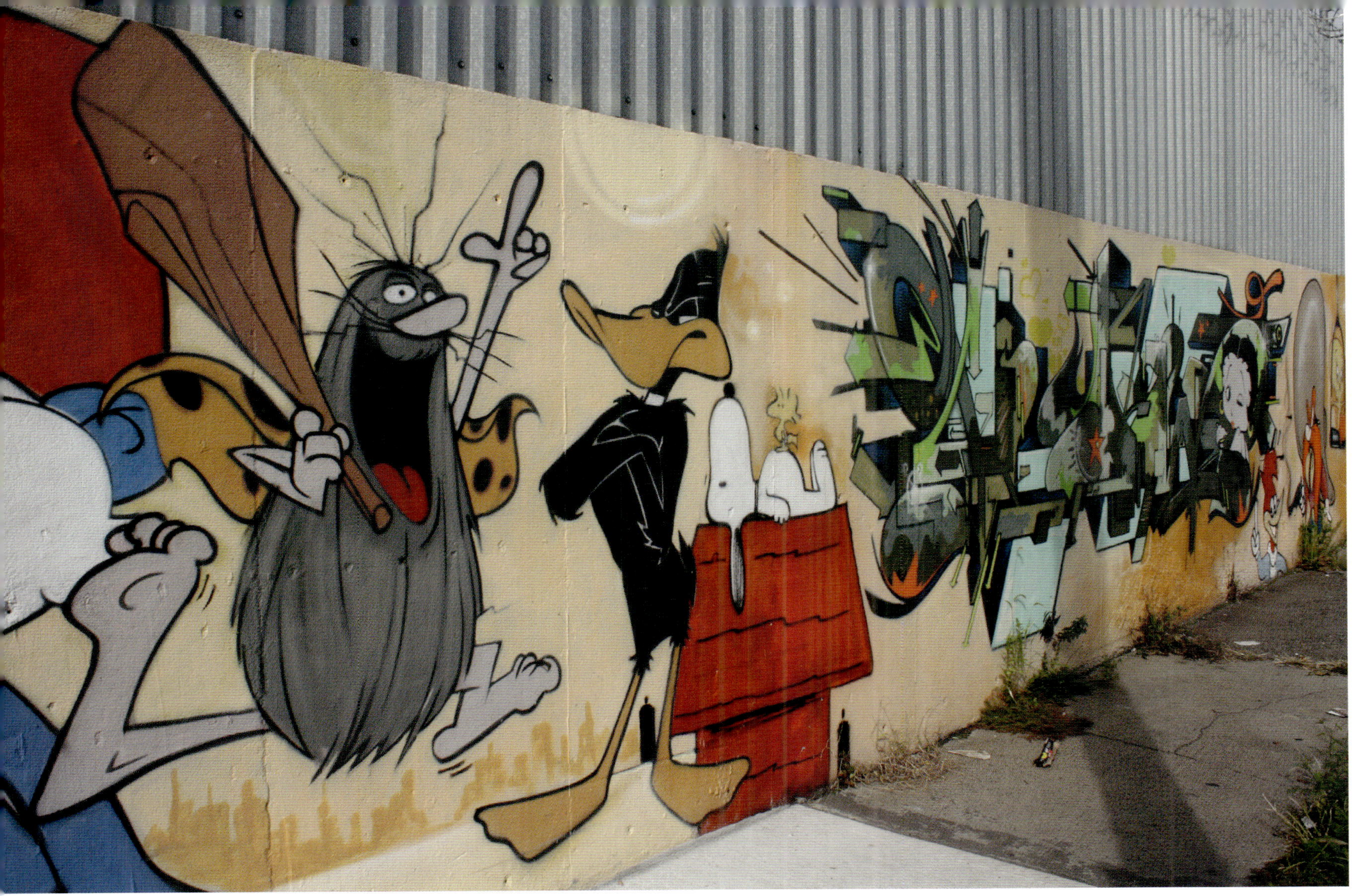

Captain Caveman, Daffy Duck, and Snoopy, by How, on Edgewater Road circa October 2010. Photo by Patrick Verel

Edgewater, Randall, and Drake, and although the face it presents to the world on Spofford is a straightforward sign with the company's name and logo, "Growing greener every day," there is a very different view on the North/South running streets of Edgewater and Drake.

Edgewater, which is a main thoroughfare for the Hunts Point Produce Market, is replete with cartoon characters such as Felix the Cat, Papa Smurf, and Yogi Bear, as well as traditional graffiti productions. Drake, on the other side of the building, is smaller and less trafficked, which is actually a shame, because that's where the real show can be found. The entire length of the building is covered with graffiti murals, including a massive, two-story-high, black, white, and red abstract piece by the twin artists How and Nosm, who are also Tats Cru members. The fence of a scrap yard across the street is likewise covered by graffiti murals, making this an especially brightly colored island in a very grey and black landscape.

Nicer, who spoke to me at the Tats Cru's office about a block or so away from the Bruckner, started painting subways when he was a teenager, but he estimates he started painting legally in 1988, when he asked the owner of a Fedco supermarket on Intervale and Fox Street if he could paint his wall. Very gradually, he and his friends got used to the idea of painting in front of people in the daylight, instead of in darkened tunnels and train yards.

> It was kind of like, the reality of life bit us in the ass. We were starting families, and we ended up having to feed ourselves, and you're no longer in this mom and pop setting where they financed everything. You're a young adult now. You have to fend for yourself. We started working 9 to 5s, and that was like a big growing up moment for us.[53]

The Tats Cru is as good an example as any of how graffiti has evolved. The Mural Kings, as they dub themselves, found a way to harness what was written off in many quarters as simple vandalism and turn it into a legitimate for-profit enterprise. Nicer feels that new reality still hasn't taken hold in New York City though, and echoes Veng's observation that the culprit is the spray can.

> A vandal can grab a spray can and do a swastika on a synagogue, or tombstones, or deface a hospital or some sacred place, and he did it with malicious intent. It could be just a kid that found a spray can, who's rebellious at the moment. He doesn't necessarily have to be a practitioner of the art form, but because of the medium that he used, he's considered a graffiti vandal.
>
> So now we use the same medium. The same tool that he used to destroy something, we'll create a portrait, or some kind of piece of art, and what ends up happening is they end up getting clumped into the same group and category. A lot of people don't have the open-mindedness of trying to filter out the good and the bad. They automatically look at the group and say they all shouldn't be respected.[54]

Nicer said they were interested in the Borax Paper building as much because of its dimensions as for the fact that its location, with its paucity of foot traffic, makes painting without interruption easier. Eight times out of ten, he said property owners they approach for permission will say yes, because they tend to be buildings whose owners are having a hard time keeping them clean, and when Nicer makes a pitch, he says they'll do something large and colorful, keep the area around the murals clean, and bring more attention to the business in the building. Tats Cru covers the cost of the supplies themselves, and the worst-case scenario is they'll paint over it if the owner finds it offensive. This, he noted, is where having a business comes in hand.

> [I say,] at the end of the day, we're not that hard to find. We have an office, we have a website, we're listed in the book. So it ain't like you're gonna have a hard time finding us. Because they're letting us use the space, it's usually a win-win situation for them.[55]

Being local also helps. Roy Mangione, the director of operations at Borax, said an employee who lives in the neighborhood referred him to

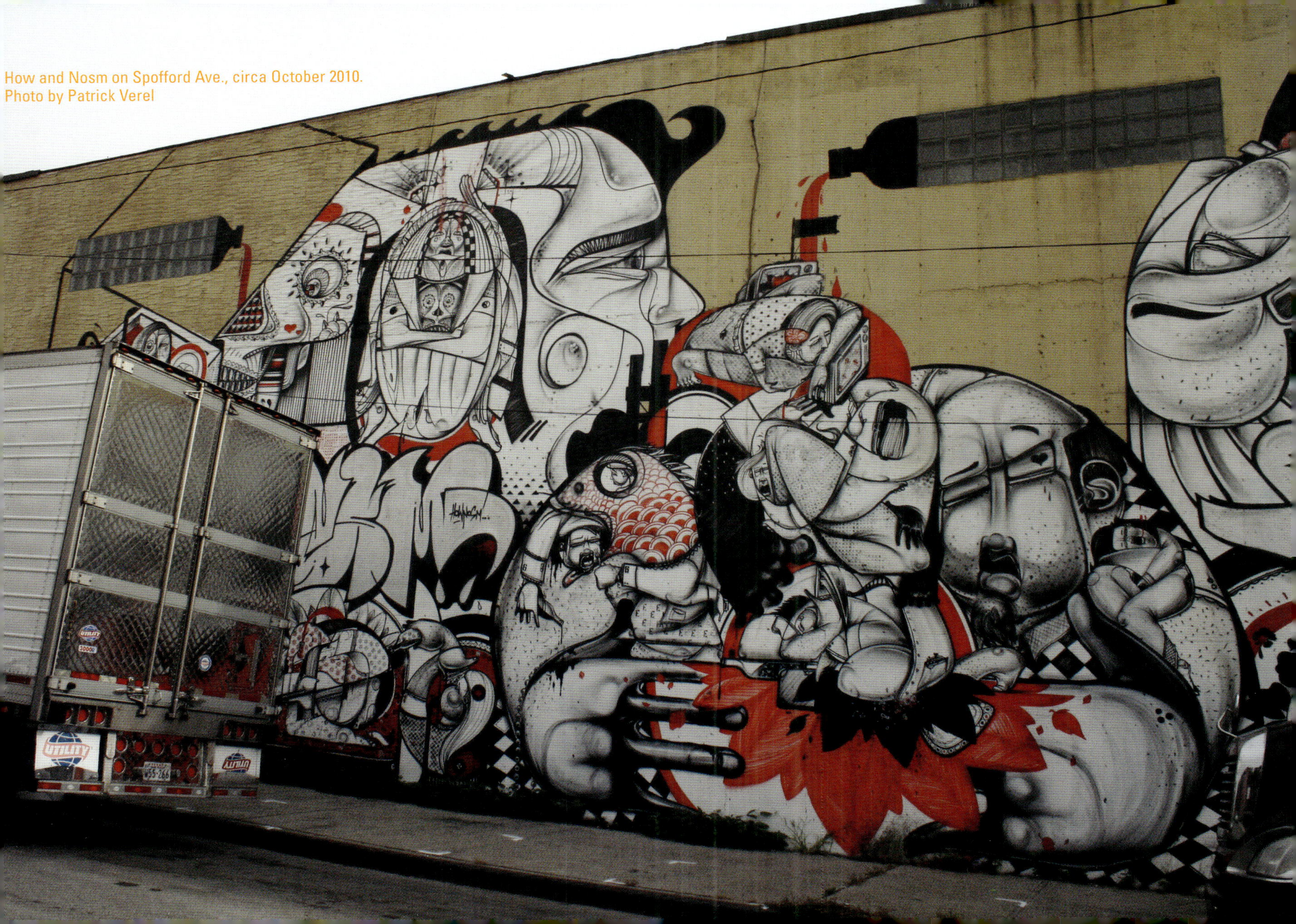

How and Nosm on Spofford Ave., circa October 2010.
Photo by Patrick Verel

the Tats Cru. The problem, he said, was the building was "getting all marked up and tagged by every miscreant."

> We gave them cart blanche on what to do as long as it was in good taste, and one of the first things they did was the cartoon wall on Halleck, and it looked really, really nice. Then we told them, "OK guys, now you can do Drake." So our landlord called us and said, "You know, you got graffiti on your building," and I said, "No, it's not graffiti, it's art." I said we're not going to get fined for it.[56]

In addition to the landlord, Mangione had to convince Mark Borak, the owner of Borax Paper, to allow the Tats Cru to paint the building. Before that, Mangione had to assign the task of painting over tags to one of his drivers, and although the cost of paint was minimal, it was still wasting the time of a worker who could have been doing something else. Now he doesn't have to worry about it.

> As long as the landlord's happy with it, I'm happy with it. Everything else is good. They did a nice job. My daughter is eleven. She thought the cartoon wall was great. I always drive around Drake to see what they do or what they've changed. One day it'll be one thing, the next day they'll have done the whole top to bottom on one portion of it. It's pretty cool.[57]

Mangione's perspective is important for another reason. When asked if he thought the city of New York was supportive of these sorts of endeavors, he volunteered that a friend is on the NYPD's vandal squad. When he asked his friend how he could catch the people who were tagging his building, Mangione said he was told that cops were not arresting taggers in the Bronx, because the district attorney isn't interested in prosecuting them. Is this really true? I don't know, but the fact is that Mangione is under the impression that he is alone in his quest to keep the property free of vandalism. The Tats Cru is part of that equation now. It's a state that Harvey would not be shocked to hear, as one could make the case that in New York City, industrial-zoned space, even in Hunts Point, is "monopoly rent deferred." Therefore, the city has less interest in responding to the needs of its citizens.

Mark Borak, who said he'll sometimes take visitors such as vendors, customers, or bankers out to the murals to show them off, echoes Mangione's comments. He also suggested during my visit that I be sure to view the New York City skyline that was painted on a wall next to a loading dock facing Edgewater; it was something that his warehouse manager was inspired to paint after the Tats Cru did their murals. Borak said he was unfamiliar with the graffiti removal programs run by the city and viewed his support of murals as a form of community outreach. The local nature of that support is what makes it so effective.

> I think it's important to support the community. These are local guys, local artists, they take pride. I think that because they're local, it's respected. So nobody messes with it. If somebody from out of town came in, who knows what would happen. So they leave it. It's respected.[58]

The only pressure on property owners in Hunts Point, given its location, is to make sure their buildings are adequate for the businesses they house; unlike in Bushwick, gentrification is nonexistent. In some ways, this epitomizes the way that Hunts Point is afflicted with the opposite of Harvey's concept of "surplus capital." Capital is invested in the area, of course, but not to such a degree that it precludes projects that are essentially art for arts' sake. This is a far cry from say, 5 Pointz, the late graffiti-covered warehouse in Queens, which I will discuss later.

Which isn't to say that the murals haven't benefitted the company in terms of external publicity. Mangione showed me a *Daily News* story on the murals, and just as Manhattan Molds and Casts's neighbor in Brooklyn asked if the Robots Will Kill crew would paint his building, so too did the owner of the scrap yard across the street from Borax offer up his fence. Mangione is certainly a fan.

> They're doing the junk yard now, because they're making them aware, you know? It looks nice. I mean, it does. Better than, you know, somebody's initials, or, you know, something

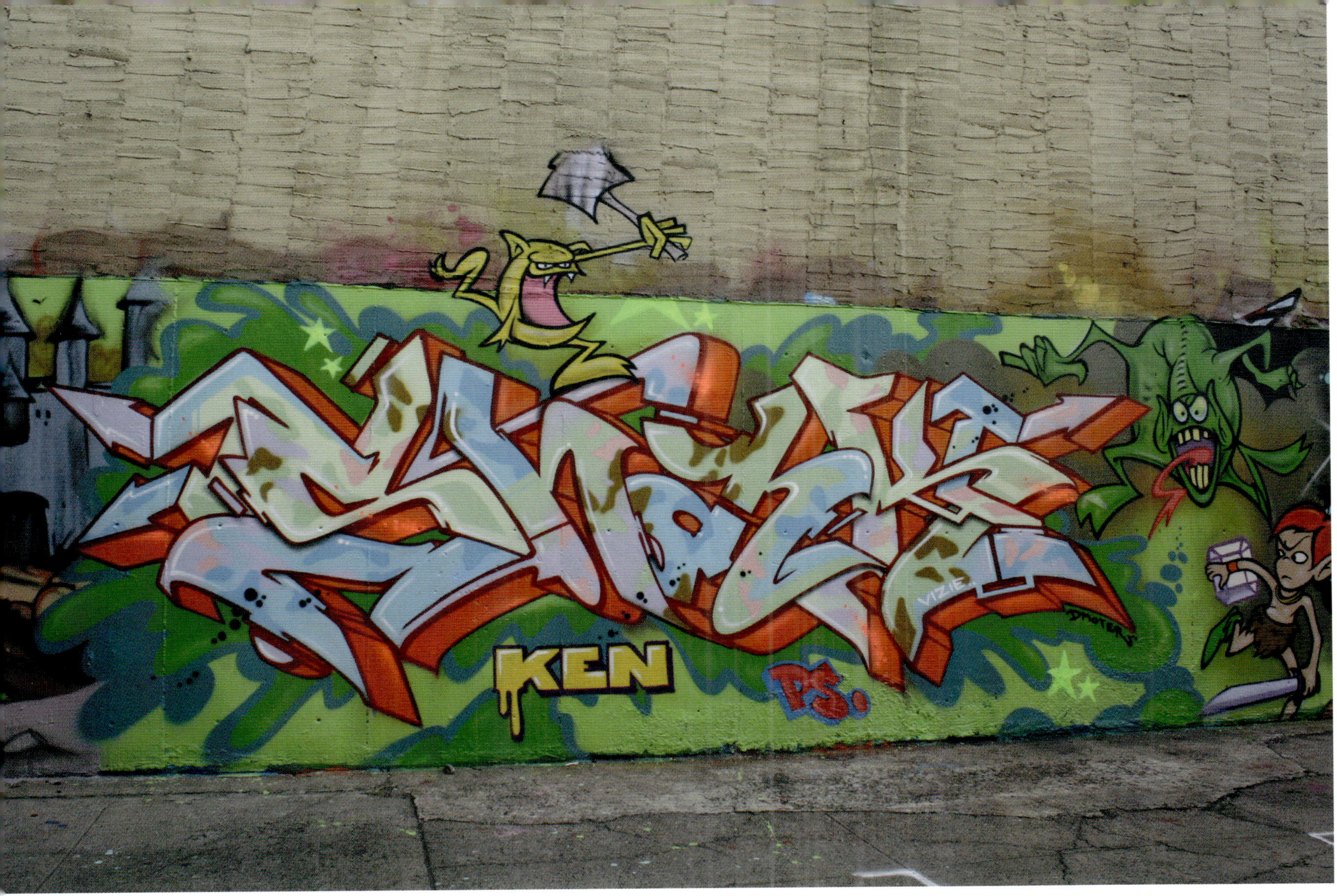

Shank piece by Dmote on Spofford Ave., circa October 2010. Photo by Patrick Verel

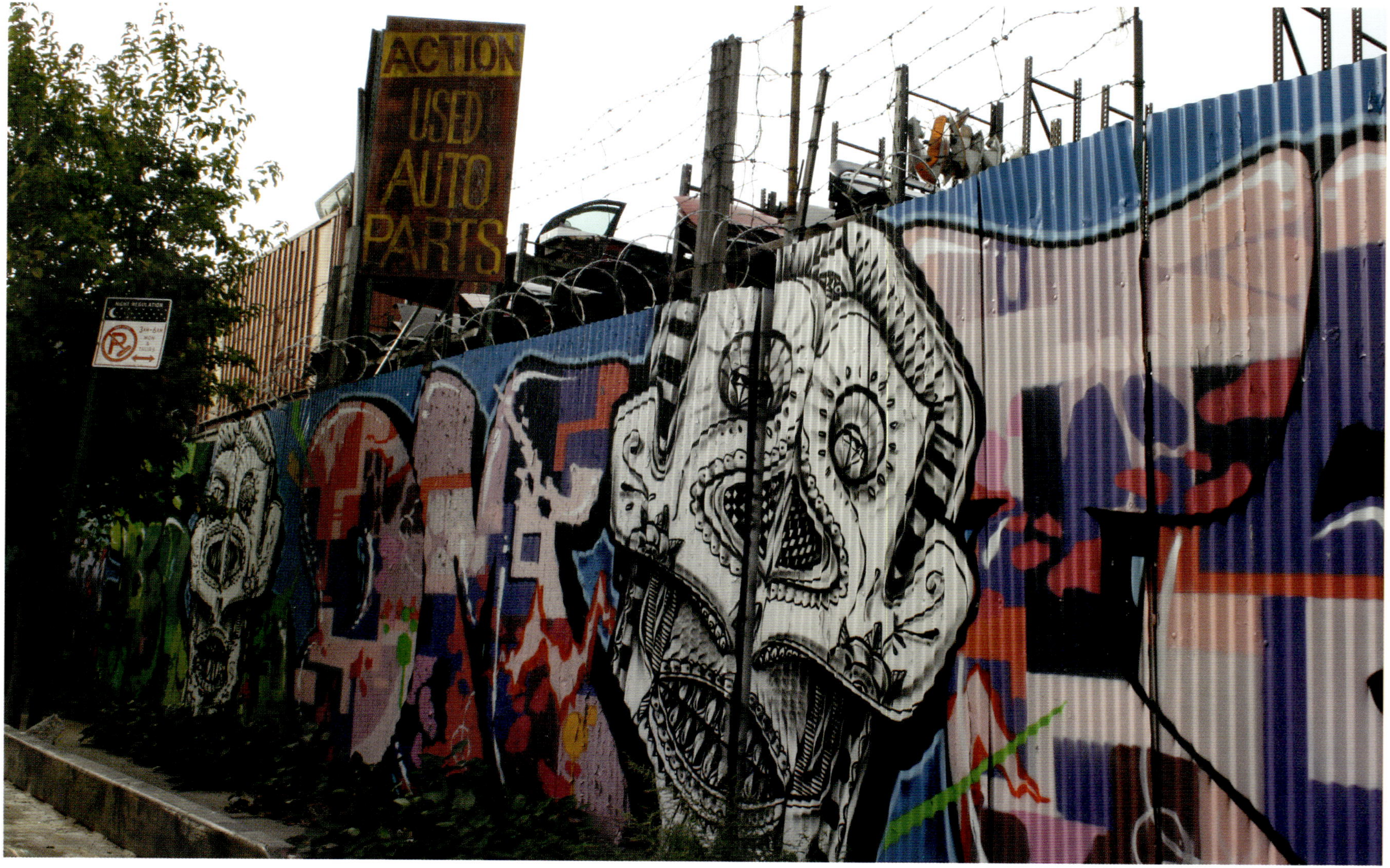

A Bio and Dmote piece across the street from Borax Paper, circa October 2010. Photo by Patrick Verel

> ridiculous. These guys are artists, man. I mean, you gotta see these guys work. I was out there for half an hour, in amazement at what they were able to create, with paint cans and stencils and…they have a whole toolbox full of stuff that they bring. It's pretty cool.[59]

Because Borax is in an industrial area, neighbors are few and far between, beyond the occasional tractor-trailer rig rumbling by on its way to or from the Hunts Point Terminal Market. On the day I visited, truck drivers Reynaldo and Frank were the only neighbors to be found. Both were parked on Drake Street near the How Nosm mural, waiting for the call to return to the market for a fresh load of produce. Frank had come up from South Texas for the first time in five years; although Hunts Point was a regular stop for six years, he'd recently been driving to New Jersey. His impression of the murals was that they "express the inner-most being of the people drawing them." He was less sanguine about tagging.

> I believe it's kind of like destroying property, you know? taking advantage of other people's property. You got logos saying about the businesses and you got all these people coming over and just painting and taking advantage of the walls. That's what I believe. It expresses who they really are, too, but I believe they shouldn't do it. If they want to do that, they should start doing it more or less like in, how can I say this…you know, I mean, get themselves in some art class or something, you know what I'm saying, instead of taking advantage of other people's walls.[60]

Reynaldo concurred, and although neither was especially verbose, the men did recognize that the murals were a topic worthy of discussion, which would not be the case if the block was flanked merely by plain brick walls and rusted corrugated metal. For at least a few hours, the way station for these long-distance truckers was an outdoor gallery of sorts.

The notion of this work taking on the appearance of an outdoor gallery is one that is very familiar to Nicer. Three days before I met him at the Point, I attempted to visit him at the site of another mural he was working on, at Whitlock Avenue and East 165th Street in Port Morris. Like Hunts Point, Port Morris is close to a highway, in this case the Sheridan Expressway, which splits off from the Bruckner Expressway only a few blocks to the south. The corner of 165th and Whitlock is also where the 6 train lurches out from underground and travels the rest of the way through the Bronx above ground. As it rises, there is a short stretch where the tracks are even with Whitlock; needless to say, it is rarely tranquil here.

I missed Nicer on this occasion due to a misunderstanding, but the visit did afford me a view of Project A.C.T., a three- block-long endeavor whose highlight is a six-panel mural that completely covers the two-story brick building facing the rising subway tracks. In addition to another one of How Nosm's pieces, the building sports a fully realized subway (with tags on the car sides, no less) rising from the ground onto a curving elevated track and a bright red "I [heart] the Bronx" framed against names of twenty-five or so neighborhoods in the Bronx. This latter image has become so popular, it was featured in an ad for Fiat featuring Jennifer Lopez. Tats Cru weren't asked for permission for use of the image in the ad and were only compensated after they threatened legal action against Fiat and the advertising agency that create the spot.[61]

It's all part of an effort to combat tagging through mural making, except in this case, it was spearheaded by T. K. Singleton, the community initiatives coordinator for Bronx Community Solutions. Singleton, who worked out of an office at the Bronx Criminal Courthouse by Yankee Stadium (she has since left), said the area had been a target of vandals who would tag the walls mere days after they'd been buffed. Instead of having cleanup crews visit it again and again, she convinced her superiors to let her put $4,000 worth of paint and supplies toward a series of murals by the Tats Cru and two other graffiti crews.

> Four years of doing these anti-graffiti cleanup projects and it still [didn't] look like we were actually doing anything on that particular

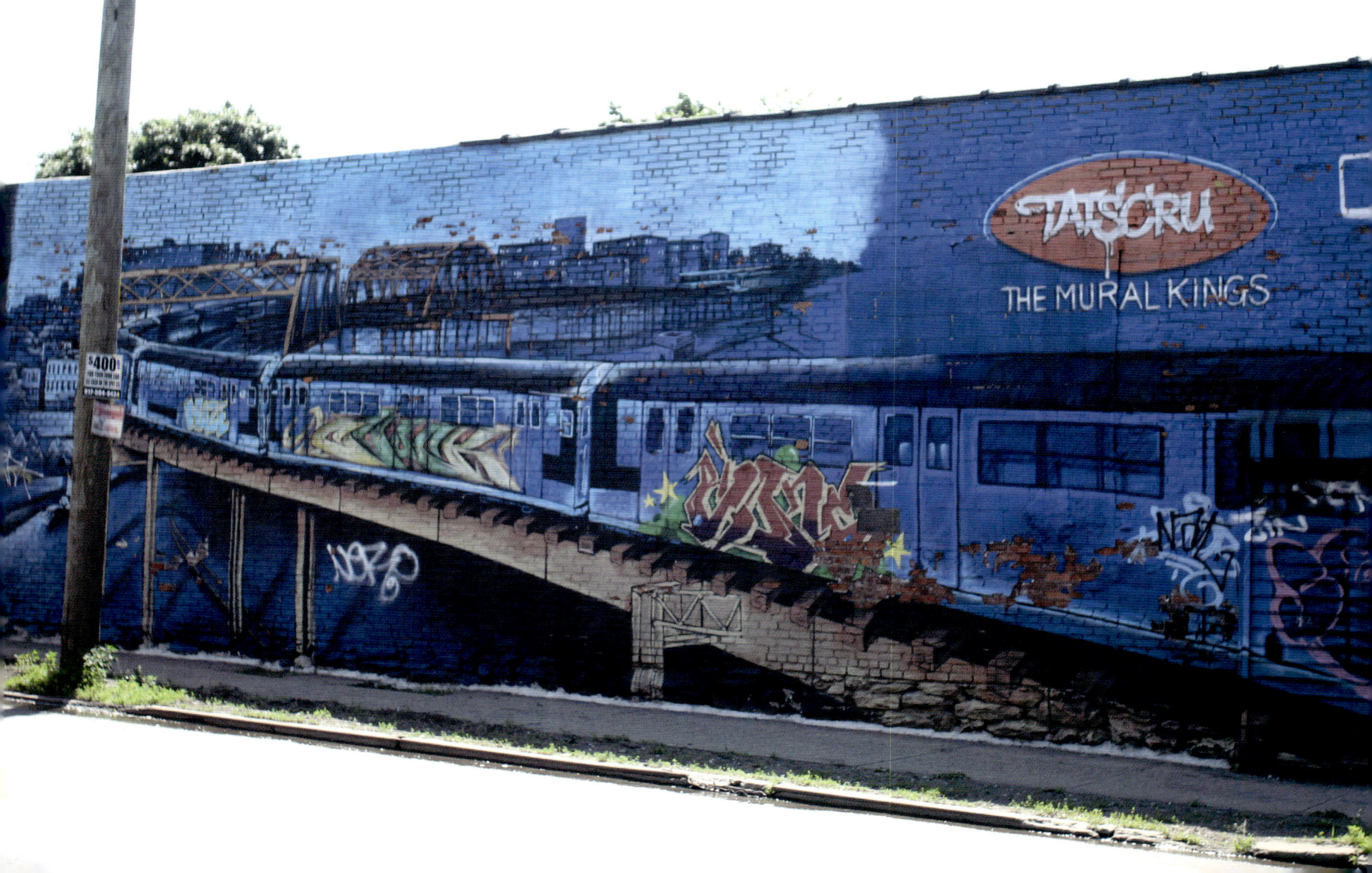

A Nicer and Bio piece on Whitlock Ave., circa June 2014. Photo by Patrick Verel

> area. [So I thought,] why not do something innovative and new like a graffiti mural project that can be respected with other artists and also the community can love it, and it can be an addition to an area that I believe, is a very cultural area?[61]

Singleton viewed the project as both a practical solution to an intractable problem and a way to boost the cultural capital of the neighborhood. She's a self-described fan of the Tats Cru, and although it took her three months to make this project happen, when we spoke, she was hopeful hopeful that she'd be able to do it again in another area. It couldn't be just anywhere though.

> It's the areas where most people will just say, 'You just can't do anything about graffiti,' like the high traffic areas, subway stations. Any street that's along those particular places where there's high visibility for a person's name, you're going to find a million and one kids willing to bomb to get their names up.[63]

Part of the reason Singleton said this area was so appealing was the fact that it could benefit the most from the increased foot traffic that the undertaking would generate. Ideally, that will make it a safer neighborhood and boost local business, too. Artists advertise their newest works online to a global audience, and that audience, she notes, will seek the works out in person. 5 Pointz drew fans from as far away as Japan, so why, Singleton's logic went, wouldn't they venture up to the South Bronx? Walter Benjamin would certainly approve of the strength of the aura of this project, set in the heart of the borough. It's fitting that an art whose roots are in the grimy recesses of the subway system is showcased right next to active elevated tracks. Singleton again:

> Graffiti is a beautiful art. It is an art form that some people may not respect, but I don't think Picasso was respected in his own time. Also, it's an art form that is begotten from the street from the community. When you leave something blank, that's exactly what it's going to be: a business area that's blank that no one's going to want to go down to anyway. Maybe the community might walk down there because of the train. But as for someone to actually go out there and look and say, "Wow, look at this art," or "Wow, look at that; how did they get it to be this way?" is totally different. What you're doing there is inviting the community out to view this. [64]

Singleton said people did come out when this project was underway, including state assemblyman Marcos A. Crespo, state senator Ruben Diaz Sr. and Bronx Borough president Ruben Diaz Jr., and all voiced approval of it when it was unveiled. The attendees' emphasis on graffiti eradication was too much for Nicer's taste ("We're the first graffiti company of its kind, so it's like going to a butcher to get a donation for a vegan workshop," he said), but the notion of creating a walking museum with alternating pieces of art was very appealing to him. It's a subtle distinction, but both Singleton and Nicer's emphasis on what is *created* in such a project contrasts with any emphasis on what is *removed*, and places them in agreement with Halsey and Young's contention that writers' motivations are not exclusively rooted in destruction. The communion, if you will, between the body and the ideal writing space, is important, too.

The location is particularly ideal in this case because outside of the Bronx Museum of Art, Nicer said there are few opportunities to see art in the borough, and certainly not in Hunts Point or Port Morris. The largest of the pieces on Whitlock can be seen from southbound 6 trains just after they leave the Whitlock station, which Nicer said makes them accessible to all.

> What do you have as the normal family setting here? The normal family setting is single-parent homes, very few full family homes. So you have mothers who work rigorous jobs, whether it's wholesale, or working retail, like clothing stores or supermarkets, or even if they have professional jobs like secretaries downtown, they're working not only 9 to 5, sometimes they're working 9 to 8, and by the time they get home, their kids are home, and it isn't like they're getting dressed and saying, "Come on, let's go to the MoMa. Let me show you the difference between a Monet and a Goya.

> Let me show you the difference between a Picasso, you know, pointillism, cubism…
>
> Not everyone in New York City really has that kind of leisure time to partake in the art culture that's out there. The stuff that we're putting out there in these neighborhoods is the modern-day Picassos and Goyas and Monets that bring arts and color to other people's lives.[65]

Although the South Bronx is about the furthest thing from a place brimming with surplus capital, it does benefit from a unique local culture that gives rise to projects like this one. It's worth reiterating that a multinational corporation thought enough of the images that it used them for a television advertisement starring Jennifer Lopez. In this small way, residents of one of the least influential parts of the city gain an element of power.fff

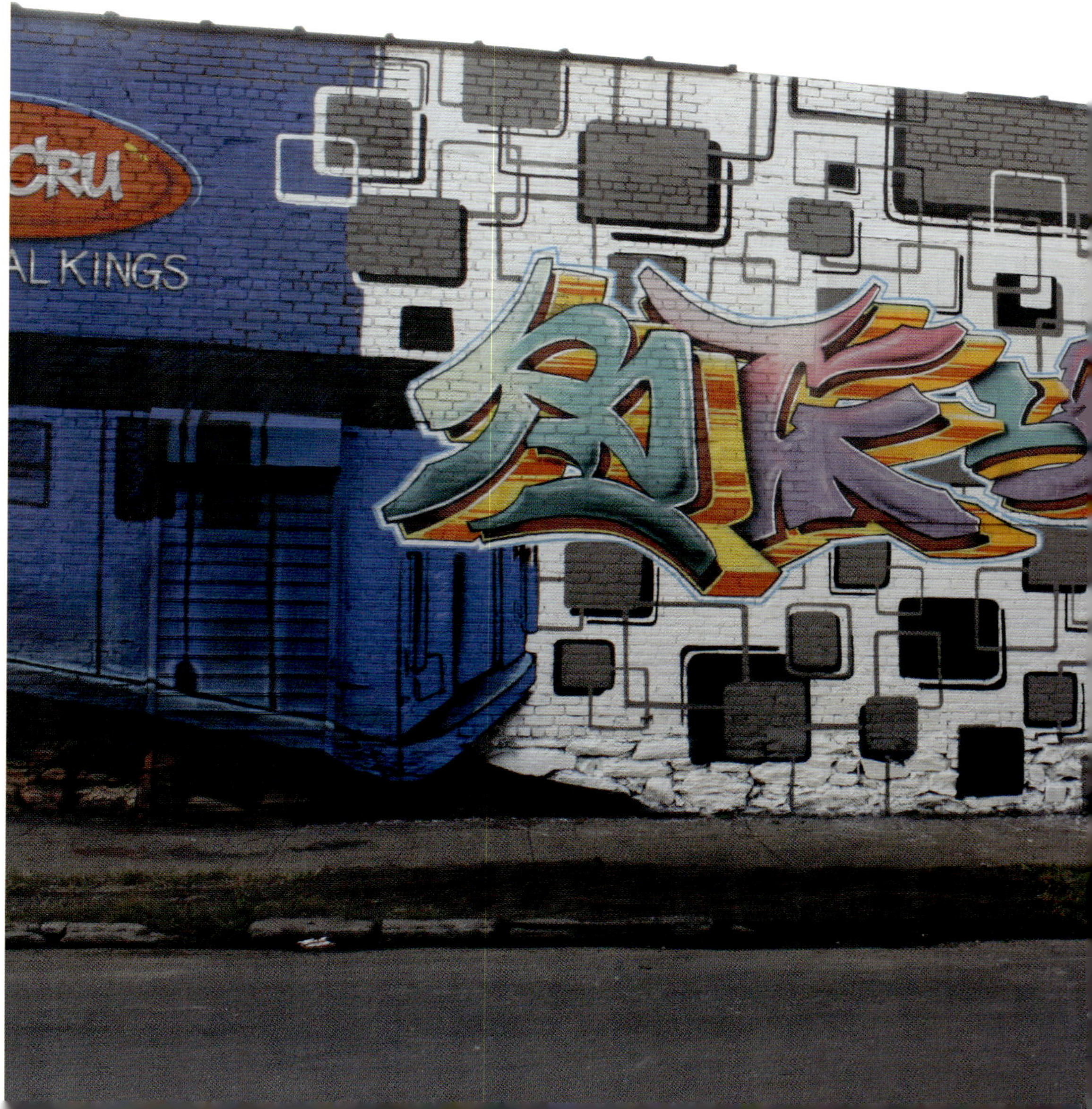

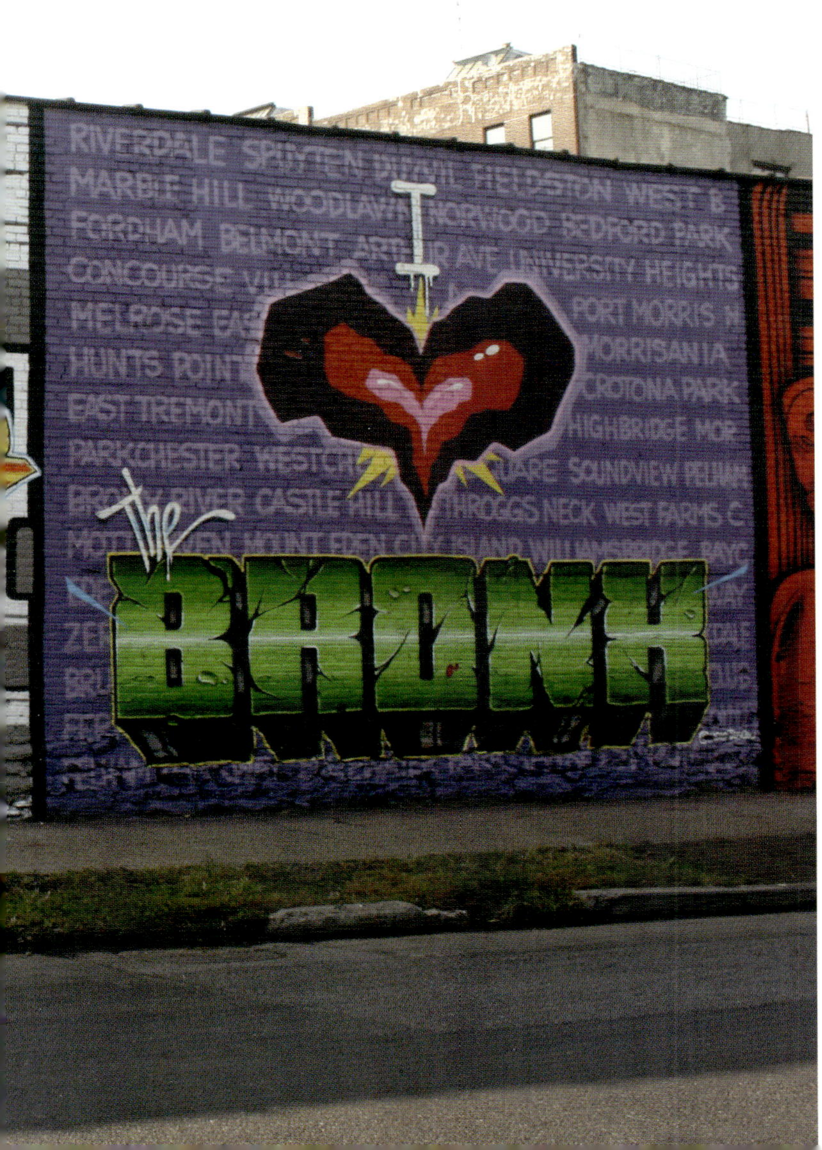

BG mural and *I Love the Bronx* by Bio on Whitlock Ave., circa September 2010. Photo by Patrick Verel

{4}

CASE STUDY

Jersey City

Human Fingerprints on the Waterfront

It may be separated from New York City by the Hudson River, but Jersey City is very much a part of the metropolitan New York region. Two stops away on the PATH train, downtown Jersey City is less than twenty minutes away from the World Trade Center site in Manhattan's financial district. The downtown, which is hemmed in by the New Jersey Turnpike to the west, the entrance to the Holland Tunnel to the north, and waterfront to the east and south, is a mishmash of historical and modern architecture.

While the waterfront sports glass-enclosed skyscrapers and condominiums that cater to urban professionals who make the short commute from the Exchange Street PATH station to jobs across the river, further inland and closer to the turnpike is the historic downtown, where new townhouses are jumbled together with older, brick tenement-style dwellings. The main street is dotted with independent merchants, empty storefronts, and the occasional bar, restaurant, or Starbucks.

A diminutive residence in Jersey City, November 2010. Photo by Patrick Verel

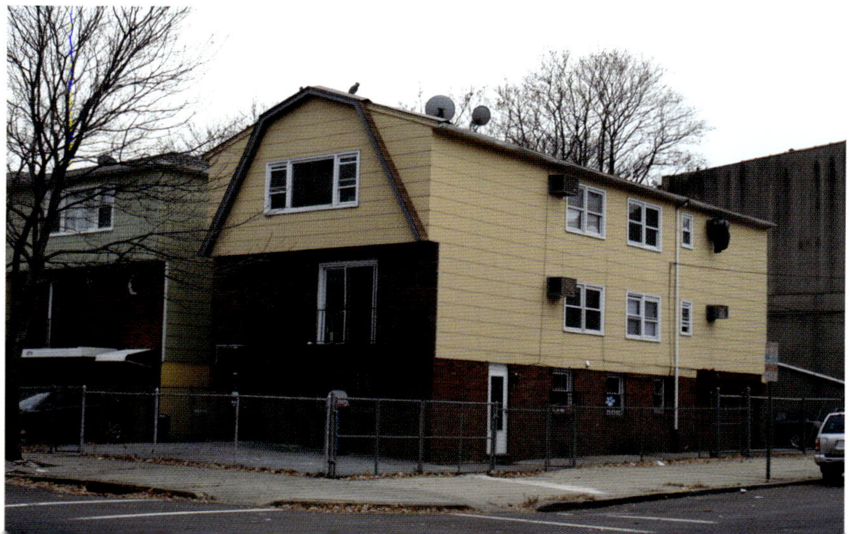

A newer residence in Jersey City, November 2010. Photo by Patrick Verel

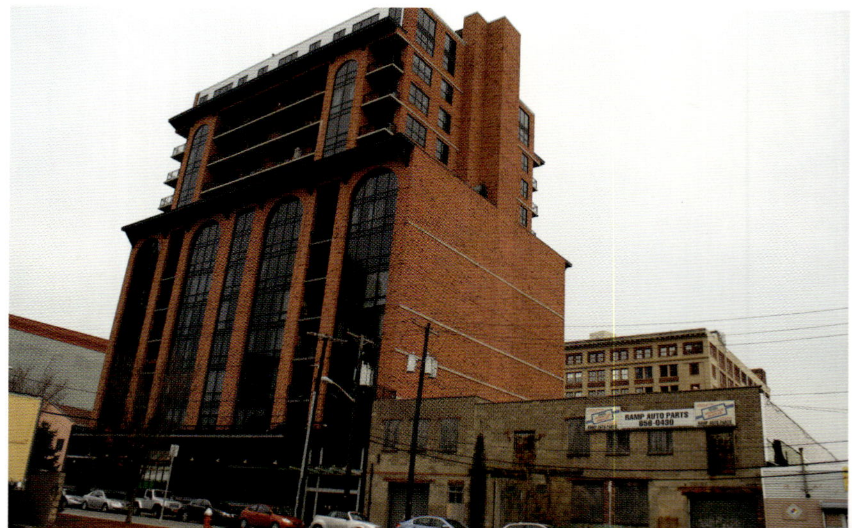

Although many of the merchants here cater to local residents, the district is still a magnet for visitors from other parts of New Jersey.

This is where I found Dylan Evans and SAGE Arts Collective members Luv 1 and Will Kaso. In an alley next to 172 Newark Ave,, a three-story, 100-year-old brick building that currently houses Palace Drugs and Liquor, Luv and Will were supervising the finishing touches of a blue whale that covered the length of the building. They were a little far from their normal haunt, as the SAGE Collective is based in Trenton, but were there at the behest of Evans, who lives in Jersey City and identifies himself as an "art curator and consultant" and "location scout for film and television." I found the group through an entry that Luv 1 had posted on the website Jersey Graf (www.jerseygraf.com) and did not expect to meet Evans, but since he was instrumental in the project, I felt I would be remiss not to include him. He described himself as a fan of art, and said that this project came about because Jerry Blankman, the owner of the building, contacted him after seeing some of the collective's work at Raw Power, a project that involved artists covering nearby 350 Warren Street with murals. Evans got the SAGE Collective involved in that project, and Luv 1 said that if another project came up, he should keep them in mind. This, Evans said, was that next project.

> I can't paint, but I really appreciate and respect what the artists do, so my way of contributing is by curating projects and just bringing what I enjoy and sharing that with the residents of Jersey City. So my strengths have just been, reach out and talk to artists, organize events and projects like this.[66]

Evans's role in this project was a combination of mediator and fixer, as he both communicated to Blankman what would be painted and arranged through the city to have the area adjacent to the building, which is both a parking lot and a driveway linking Newark Avenue to another parking lot, closed to traffic. He also oversaw the procurement of supplies and picked up the tab for lunch, too. The design, which was proposed by the collective, was originally going to be an underwater theme with jellyfish and divers, but it morphed into a single whale, with additional elements to be added later. Evans tries to convince building owners to give artists creative freedom and steers artists away from controversial pieces. It can still be challenging to get building owners on board, though.

> Some owners assume that all public art is graffiti. They don't understand the value that it can bring to a neighborhood. So it can be tough. I do get nos from some people, but then I also get yeses from some people. Hopefully the neighborhood and the owners are happy with it, and that it does more good than bad. I mean, I think any art on a wall that isn't offensive is better than a blank wall. Maybe there's even room for offensive art some place, but that's not what I want to bring to Jersey City.[67]

Like Veng and Crane, Evans pitches to owners that if they allow him to commission a painting, "street kids will respect it more, and tend not to tag over it." This is true especially if the wall he's asking to paint already has tags on it.

> I'm thinking of the projects I've done, they've all been pretty well received and not marked up. I don't know if it's been an effective selling point, because you know, there are still some owners that I'm working on, getting permission. But yeah, that is something I try to use, that it will prevent further graffiti.[68]

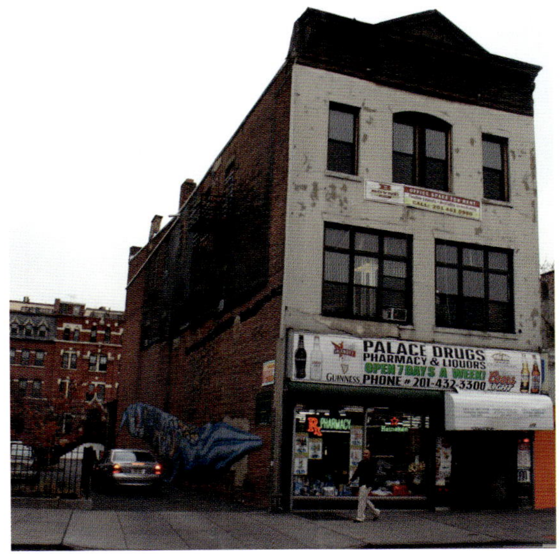

The front of 172 Newark Ave., November 2010. Photo by Patrick Verel

Luv 1 estimated that he'd been painting on the streets for three years, even though he said he'd been doing art his whole life. At first, he started doing graffiti illegally in out of the way places, where he could "learn the craft" before doing higher visibility pieces.

> It's a natural thing for myself that I just do. It's therapeutic to me, I would say. But I think art in general is therapeutic. Switches up the monotony. To me, I don't see enough human fingerprints when I travel the world. I see corporate fingerprints all over, but I don't see, you know, like the people of the community. That to me is important.[69]

Luv 1's emphasis on "human fingerprints" again brought to mind Halsey and Young's ruminations on writer motivations. He doesn't look at a space that is blank or recently buffed and focus on what's there, but instead imagines what it could be—a rejoinder to what he sees as excessive commercialism. Halsey and Young make a case that the allure of the ideal writing space is a strong counterweight to the penalties that await taggers; in Luv 1's case, a similar desire to leave "human fingerprints" is stronger than the bureaucratic hurtles that accompany legal graffiti murals.

As noted earlier, Jersey City is a relatively new space for the SAGE Collective, and as I would discover later, Trenton, where they hail from, is a very different community. When reflecting on their experiences, both Luv 1 and Will Kaso often harkened back to Trenton. Evans said he tapped them for this project because he considered Jersey City to be a bit of a "dry well" for high-quality graffiti artists, and in any case, Luv 1 and Will do not limit themselves to one area: Trenton, Hopewell, and Bedminster, New Jersey; Philadelphia; Washington, DC; Brooklyn; and Harlem are some of the spots they've painted.

In Trenton, they target abandoned buildings for their work as often as inhabited ones, and in many cases they've taken a "paint first, ask permission later" approach. This lends a certain amount of tension to their work. When asked about the first time they painted a wall with an owner's permission, Will Kaso launched into a lengthy story about how in July 2008, they painted an entire city block in broad daylight, and when confronted by a resident about the legality of their work, they bluffed and said the city had given them the OK. After they finished, they succeeded in petitioning the local residents to let it stay, but this is obviously not a strategy that most would get behind.

If the SAGE Collective comes across as slightly disrespectful of authority, the same does not extend to local residents. Will Kaso likes to call their work "conscious graffiti," and Luv 1 notes that even though their first mural was unsanctioned, it was primarily Dr. Seuss imagery that they figured would appeal to the community.

> I think what's different about what we do is, we do it with the community in mind; it's not just to put our names up. We're doing stuff to brighten the community, and I think that's what makes it different from graffiti, and maybe it's art graffiti, just street art, or aerosol art or something.[70]

In addition to the purely aesthetic improvement that a mural provides, Luv 1 and Will Kaso's experience shows how their actions can produce unexpected consequences. Asked if preventing vandalism was ever a motive for building owners to employ their talents, Will Kaso volunteered that he'd once painted two images of the musician Nina Simone on an abandoned building in North Trenton (it has since been torn down). A few weeks later, a friend who lives nearby told him that the drug dealers who'd normally hang around that lot had dispersed because the mural was drawing too much attention to the spot. He's proud that none of SAGE's works have been vandalized, but both he and Luv 1 are skeptical of the possibility that good work alone is a deterrent.

> **Will:** I think it depends. Like, I work with the Philadelphia Mural Arts Program, and when they put murals in areas that are heavy with graffiti, a lot of their murals don't survive. Then it becomes a point of, well, who's doing the wall? A lot of the times, the people doing the walls are outside of the whole scene. So if you put cats on these walls and they have a name…

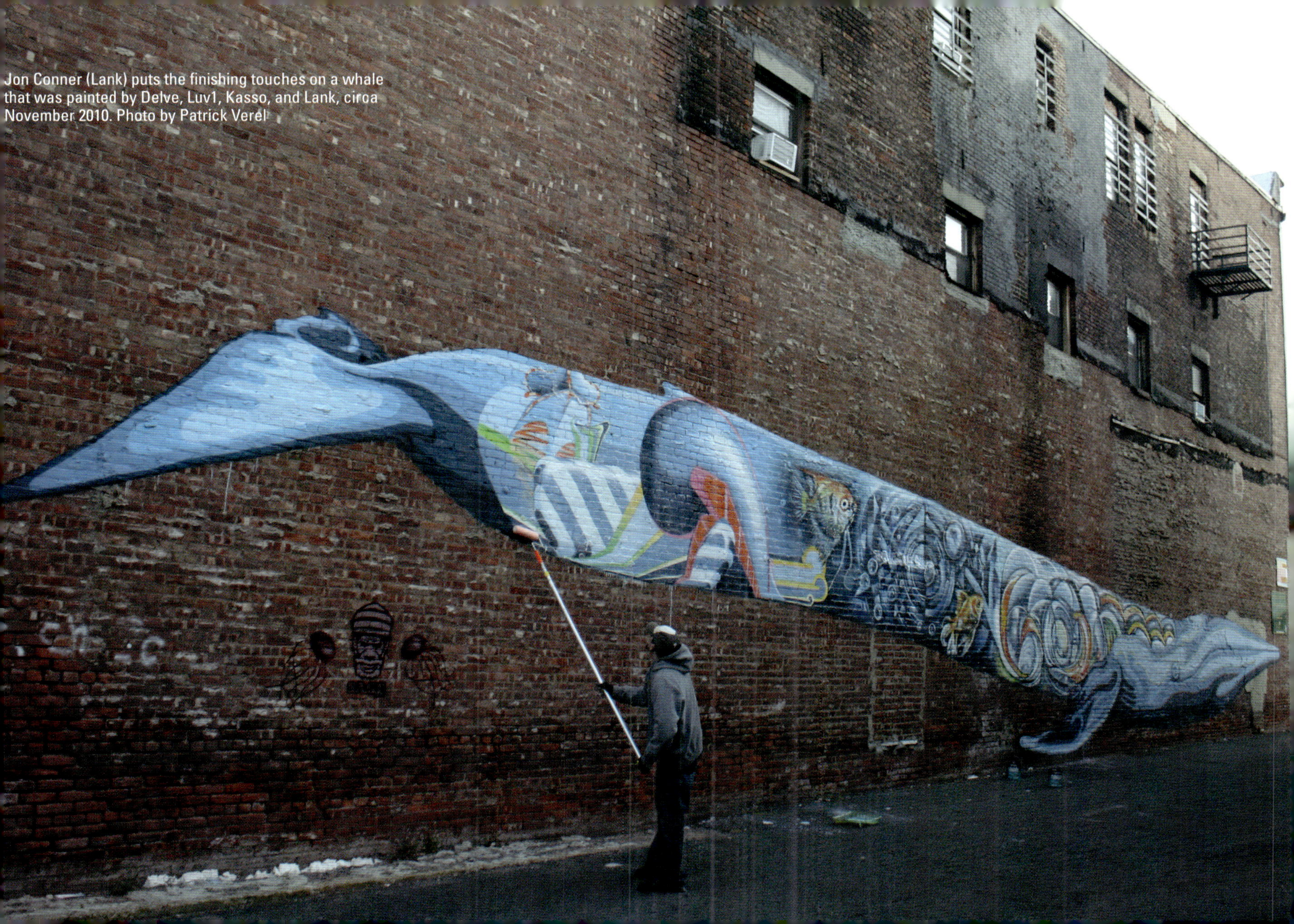

Jon Conner (Lank) puts the finishing touches on a whale that was painted by Delve, Luv1, Kasso, and Lank, circa November 2010. Photo by Patrick Verel

Luv 1: ...If they're respected artists, then they don't touch it.[71]

This is an important acknowledgment of an essential point: It matters not only where graffiti murals are placed but also who creates them. The impression that one gets from talking to Will Kaso and Luv 1 is that there is a very thin line between being stylistically true enough to street life so that other writers respect their murals and antagonizing the authorities and suspicious neighbors. It is clearly something that irritates Will Kaso.

> About a month ago, I was doing a permission wall for a friend of mine, at his art studio, and one of the residents there called the cops on me. He was like, "He's out here doing graffiti." The cops came, and they were like, "This doesn't look like graffiti," and I was like, "It isn't. I'm just painting." And then I told them who I was, and they was like, "Oh yeah, we've heard of you." I'm out there for hours, just hanging out with the police officers, talking about art and all this type of shit. It gave me an opportunity to really get to know these guys, and for them to get to know me. But at the same time, how many walls do I have up here, and you're still fuckin' with me? Like, seriously?[72]

Jerry Blankman, the owner of 172 Newark, greeted me at his offices at the Jersey City Special Improvement District at Journal Square, which is one stop past Grove Street on the PATH. He explained that he found Dylan Evans via Rebecca Feranec, the studio tour coordinator for Pro Arts Jersey City (she has since been promoted to executive director). Evans has been a second-tier supporter of the artist tour for about the last ten years. Since he doesn't have the funds to fix up his 100-year-old building, he figured this would be one way to spruce it up. The whale is just the start though; his ultimate goal is to turn the building into a canvas for artists of many stripes.

> As my capital builds up and I find the rental income that I'm looking for to do this, every phase, eventually, I'd like to have something where my entire building is nearly covered in some sort of an artistic mural. I think it works for all concerned, and the more the better, as far as I'm concerned.[73]

Blankman's roots in the area go deep. The building has been in his family since 1925, when his uncle started the drugstore there. His father worked there, and when he was thirteen, he worked there too. When his father died in 1996, he took over, and he ran it for eleven years before selling it to investors, while retaining ownership of the building. He doesn't visit the space as often as he did when he ran the pharmacy, but he did swing by to see the whale and ran into lots of people he knew; he said all praised the work.

> Dylan and I worked out ahead of time, that the artists would have full creative control, but I didn't want anything that would be offensive to any race, gender, anyone like that. I didn't want anything that was adult in nature or content, and as it turned out, my two sons are great lovers of the sea and of the ocean, so the aquatic theme fit right into something that I could quickly relate to. But that was my only feedback, was people walking past and thinking it was a really cool thing.[74]

If there's one person who understands the graffiti as vandalism versus graffiti- murals as art, it's Blankman, who as chance would have it, supervises a graffiti removal program in the Special Improvement District (S.I.D.) at Journal Square. He founded and was president of the Special Improvement District that 172 Newark resides in, and does not have patience for people scribbling their names on things.

> Graffiti's illegal if you're tagging somebody's building without their knowledge, whether it's beautiful or not. In many cases, it's not. In some cases, it is. Regardless of whether it's beautiful or not, if you have someone's permission, I think it's great. I think its part of the urban culture and the fabric that we live in in an urban environment, and I think that's great. But we spend a lot of time in the SID combatting illegal graffiti, so I think there needs to be a line. If we're just going to say graffiti, that's a very general term. There's a huge distinction there.[75]

Like Luv 1 and Will Kaso, he's skeptical of the power of murals to deter vandalism, noting that he'd recently commissioned an artist from West Orange to paint abstract art on a utility box a few blocks away. The day after it was finished, he and his assistant went out to take a picture, only to find that someone named "Marian" had written her name in white on it. Could it be that the art was disrespected because the artist was from somewhere other than Jersey City? Blankman wasn't buying it.

> There wasn't any real artistic graffiti on this particular box to begin with, so I'm not sure it was territorial. I think it was someone just being rude. I was disappointed because I thought it was a really nice piece of art.[76]

Blankman is upfront about his motivations at 172 Newark. Asked why he thought the whale might be an improvement over a blank wall, he returned to the fact that his building is in disrepair, and although he's a supporter of the arts, the side benefit for him is a building that is simply more attractive now than it was before. In a sense, it's a win-win, because he believes that even if a mural is not a direct link to an increase in tenancy, a strong and vibrant artist community contributes an indirect financial benefit. Even if he doesn't fill his vacancies, he notes, his building is still worth more than it was a month ago.

> The culture of Jersey City in downtown is extremely important to me because my family's been there for almost a hundred years. But I still have two kids in Basking Ridge who need to be fed at night, and the financial aspect never leaves my mind. I'd be disingenuous if I said anything else.[77]

In fact, Blankman looks down to the riverfront developments that have transformed that area of the city and wonders when the area where his building is located will change, too. Following a script that countless real estate owners have

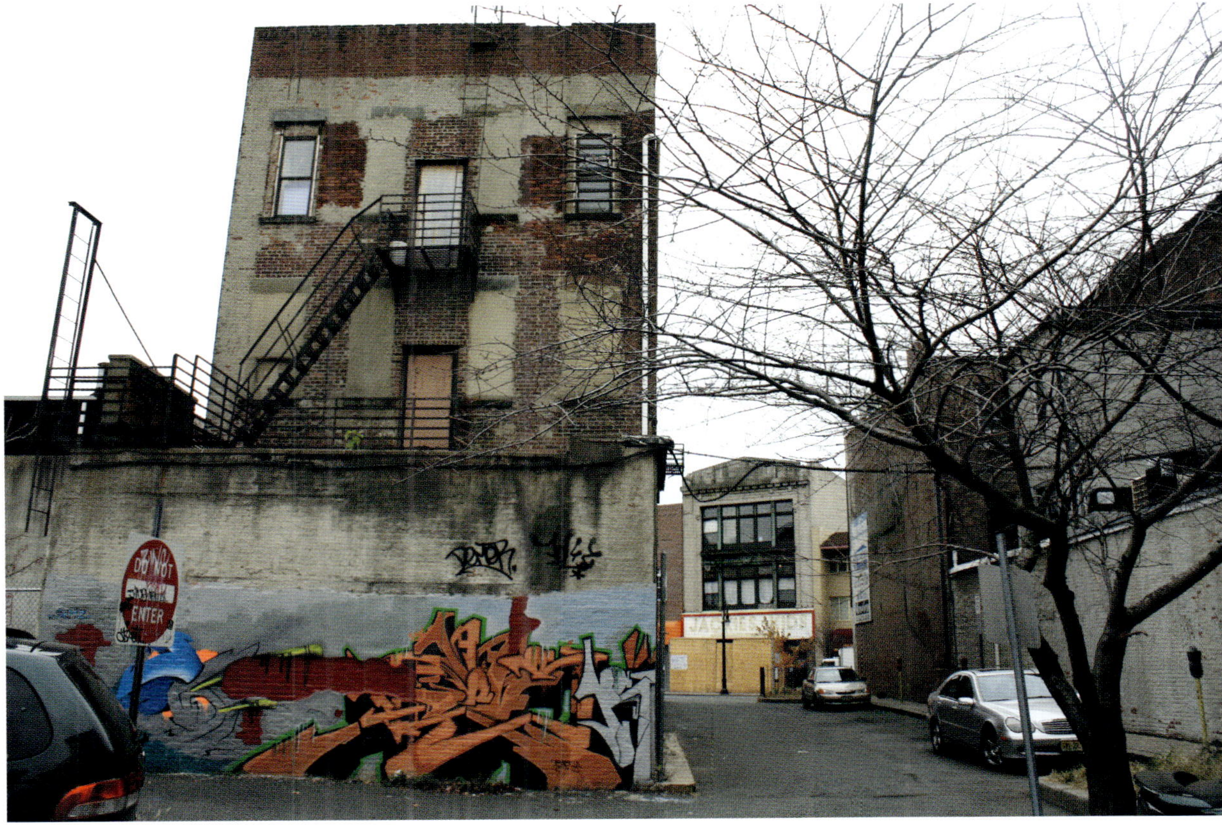

Col and Demer adorn the back of 172 Newark Ave, facing a parking lot, circa November 2010. Photo by Patrick Verel

before him, he's attempting to help usher in that transformation by making the area more appealing to artists.

> It hasn't made it to my street yet, so the rental income and the property values are not at a point where people can pull equity out of their buildings and really renovate them so that they look beautiful. It hasn't come to that yet. So this is sort of, a way station, where I can get some work done, make it look nice and hopefully we do experience the boom that the waterfront has.[78]

Of all the cases studies, Jersey City perhaps best epitomizes Harvey's notion of "creative destruction" in the service of excess capital. Blankman is a bone fide supporter of both the arts and his local community, and he freely admits that both can be put into the service of raising capital for himself. Few would begrudge this strategy; as he noted, he has children to look after. And yet, it's difficult to hear gentrification spoken of so excitedly. On the one hand, Harvey might applaud a piece like this as a "mark of local distinction." At the same time, if the murals Blankman plans to install do what he hopes they will, then the monopoly rent he extracts from this unique space will by necessity be directed to efforts to further increase his capital. Improvements he makes to the building will be accompanied by higher property evaluations, which will lead to higher tax assessments from the city, and Blankman will be forced to raise rents on his tenants.

This cycle of "creative destruction" that results in the eviction of the poor, the underprivileged and the marginalized, is at the heart of the tension that Harvey explores in *Rebel Cities*, and it's not hard to envision elsewhere either. With both Jersey City and Bushwick, it's not hard to imagine a scenario where artists do move in, displacing the poor, only to be displaced by young professionals, and so on, until a state is reached whereby graffiti murals are no longer appropriate. That day is still far off for Jersey City, but it is an example of why, when it comes to graffiti murals, a case can be made for government-sponsored promotion. As Harvey notes, the market values marks of distinction for the monopoly rents they stimulate, but there is always a risk that those same marks of distinction will be overwhelmed.

In the meantime, with its location in the middle of a busy commercial district, the whale draws a range of opinions from bystanders. Ronnie, a white woman in her late 50s who has lived in Jersey City her whole life, said she sometimes found herself tired of "seeing half buildings or blank, empty walls," but she didn't consider herself a fan of tags, either. Asked if she felt the whale improved the neighborhood, she gave what would seem to be a positive response:

> It gives you something to look at. When you see something like this, you know somewhere, someone has an interest. When you see people have an interest in a building, you feel a little safer. [79]

Zimbardo would be proud. The crucial part of her response is the first part. One could easily say that a building that has been scrubbed clean is, like 172 Newark, one that that has an owner who has an interest in it, but that interest is simply an economic one, nothing more. A mural means a lot more: in this case, change. Ronnie described the neighborhood as one that's gone through a lot of transition. Once exclusively Italian and Polish, it is a now a mix of Latino, blacks, Italians, and Polish, along with newly arrived New York City expatriates. It feels like a safe neighborhood, she said, and one of the reasons why is community art like the whale mural.

> When it's general art like this, or you know, urban art, it's different than when you walk into a wall with tags. You don't want to see TAZ and Q's, you know, it's different. This is art. It's not like the subway art. We've come a long way.[80]

Not everyone is a fan. Rama, for instance, seemed incredulous that I would even want to talk to him about the mural. A 50-something man of Southeast Asian descent, he had traveled from Edison to visit the pharmacy. He said he would rather see a clean wall than a mural, even if it was not explicitly connected to graffiti.

> **Q:** What's your impression of it? Do you like it?
>
> **A:** I don't know anything this…It looks like, ugly. I don't like it.

Q: You don't like it? How come?
A: I don't know. It looks, these kinds of things on the wall, writing on the wall, this and that, I don't like it.
Q: So. OK. Um, do you feel like it makes the neighborhood look worse or better?
A: Yeah, it looks worse.[81]

It is possible that Rama didn't fully understand the question being posed; English was obviously his second language. But even if he did, and he genuinely felt that a blank wall would be preferable; he did say at another point in our conversation that he felt the neighborhood was improving, with the foot traffic around us serving as proof. So even if he is not affected in a positive way by the mural, it can be said that he is affected by others, like Ronnie, who do see it in a positive light.

Michelle, a 30-something black woman who had driven into town from Bayonne with her daughter to do some shopping, certainly appreciated it, and like Ronnie, she drew a contrast between it and tagging, which she equated with negativity. This downtown spot could use less of that, she noted.

> It gives the people something to look at as they're walking through. It's an alleyway, and most people are skeptical to walk in an alleyway, because sometimes it's occupied by people who like to drink and do drugs. I'm surprised they're not out here today. But to look at something creative and not just tagged up there, it's a good sight.[82]

With this observation, Michelle echoed Will Kaso's assertion that in some cases, the presence of a mural can actually deter questionable behavior. Tags have the opposite effect, though, she said, because she's seen profanity and "not so decent pictures" along with them. Once again, it's a case of symbolic interactionism. Michelle again:

> Tagging is usually done out of vengeance. You know, you're mad at someone, you're mad at the person in the building and you just want to tag something, just to let them know that you was here, and you really don't care if it's painted over or if it's clean, you know, when the bricks are clean. But when you do a mural like this, you're really putting your heart into it. So it's totally different.[83]

Finally, there's Junior, a Hispanic man who has lived all fifty-two years of his life in Jersey City. He was familiar with other instances of graffiti artists being asked to take part in sanctioned public art projects, and like many others I spoke to, he framed the issue as one of a private property owner's prerogative. This perspective is more often associated with the right of an owner to keep their property free of tags, but it can be applied in this instance, too, as illustrated by his answer to the question "Why do you think this is better than a blank wall, which is what was there before?":

> It gives people something to look at, something to talk about, something to attract them and if the building owner is OK with it, who am I to say they can't do it?[84]

His impressions of the neighborhood would also please Blankman, as he said it's gentrifying as more upscale restaurants and bars open.

> It's changed over the last twenty years, dramatic change, dramatic improvement. I've been here when downtown Jersey City was pretty much the slums, and today it's a nice place to live.[85]

{5}

CASE STUDY

Staten Island

No, Really, Staten Island

As removed as Jersey City might seem to be from New York City, it's a trifle compared to Staten Island. My journey to locate graffiti murals in the city's most suburban of boroughs brought me to Stapleton, a neighborhood on the northeastern corner of the island, three stops from the Staten Island Ferry on the Staten Island Railroad (SIRR). Like nearby Brooklyn, Stapleton has an urban feel to it, thanks to access to public transportation and the Stapleton Houses, a public housing project that many members of the hip-hop group Wu Tang Clan called home.

It is also the home of NYC ArtsCypher, a nonprofit group whose mission is "to promote positive values through arts and entertainment programs, projects, & events with a focus on emerging artists and teens."[86] Charlie Balducci, the group's founder, met me at NYC Arts Cypher's Broad Street office. Although Balducci has supervised the painting of murals around Stapleton, including one visible from the elevated SIRR platform, he was most interested in talking about a project that was just getting underway about two miles inland, next to St. Peter's Cemetery.

Leewood Real Estate, a prominent developer on Staten Island, was looking for a way to jump-start a stalled development for a twenty-four-unit condominium in West New Brighton that had been languishing behind a beat-up construction fence since 2007, and one of the ideas the developer pursued was having the fence, which stretches 200 feet, repainted with a mural. Wayne Miller, who joined Leewood in December 2010 as vice-president of sales and marketing for The Clover Club, as the development is called, knew Balducci from grant proposal meetings they'd both attended—Balducci for NYC Arts Cypher, and Miller for the Staten Island Shakespearean theater company, where he served as producing artistic director. Balducci took the idea and ran with it.

> [Miller] had initially thought of just doing a mural, and I twisted it and made it a lot more complicated for myself and the organization by incorporating a program where it's not us just doing the mural, but we would team up four kids with four artists, and sketch something out with the kids involved and then have the kids be there to help with the actual creation of the mural, because it runs hand in hand with what our program is.[87]

Balducci lined up artists to paint the fence, and he also worked alongside the New York City Department of Probation to find teenagers who'd been arrested for graffiti. The intention, he said, was to show them "the positive side of graffiti, the consequences of vandalism and to give them an opportunity to have an outlet to express themselves in a safe environment."

The project cost $5,000, with $1,500 going toward the paint, $500 to $600 for each artist and the rest going toward a videographer and transportation. Balducci viewed it as a proving ground for his organization, to show how it can

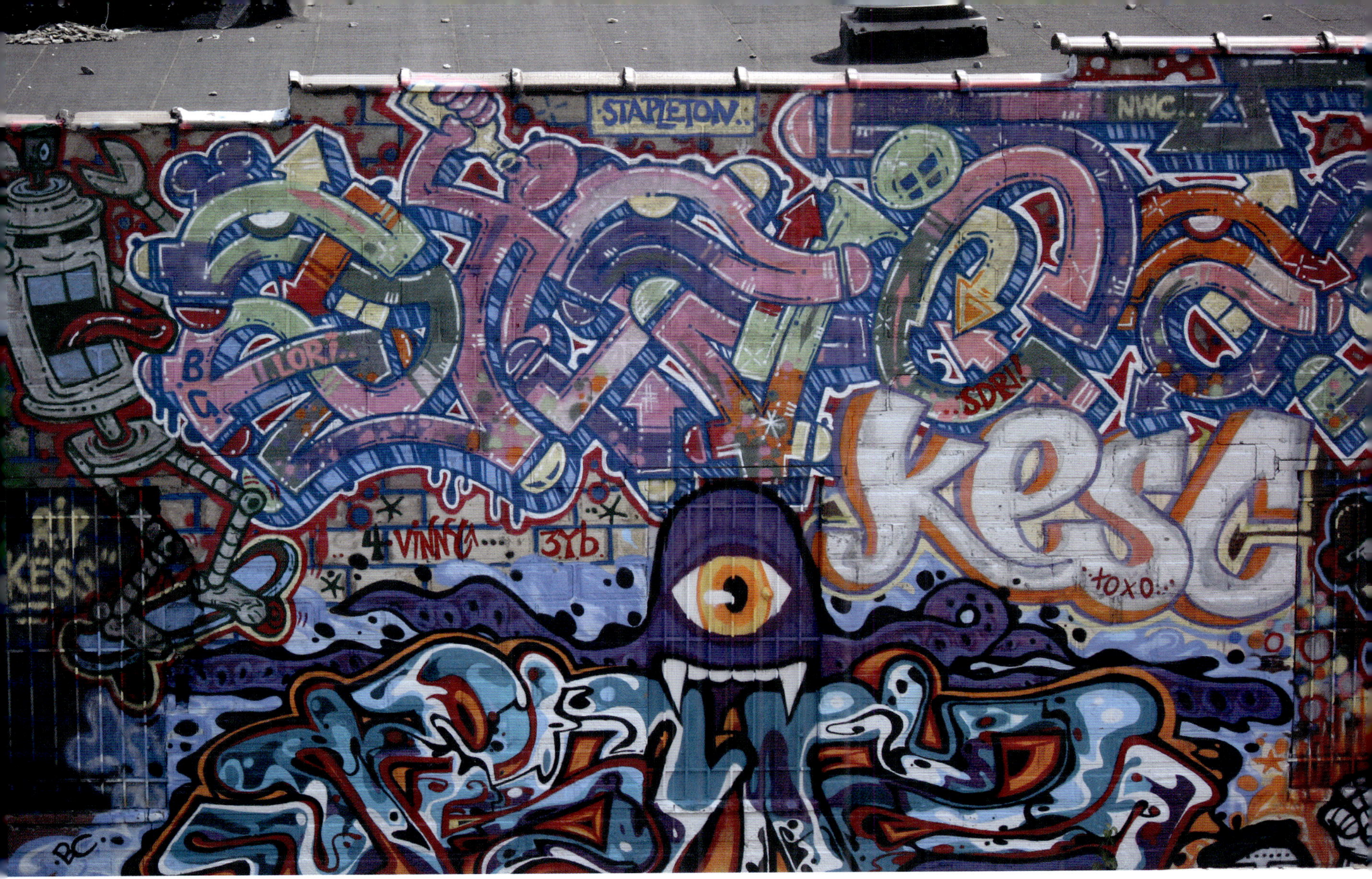

A close-up of one of the many productions on the wall next to the Stapleton station of the Staten Island Railroad, featuring Strider, Kesc, and Dems, circa July 2014. Photo by Patrick Verel

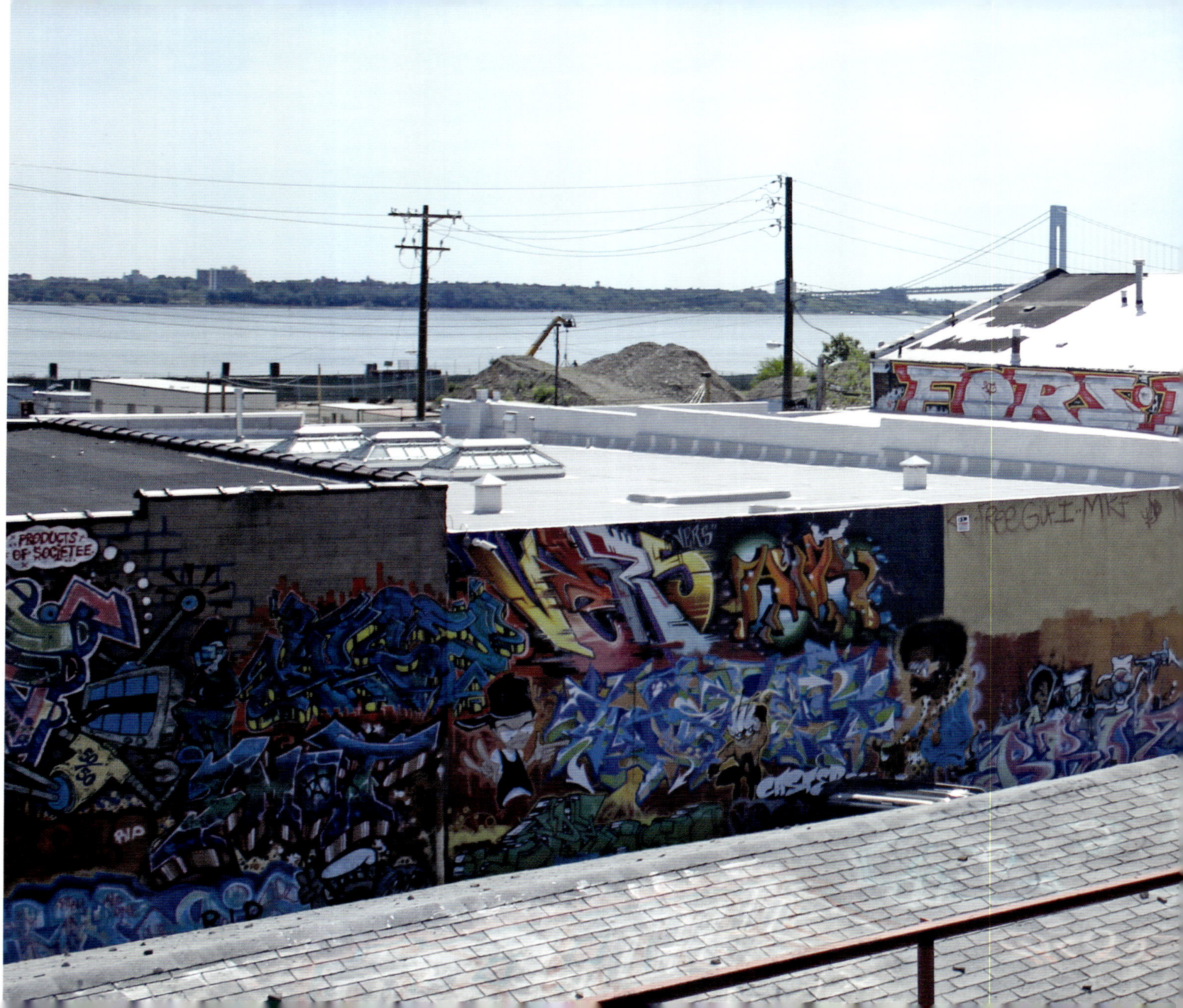
PRODUCTS OF SOCIETEE

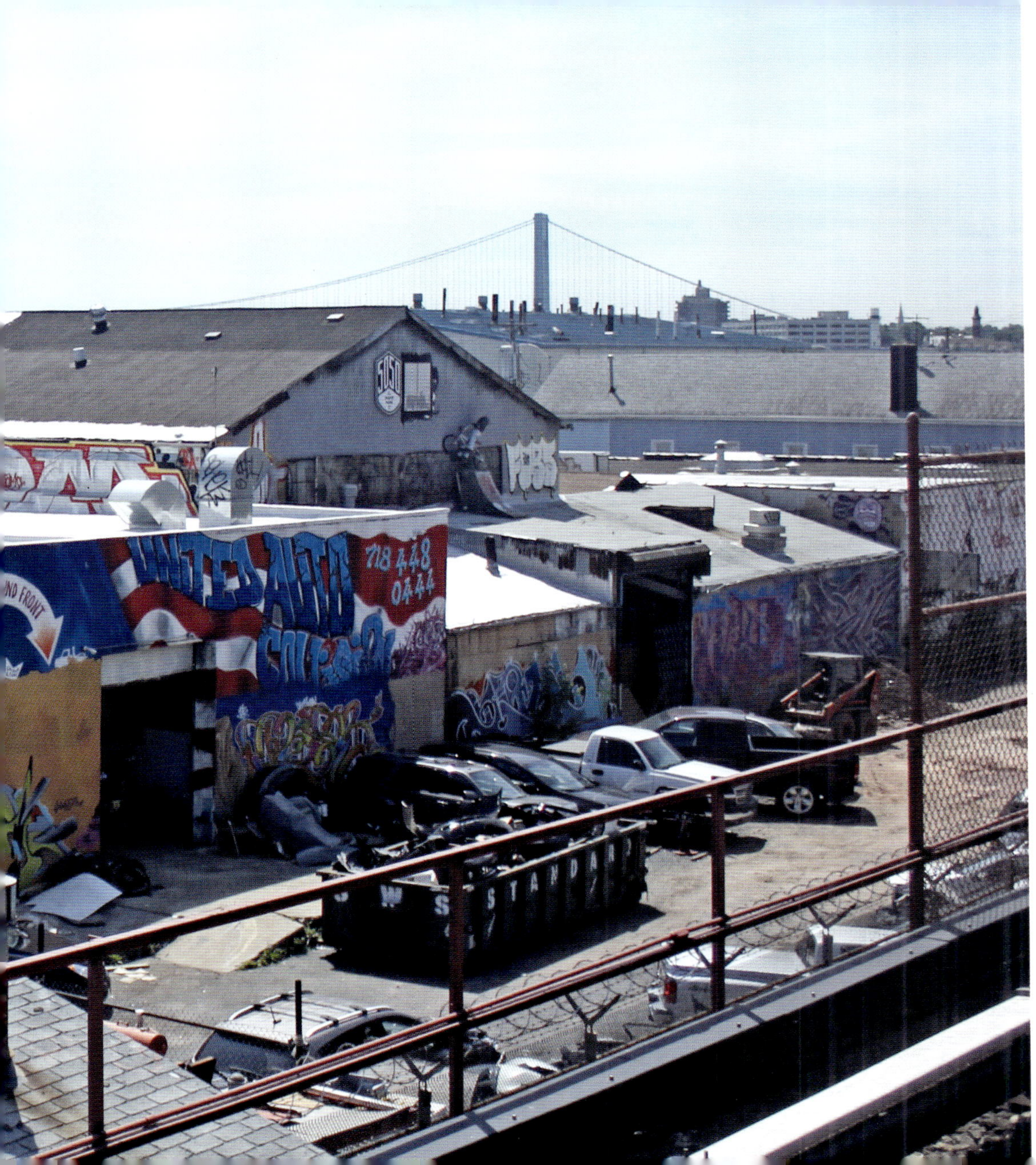

United Auto Collision and the Verrazano-Narrows Bridge, as seen facing south from the elevated platform of the Stapleton station of the Staten Island Railway, circa July 2014. The wall was organized by NYC Cypher. Photo by Patrick Verel

work in tandem with people who would normally be leery of those whose main tool is a spray can.

> They'll bring the attention to the site, my artists will get the opportunity to use this big showcase of work, the organization of course put it together, so we get the kudos, and everybody involved really just benefits from the quality of life. Those particular construction sites always look ragged and run down and water logged and splintering. We're gonna beautify that, and so I'm hoping that it also starts a trend.[88]

When we spoke, Balducci was just gearing up for a new season; he estimated that the previous summer they had done ten murals. Half were requests from owners; the rest came from his solicitations. Of all the people who are involved in promoting the art, he is the most adamant in emphasizing the collaborative aspect of his work, even going so far as to distance himself from the "selfishness" inherent in the pursuit of "throwing your name out there," which he said was the essence of graffiti. In a way, Balducci is on the far end of the spectrum of those I interviewed, because he equates the word graffiti with a concept that is strictly illegal.

Construction fence with work from Gano, Trace, Prez, Geoff Rawling, and kids from the NYC Arts Cypher MURAL program, circa April 2011. Photo by Patrick Verel

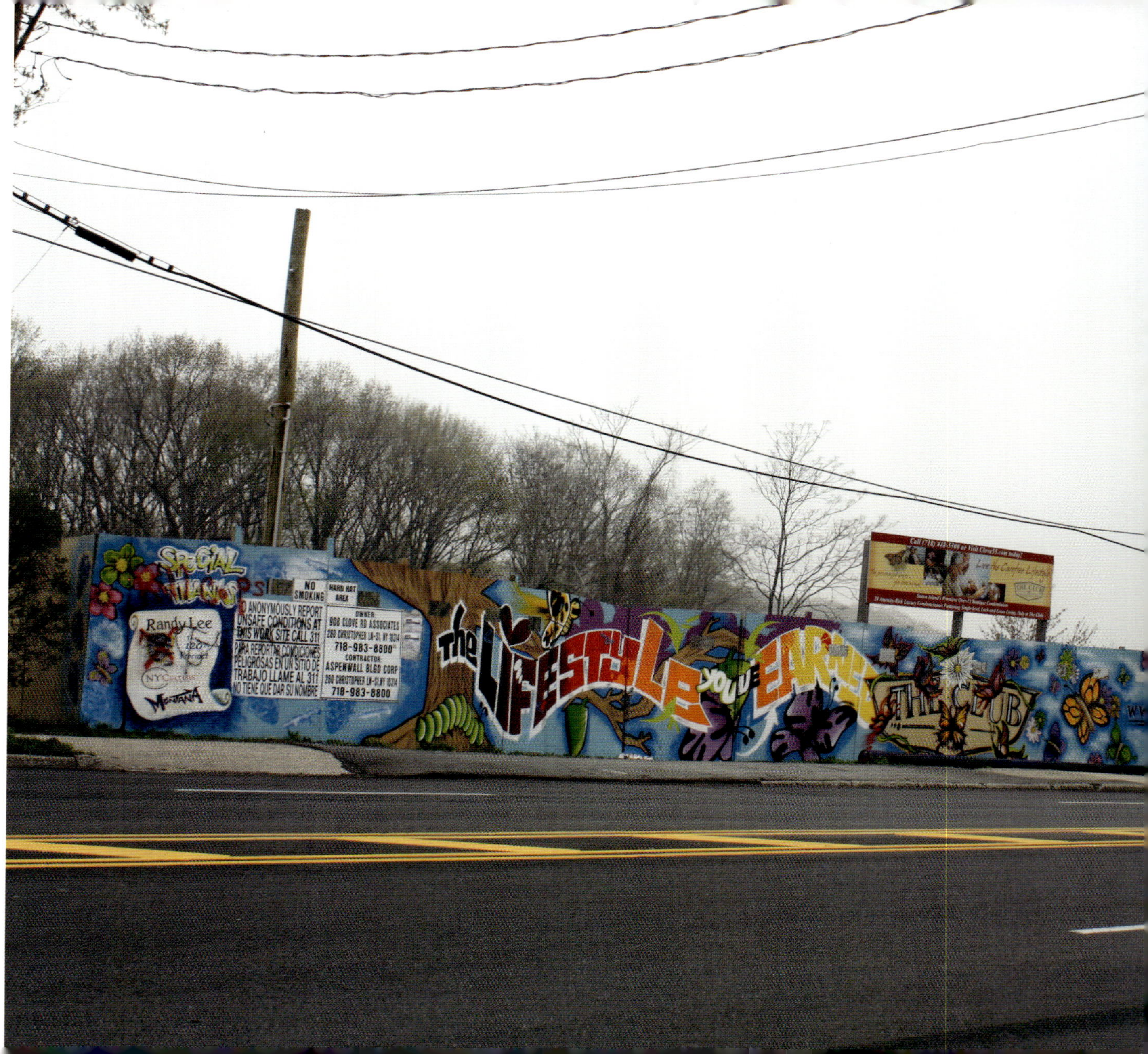

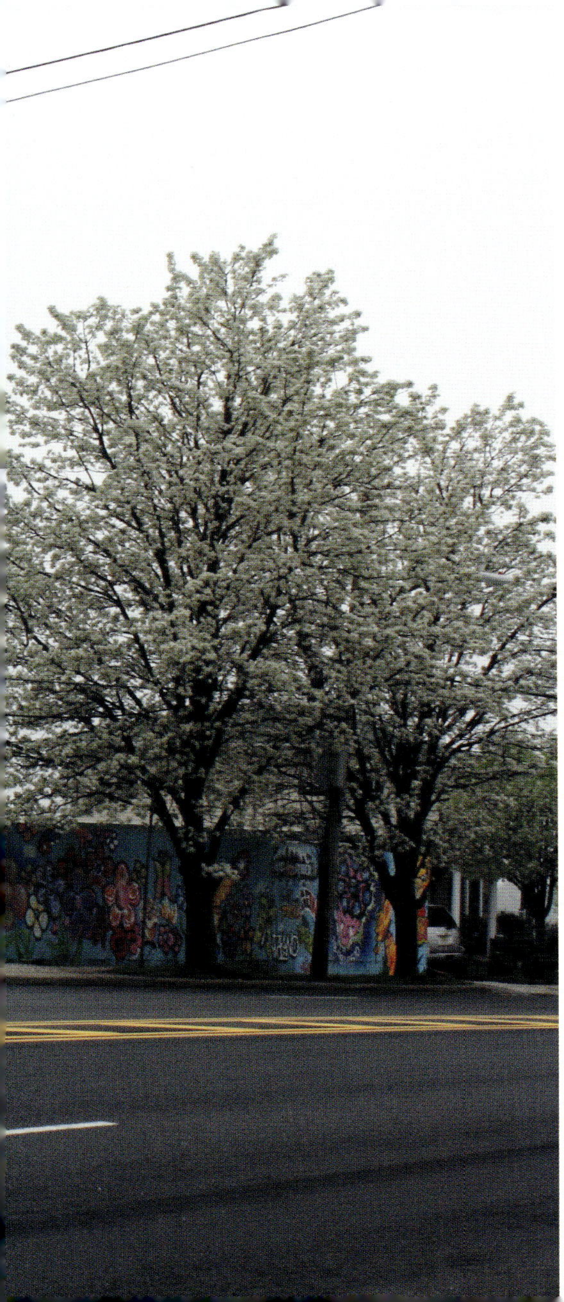

> The graffiti art is all about self expression and putting your name out there and getting known and "getting your ups" and stuff like that. We don't approach it that way. We approach it more like, "Well what would you want us to do?" I think that allows a lot of sensitivity for it, because we're not coming in with the attitude, or to be stand offish. We're coming in the premise of, "OK, you've got a wall. We acknowledge that. You have a business; you own a hardware store. Why don't you let us do something that advertises your hardware store on this wall, and at the same time, we can put in some imagery or things that promote our business and promote those particular artists?"[89]

Anyone who glanced at the construction fence at Clove Place would understand that there was a lot of negotiation with the property owners; save for the six signatures of the artists involved, there is nothing that resembles traditional graffiti murals. Rather, the fence is a mixture of butterflies, flowers, and the slogan of the development, "The Lifestyle You've Earned." Even compared to the blue whale in Jersey City, it's tame, to the point of almost being anodyne. And, as in Jersey City, graffiti style art is in the service of marketing of real estate, with the goal of gentrifying the area.

In any case, painting is just one facet of what NYC Arts Cypher promotes, along with dance, film, and music, and the mural the group organized by the Stapleton railroad station illustrates how they are also involved in promoting traditional New York style graffiti. What's just as important is how Balducci views his larger role in Staten Island.

> I look at everything as something that can be better. I always look at things to be progressive and to move to the next level. I feel like a blank canvas is just something that needs to be painted. So I drive around the neighborhood and I look at walls and architecture and different textures, like stucco and concrete and brick, and I'm thinking "How can we create something on there that would beautify the neighborhood and would help people promote things?" [90]

Wayne Miller said the mural is meant to evoke a "mid-'60s kind of psychedelic painting," that will hopefully remind the sixty-five-and-over set of the summer of love in 1967. Aside from that theme, Miller said they asked that the name of the development be included, along with a monarch butterfly, which is a key part of the branding within the club (the Monarch Club, the Monarch Roof, etc.). He takes pride that everyone involved got to include some input.

> It was a rare opportunity for the business community to partner not only with at-risk kids, but with the art world, and this has been very well received by the Council for Arts and Humanities here on Staten Island. A lot of artists have commented to me personally about what a fabulous thing we were able to do. We served a lot of

> constituencies, and we've been very happy with the response to the building project, where people have actually called up and said, "Hey, that's really gonna go on, isn't it? It looks interesting. It looks like the kind of place I want to know more about." So we've accomplished all of our objectives.[91]

Miller is appreciative of graffiti as an art form, having gone to art school and grown up around theater. In particular, he recognizes the need to guide the teens who have an artistic ambition to an outlet and "utilize that talent and that creative urge that's burning inside of them." To him, tagging is not necessarily the sign of a wayward soul lashing out at the world—it's the sign of a need for an outlet.

> Most of the people I know say, "Graffiti? Vandalism. Put them in jail." It's very cut and dry. That's why I was so happy to be able to bring this to fruition, because I think that if you look closely at what we've done here, you can see the young people who worked on this are really talented. This gave them an opportunity to put forward their creativity in a positive manner.[92]

Once again, Kramer's assertion that there is a gray area, where authorities only see black and white, which comes into play when the question is one of urban vitality. It's much easier, from a political standpoint, to stand firm on harsh sentencing rules for graffiti vandals than it is to recognize the validity of, as Miller puts it, "the creative urge that's burning inside of them." But if they did, it would naturally lead to a realization that those talents might be harnessed for good, via the graffiti mural.

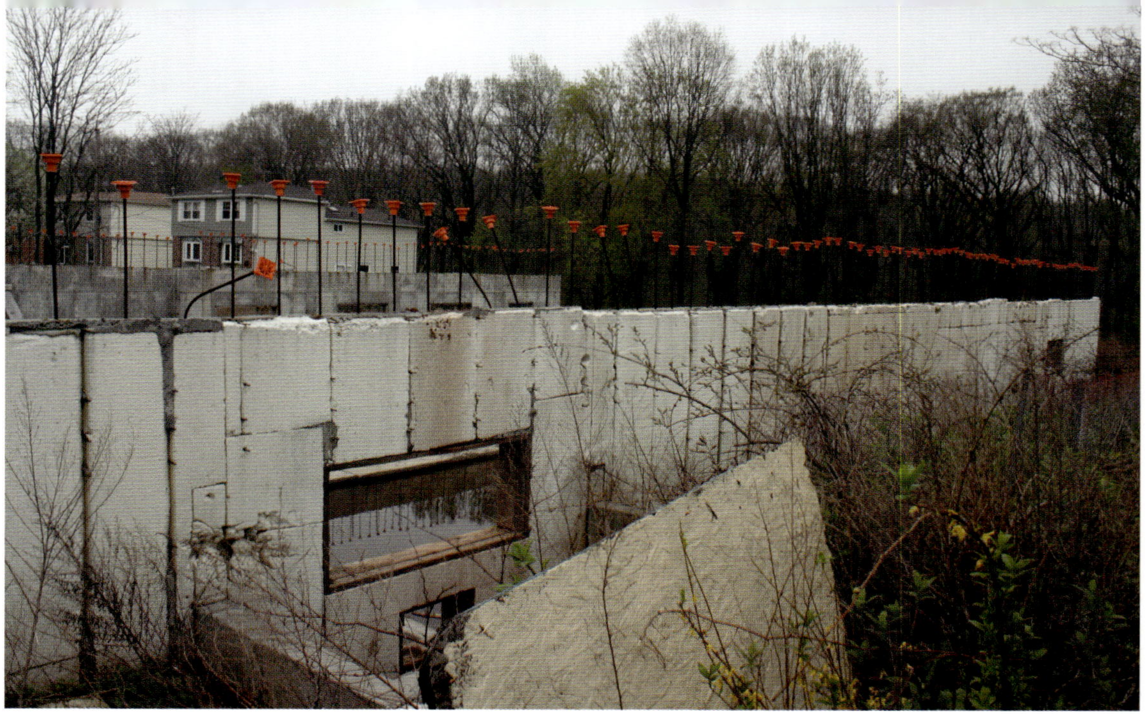

A side view of the construction, with houses on Clove Court in the background, circa April 2011. Photo by Patrick Verel

This is the first time Miller has worked with Balducci on this kind of project, and he said that Balducci's prior experience with others, such as an optometrist Miller counts as a friend, helped a lot when it came time to convince Leewood executives to give them a shot. The fact that it's a partnership between "at-risk kids with spray cans in their hands" and "guys who drive Lincolns and build real estate projects" makes it interesting for him. There's also civic responsibility. Asked why his mural is better than a plain wooden fence, Miller fell on the realm of perceptions. The weathered, ill-kept fence signified that the project had stalled in a weak economy, was a blight on the neighborhood, and was a "constant visual marker for the bad time the United States is in right now." A mural is a rejoinder to several preconceived notions.

By doing this, you're putting a piece of art in the community. You're reminding the community that things aren't all that bad, that there are good kids. And you know, this is Staten Island, which is a conservative, blue-collar community. To show that community that the kids with their baseball caps on backwards and their pants rolled up and hanging around their waists with a can of spray paint in their hand are capable of doing good work, and good things that not only help business but beautify the community, is kind of what made this all worthwhile.[93]

By the time I visited the site, the fence had already been painted, but if the fence was anything like the construction site itself, it's easy to see how it could be construed as blight. The foundation of the development had been poured and the first floor had been started, but the standing water and overgrown vegetation on the site attested to the amount of time it had sat untouched. Where once there stood two houses and a flower shop, there now was only deferred progress.

Geoff Rawling, one of the artists Balducci recruited for the project, met me at an Italian restaurant near the Jersey City waterfront. Rawling, a white fifty-one-year-old Rockaway, Queens, resident who grew up in England, does not fit the profile of a traditional graffiti artist, nor does he consider himself to be one, even though he appreciates graffiti style. Instead of writing a tag, he excels at creating illusions that make it look like there are holes in solid surfaces. He likes to tell a story about getting caught painting on the side of the Berlin Wall in 1979. One of his first jobs as a teenager was painting a sign for the very first Tesco store on Well Street Market, Hackney, in the East End of London. The neighborhood had deteriorated since the store first opened in 1919, but the store was still there in the '70s when Rawling found work there.

I painted all kinds of Jamaican, Pakistani kind of foodstuffs and stuff on the outside, because that was what the neighborhood was like, mostly. We had a big Jamaican market called Ridley Road. So it was very colorful, bright stuff. I actually had a job in the warehouse there, which lasted about six weeks, and they realized I was useless at that, so it was better to pay me to paint instead. I learned very young that once you do one painting, everyone else hires you. They say "Oh, this guy is painting this," and next thing, you're doing the dentist's office, and you're doing the pet store, and you're doing everything in that neighborhood.[94]

Rawling's London pedigree made him an outsider in New York City when he moved here, and he recalls being called a sell-out by fellow Lower East Side artists both because he was willing to work for payment and because he used brushes along with spray cans. As versatile as an artist can get with different size spray can caps, Rawling said that for detailed work or 3D pieces, he prefers to use a brush. For him, spray paint is best used for filling in big spaces.

A lot of guys didn't like that because they'd see it as some kind of...you know, graffiti to them was the spray can and it was doing it for your love and your neighborhood and all of that stuff. You know, I totally understand, but I came across the Atlantic, and I have to make a living.[95]

Like Veng in Brooklyn, Rawling has as much, if not more invested in traditional, canvas-based art. He considers his murals to be a form of publicity that he hopes will generate buzz for his commercial work. He doesn't do outdoor murals for himself anymore, but he does appreciate the desire to be out in public, noting that graffiti is a true art when people can express themselves freely on a wall, and the best place to do that is "in a neighborhood where there's a lot of big gray ugly walls that no one cares about." Where better to, in Walter Benjamin's words, "shock, amaze, inspire, or impress?" He sees his role as a mentor to teens who want to stretch their creative wings but who either don't appreciate the severity of their actions or understand the alternatives.

What I teach the kids is, if you go up to that guy who owns the lot there and it's a big old dirty lot, and you say, "I wanna paint that wall," he's ninety percent gonna tell you, "Go ahead.:

As long as it's not his frontage, you know? The trouble is, a lot of these kids, they don't think like that; they want their name out there. And those to me aren't the real graffiti artists. Some of these kids just want to put their name out there. That's just territorial. They don't have an art form, they're just being, "Yo, I'm here."

And if they do it on the front of your business, I understand why you'd be mad. Even as a kid, I wouldn't have done that, because I understand. Why would you want someone writing graffiti on the front of your building when you're trying to sell pizza? It doesn't appeal to the business. But if that pizzeria has a wall against the subway, which the subway goes by every day, and you say, "Guy, I'll paint a big pizza pie, and I'll do a whole freestyle artwork," they'll love you, they'll probably pay you. So there is a fine line there.[96]

Rawling provides an excellent role model for aspiring artists, but he has no delusions about the motivations of the teens who illegally write and spray tags around town. He knows there's a certain badge of honor for being "the graffiti kid" in school. He also scoffs at the notion that harsh penalties will deter them, because by virtue of their age, they're not considering the consequences of their actions—even if a felony awaits them down the road. To that end, he echoes Halsey and Young's assertion that it's fruitless to simply forbid the writer from tagging. Give them an outlet, though, and murals like the one at Clove Place become not just an alternative to tagging, but a tangible goal for erstwhile taggers.

I've seen the shyest kids who were really talented, sit down in a group and do absolutely nothing verbally, or eye contact, but if you get them drawing, they start going, and they're listening to you. They don't even want to look at you, because they're ghetto kids; they've got too many issues. But they can let it out, and they are listening to what you're saying, you know what I mean? [97]

Jeff Li, Leewood's vice-president and project director, echoes Miller's emphasis on giving teenagers an outlet. First and foremost on the company's agenda is to stir up excitement for the project. But Li is also versed enough in the world of street art that, when asked what his general impressions of graffiti were, his response was that "in the right context, it can be an art unto itself." He noted that Jean-Michel Basquiat, an artist who started out doing graffiti in the 1980s, for instance, ended up teaming up with Andy Warhol.

One of the things that we liked was that Charlie's taking kids who've had run-ins with the law prior to that, specifically for graffiti, and they're providing a place where they can learn their art yet at the same time provide a venue where they can do it legally.[98]

Li also agreed with Miller's assertion that Staten Island is not like the rest of New York City. Aside from being more suburban in nature and conservative politically, he said one does not see graffiti on Staten Island in a "positive way." Until Charlie Balducci came along, he said he hadn't seen "quality graffiti" either, which is another indicator of the fluid interpretations that graffiti can elicit. Where the interview was really the most revealing was when I asked Li to be more specific with regards to the right context for graffiti. There is a difference between graffiti that is intended to be art and graffiti that is intended to be defacement, he said, but identifying where that line exists is hard.

If you see graffiti that's just all over a mailbox and has no artistic content to it, then it's more of an issue for me. I think it has to be respectful of people's property. Certainly an active business that is trying to maintain a clean storefront, I don't think that's appropriate. I don't know that you could call that graffiti, but those space invader aliens… you see those all over the place. There's one right over by the Highline Park.

And that guy's gotten pretty famous. It's pretty small, it's pretty unobtrusive, and it's all alone there on the corner of 14th. So is that appropriate? It looks nice there by itself, but if you start tagging the entire Highline, I don't think they'd be very happy with that. You see stuff like in the pavement, with the robot man stuff. Again, is that

> appropriate? Some guy probably has to dig that out when they do the streets.
>
> So the appropriate… It's like the Supreme Court says with obscenity. I'll know it when I see it. [99]

Li was referring to the works of Invader, a French urban artist who embeds ceramic tiles into the walls of buildings to create small homages to the 1978 arcade game Space Invaders, and Stikman, who embeds tiny stick figures in pavement. That he would cite this type of art as an example is not terribly surprising, as the medium of street art, be it in the form of wheat pastes or stencils, has become much more popular since the release of the 2010 Oscar-nominated documentary *Exit Through the Gift Shop*, which featured Invader. The intention of the creator of a piece of street art, which is what Li was wrestling with, is a tricky concept to fully explain, and while it's not surprising that someone who is a property owner would shun vandalism, it's instructive that Li is willing to consider that not everything that is unauthorized is necessarily vandalism.

As chance would have it, Clove Place was the perfect space to see that very divide. While interviewing Miller at the site, I noticed that a section of the fence where Balducci had thanked Randy Lee, the NYPD 120th precinct, Montana Paints, and the New York Department of Cultural Affairs had been defaced. A red "X" had been spray

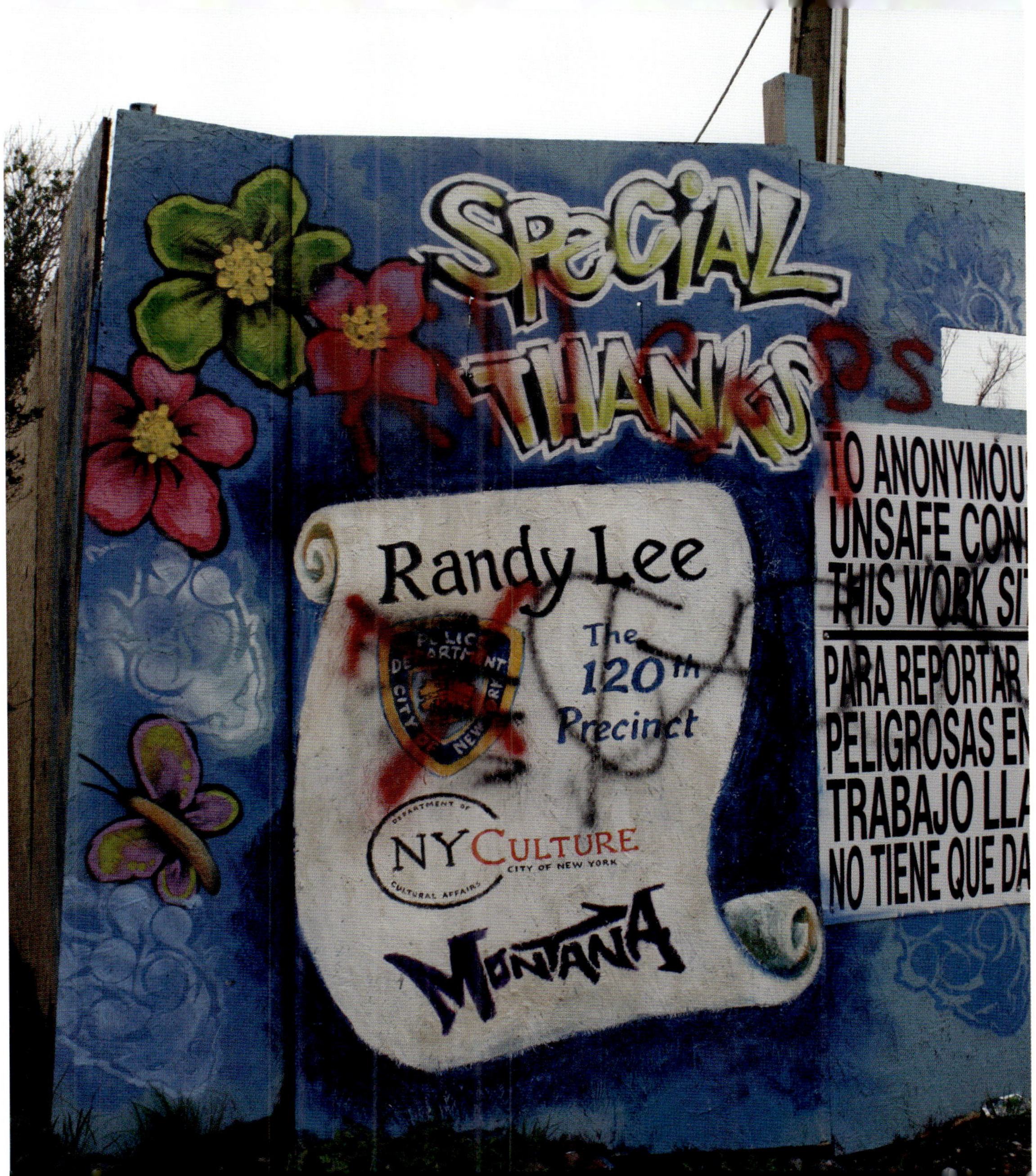

The defaced section of the mural, circa April 2011. Photo by Patrick Verel

painted through the NYPD shield, and "Kill Cops" covered the "Special Thanks" section. While Miller got on the phone with Charlie Balducci, a woman walking a dog nearby told me that there was more vandalism just down Clove Court, the U-shaped street next to the development.

Miller and I found the development's shared mailboxes had been defaced with a crudely drawn red five-point star, heart, and tag "Marz," and a unintelligible black scrawl. A fence nearby likewise had black spray paint of what appeared to be the word "Penas." In less than an hour, Balducci arrived, and armed with white spray paint, covered over the offending works on both the construction fence and the mailboxes. It was a vivid illustration of the fact that when it comes to vandalism, there can sometimes be no deterrent strong enough to discourage someone with an axe to grind. There were few obvious "releaser cues," of the sort that Phillip Zimbardo spoke of, for instance. The Clove Place construction site was not in the best shape, but the neighborhood, while not terribly flashy, was tidy and well maintained. It's also worth noting that the vandalism was directed at a part of the mural mentioning the police, not all of it. It's possible that this was precipitated by someone lashing out against the harsh measures the city promulgates as part of its "broken windows" theory, or it could be any number of reasons.

But the important take away from it, as far as I'm concerned, is that the vandalism was directed at a very distinct symbol of power, and not at the flowers, butterflies, or other aspects of the mural

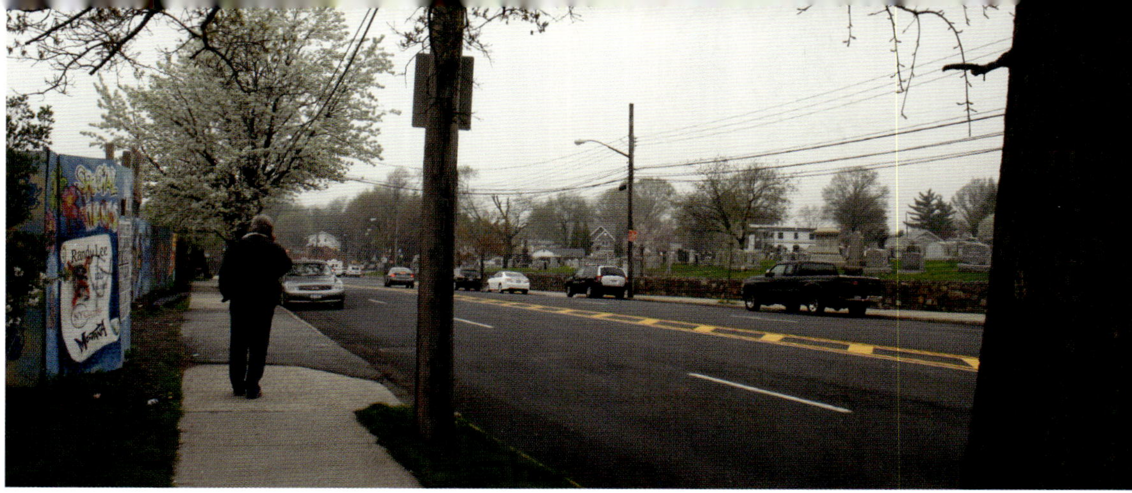

The development's most prominent neighbor is a quiet cemetery, circa April 2011. Photo by Patrick Verel

The defaced mailboxes, circa April 2011. Photo by Patrick Verel

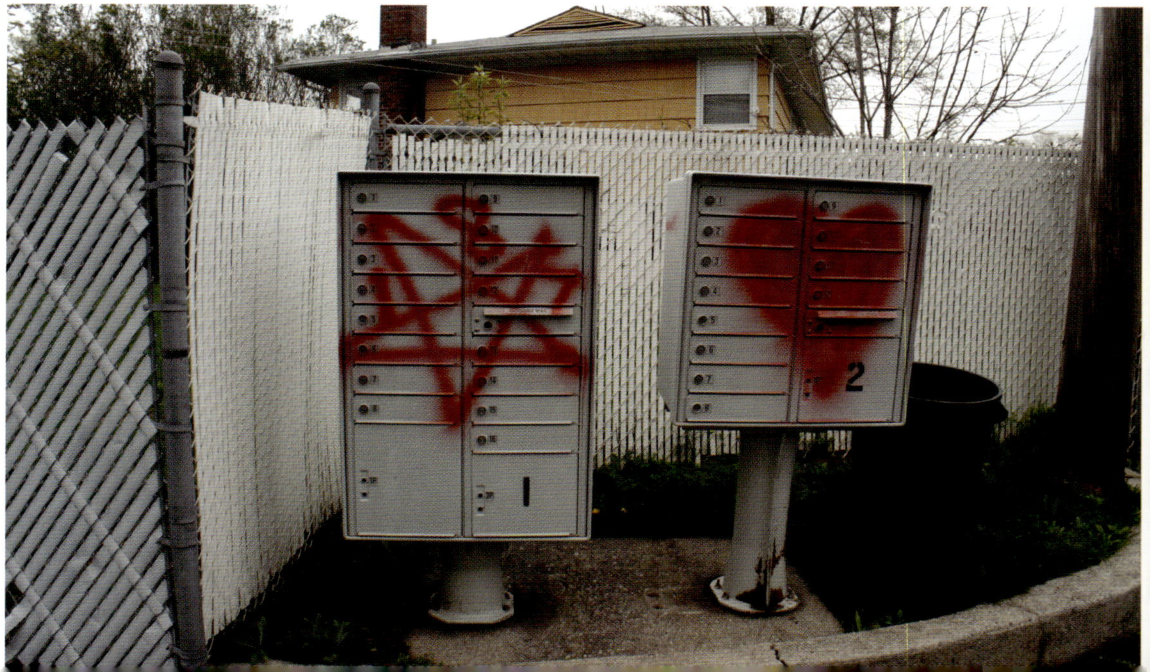

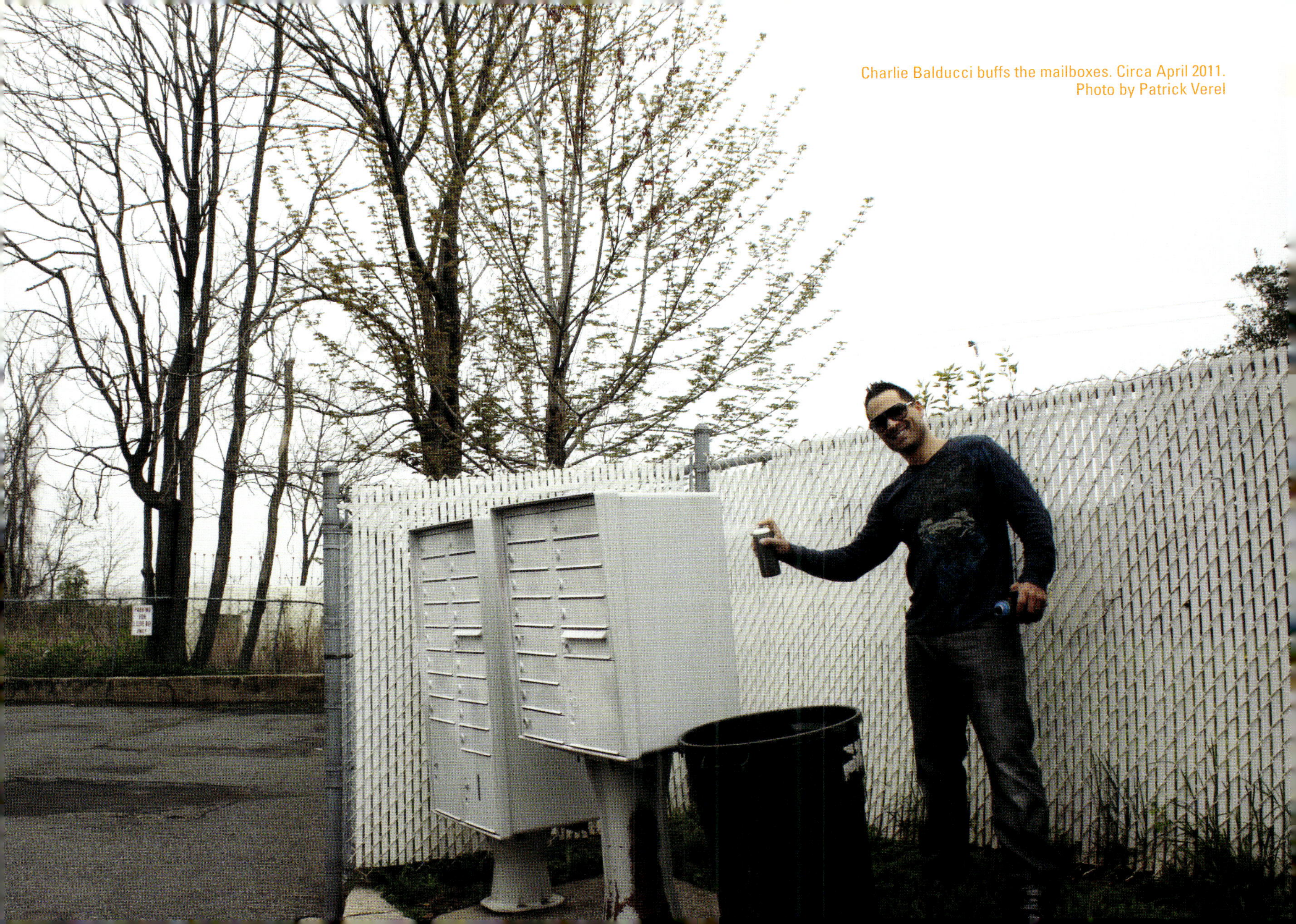

Charlie Balducci buffs the mailboxes. Circa April 2011.
Photo by Patrick Verel

that the teens worked on. Miller's reaction, and Balducci's rapid response, also makes a compelling case for anyone who doubts that mural makers take ownership of their creations.

Kent, a white man in his forties who had lived for the last two years with his girlfriend in the house that abuts the site on Clove Road, approved of the way the mural caught the eye, noting that he first thought it was graffiti because their house had been tagged before, but "then you take the step back and you see the beauty of it, and the detail that went into the work."

> I don't know if I want to say calmer, but it catches your eye. It takes you into a better place, with the butterflies and the...It just puts your mindset in a different space.[100]

Kent noted that the neighborhood was both figuratively and, with its proximity to a cemetery on two sides, literally, dead. He moved to the house after the development had broken ground, and said he'd wondered if construction would ever start again. He guessed that the tags on the mailboxes and the "Kill Cops" had been done by someone on Clove Place, although he declined to say who he thought it might be. Asked whether the mural made the neighborhood a better place, he said that it gives it "an asterisk."

> Not that it's a bad place, but it definitely... It brings a little bit of life to this little area right here, with the cemetery. The colors and all definitely brought it up, especially during the wintertime.[101]

Down on Clove Place, Tom, a white man in his sixties who had lived there for twenty-six years, begged to disagree. Although his wife, who was the one who tipped me off to the vandalism on the mailbox, insisted that I speak to him about the mural, our conversation lasted a mere ninety-six seconds. He didn't like it, he didn't consider it art, and his general impression of all graffiti was that it's "a mess." That last observation was revealing because as straightforward as the flowers were, to him they still held an aura of edginess that was too much for him.

> **Q:** What do you think of it?
> **A:** I don't really like it. I don't know...I would just rather see a plain fence. I don't think its art, for me. It looks like graffiti to me.[102]

Louise, also white and in her sixties, was more open to the mural. A resident from across Clove Road for the past six years, she was on her way home from the gym when I spoke to her. She wouldn't go so far as to say the mural made it a better place, as she preferred to see actual houses at the spot, but it was an improvement over a yellow fence with random tags on it.

> When I see graffiti, it looks like it's kind of a low life neighborhood, you know? It doesn't look good, no. I don't like it. You're talking about the graffiti and the scribbling and all that? Yeah. But something like this to me is artistic. Somebody's expressing themselves.[103]

{6}

CASE STUDY

Trenton

Art That Lifts a Struggling City

Trenton was not in the original plan. The city, which is sixty miles southwest of New York City, is within the New York Metropolitan region, but its central New Jersey location puts it much closer to Philadelphia (thirty-four miles). When I first started visiting murals, I focused on New York City and its immediate environs because the city occupies a singular place within the realm of graffiti. But while perusing njgraph.com for a contact in Jersey City, I stumbled on a video report from CNN about an annual party thrown by a company called TerraCycle. It was sort of a block party, except instead of pony rides and clowns making balloon dogs, the entertainment was a slew of graffiti writers unleashing their best swoops, swooshes, and twists with spray cans. I knew I needed to learn more about this place.

As it turned out, the organizers of the graffiti writing at TerraCycle were the same ones I'd interviewed in Jersey City: The SAGE Collective. Will Kaso and Luv 1 weren't available for interviews, but fellow SAGE member Leon "Rain" Rainbow was extremely helpful, going so far as to give me a tour of the collective's many murals around Trenton. TerraCycle, where we met and spoke, was in a desolate industrial section of town, sharing space with a car impound lot, a power substation, and a few forlorn houses, including a clearly abandoned one with only half its aluminum siding still attached.

I also met former TerraCycle spokesman George W. Chevalier III there. The company started at this location in 2003, and they started allowing artists to paint on it shortly after. In 2007, they started throwing "graffiti jams," and every year since then, they've buffed the entire two-story building clean before opening it up to the community. The rest of the year, the outside of the building facing the street and the expansive courtyard behind it is open to a cavalcade of artists both green and experienced. On any given weekend, young men and women can be found milling about on the grounds, working on pieces, refining techniques, and trading ideas about future projects. Graffiti is not just a feature of the building's exterior—it's on the interior walls, too.

Chevalier said the company's embrace of graffiti goes deeper than mere aesthetics. TerraCycle's business plan revolves around collecting products like used plastic pens and juice pouches and repurposing, or "upcycling," them into useful products like bags, pots, ice melt, fertilizer, and a sundry of other products. As the company notes on its website, "Graffiti in fact is a form of waste as people typically pay to remove it and at TerraCycle we embrace all forms of waste!"[104]

Chevalier expanded further:

> Trash is something that people just like to push away and not think about, and graffiti is kind of a scourge on the urban landscape. Most people just want to kind of paint over it and not think about it. We said, you know what? These guys are talented, why don't we

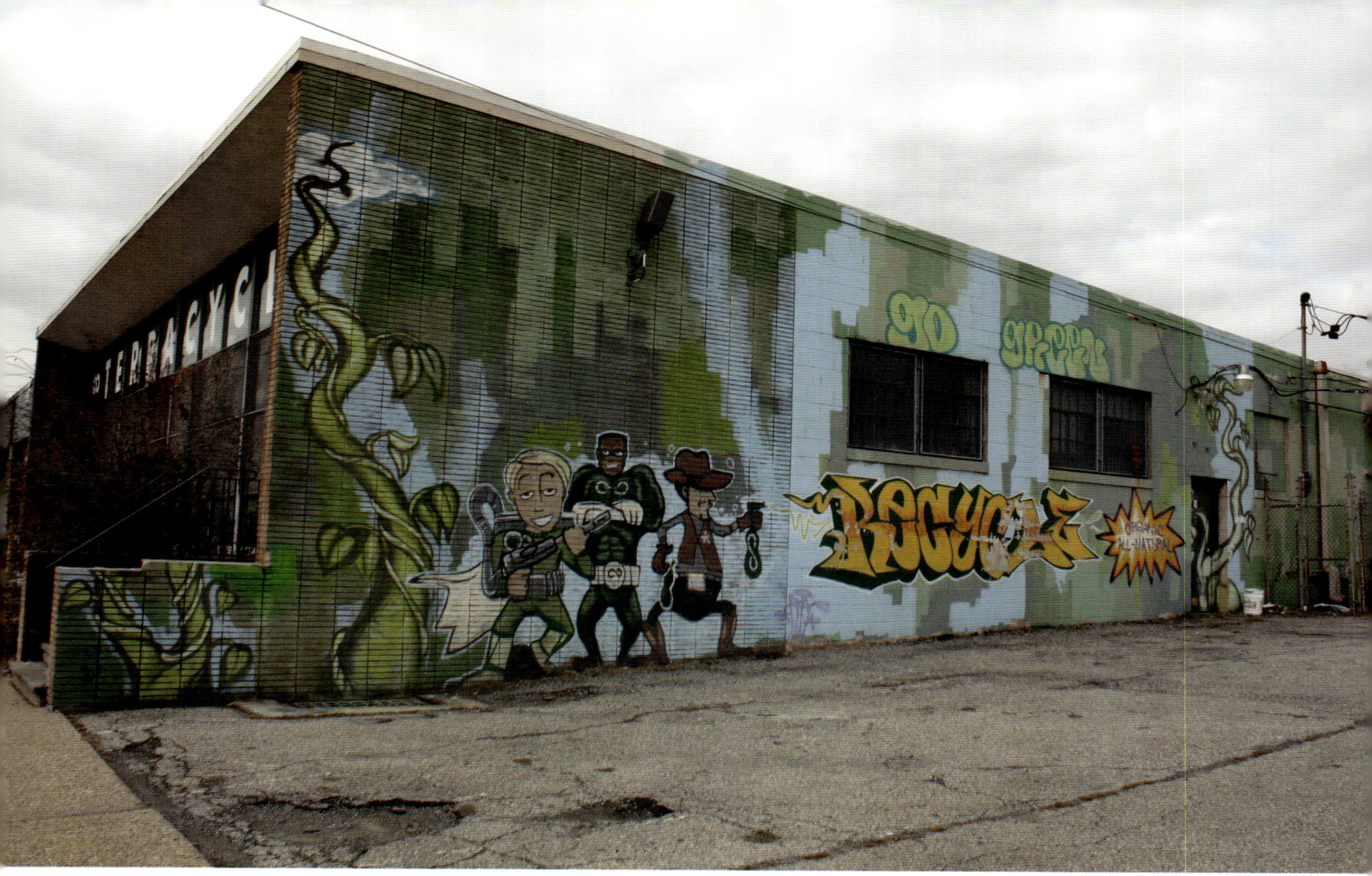

TerraCycle's offices, as seen from Hillside Ave. Mural by Rain, circa March 2011. Photo by Patrick Verel

embrace it? But if they're throwing up a quick hand, and its basically defacing property, that's shitty. If they're coming in and we're embracing it and giving them an opportunity to spend some time on it, the results, they speak for themselves.[105]

When TerraCycle started out here, in what was once a distribution center for *The New York Times*, it had all the room the company needed. They expanded into other facilities in Trenton over the years, and today, the space is mostly used as offices. The neighborhood is as utilitarian as one might expect in an industrial corner of a town where thirty percent of the residents live below the poverty line.[106] In this sea of grays, blacks, and browns, there is the flash of green accompanying a posse of whimsical cartoon super heroes, red surrounding the second half of the phrase "Eco Friendly" and purples, oranges, and blues of the pieces adorning the front of the building. Chevalier said artists are given free reign in the courtyard behind the building, to the point where he once felt compelled to have a bikini added to a drawing of a busty woman in the court yard when a group of fifth graders visited on a tour. The anything- goes attitude works there, because the courtyard is hidden from public view. Not so for the sides of the building facing the public.

> That's where visitors see us and get their first impression. So it's a little bit more toned down. It's not quite corporate, because it's still graffiti, but it's a little bit more, I think, digestible to the random various guests that we get. I mean, we get business people coming in. We don't want to jar them too bad.[107]

Front/back distinctions aside, Chevalier said his company sees itself as young and fun, and as such, the original tan and white scheme of the building would be a mismatch.

> It didn't fit with our energy and our style, and also, it's a little bit drab, just because like I said, it's a post-industrial scene here. So we figured it would be a good way to brighten everything up and make it a bit more cheerful and express our personality a little better.[107]

TerraCycle's closest neighbors on New York Ave., circa March 2011. Photo by Patrick Verel

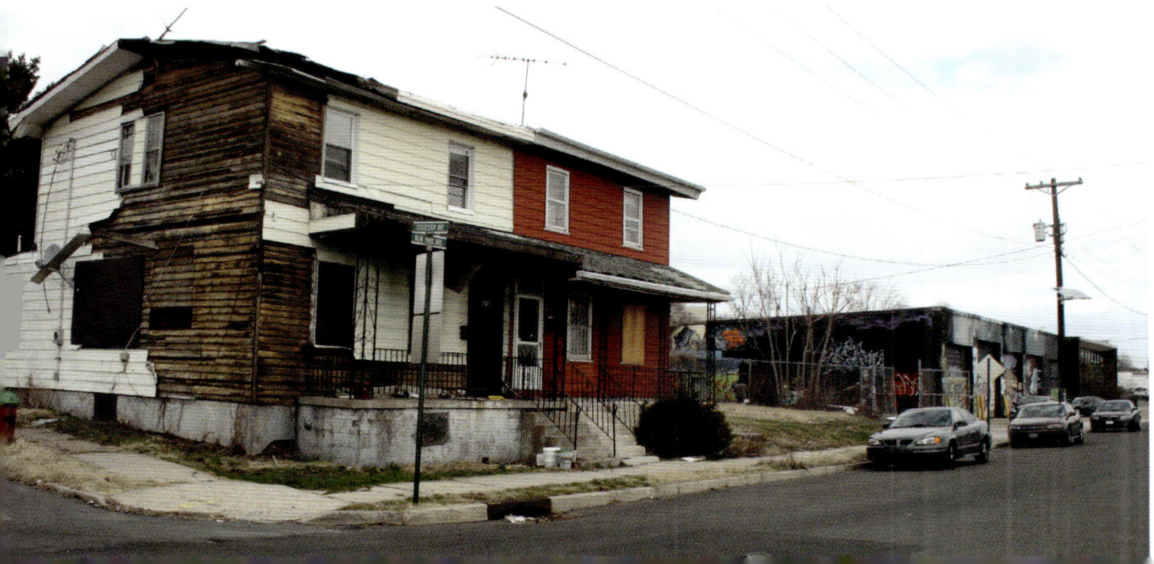

TerraCycle has developed a relationship with several artists that is tight enough that they have been given keys to the courtyard for after-hour access. One of the employees, who is himself a writer, photographs many of the finished pieces, and Chevalier said they're considering publishing a book of the photographs. In addition to the exterior walls of the building, an unused trailer and an old loading dock are fair game for writers; the varied surfaces make it an exquisite environment for graffiti. The recycling ethic of the company even trickles down to the writers; during my visit, one 20-something gentleman volunteered that he paints used spray cans and gives them away as gifts. Chevalier said it's nice to be associated with such a hip young crowd, and it also brings them closer to the community.

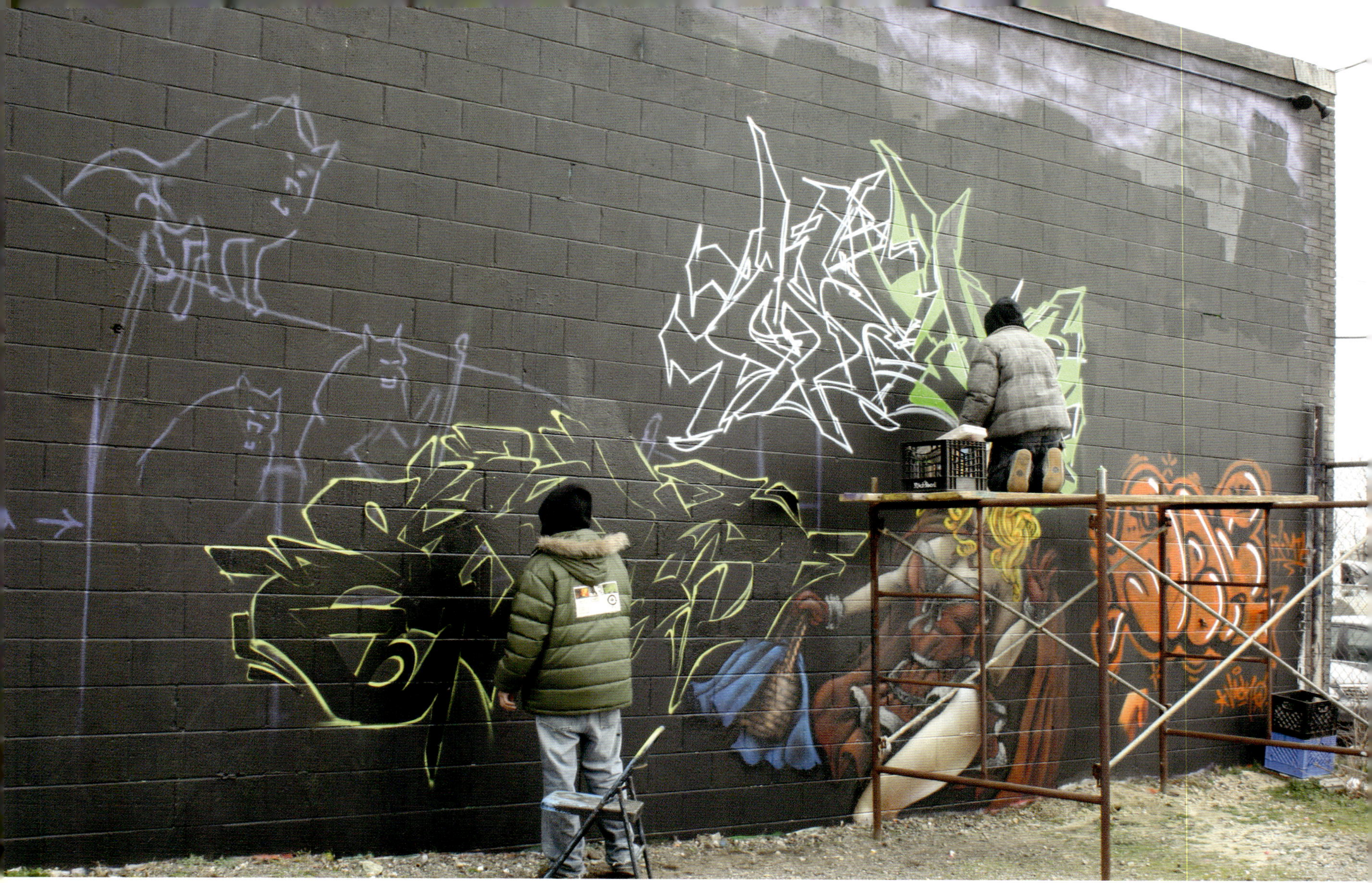

Writers Mek and Evak at work on pieces at TerraCycle, circa March 2011. Photo by Patrick Verel

They do lots of good stuff in the community, and they do lots of good stuff for us. They're instrumental in the graffiti jam—they actually do graffiti classes. They don't approach it from the standpoint of "All right, this is how you become a vandal." They approach it from the artistic standpoint. They literally spend classroom time doing sketches, working on style and all that, and then they use our walls. In doing that, we're kind of a part of that. More people in the community get to hear about TerraCycle. So it does work both ways.[109]

That connection came very early on. Rain recalls meeting TerraCycle CEO Tom Zachy at a party between 2000 and 2003.

> I hadn't seen him in a few years, and then one of my friends, a dude that I knew that worked there, was like, "Oh yeah, he got this warehouse down in Trenton now." And he was like, "Yeah, you should come down. He might be open to, you know, having you guys paint down there, or doing some projects with you.'[110]

That was in 2005, and like the Tats Cru's arrangement with Borax Paper, it started with a sign for the business. In an arrangement that would please David Harvey, the company leveraged cultural uniqueness in the service of the bottom line. But when it opened the gates of the courtyard to writers of Rain's ilk, they didn't just make available a space to while away the hours. They also embraced what Harvey touts as "collective symbolic capital, to which everyone has, in their own distinctive ways, contributed," in a way that is not obviously tied to their bottom line. Unlike the construction fence mural in Staten Island, the graffiti murals at TerraCycle are a permanent feature of the company's physical landscape, and as such, a vehicle for Trenton's still-evolving graffiti scene. As Rain tells it, this space has allowed writers to practice their own styles and learn new ones from others, be they locals or visitors from New York or Philadelphia. He said TerraCycle understands the benefits of their work.

> I think TerraCycle's one of the only companies that really, really capitalizes on having legal walls. I think it really works because they're a young, hip company and they're trying to show that. Like, "Oh, we're different, we're not the standard corporation."[111]

Rain got his start young, writing in books and occasionally tagging when he was thirteen. He started seriously painting in 2003, doing productions, organizing events, and teaching classes on aerosol writing. He estimates that he works twenty-four to thirty hours a week for a web design company, and thinks of graffiti murals as part of what he does.

> There's definitely money involved with certain things that I do. I do commercial work, and it's not always what I want to do, as far as I might be painting somebody's logo, which is fine. But that wouldn't be something that I would normally do. I think that I enjoy using aerosol. I enjoy painting with the guys I paint with.[112]

He still writes illegally, at what he calls "chill spots," which are lower-risk painting areas like dead train lines or abandoned buildings. Up until recently, he also had access to two sides of a TerraCycle warehouse at the end of Roberts Avenue. The bulk of that space faces a wooded area and a culvert, but another side of the building is visible from the railroad tracks that carry Amtrak passengers up and down the East Coast. This location provided a high-profile perch for the group until July 2012, when the company that TerraCycle had been renting it from changed its mind and restricted access to the site.

This hasn't deterred the group, though. For example, from September 21–23, 2012, they organized "Windows of Soul," a block party featuring artists painting on abandoned buildings in downtown Trenton. This is the niche that the SAGE Collective, which is a registered 501(c)(3) nonprofit, has carved out for itself.

> Most of the community embraces us as far as when we do legal walls in the city. We're in some of the worst areas of the city. Places where most people wouldn't go, we go and paint. A couple years ago, we did a little schoolyard in a real cutty alley, but there was kids that came to that park every day, you know what I mean? So it's like, you

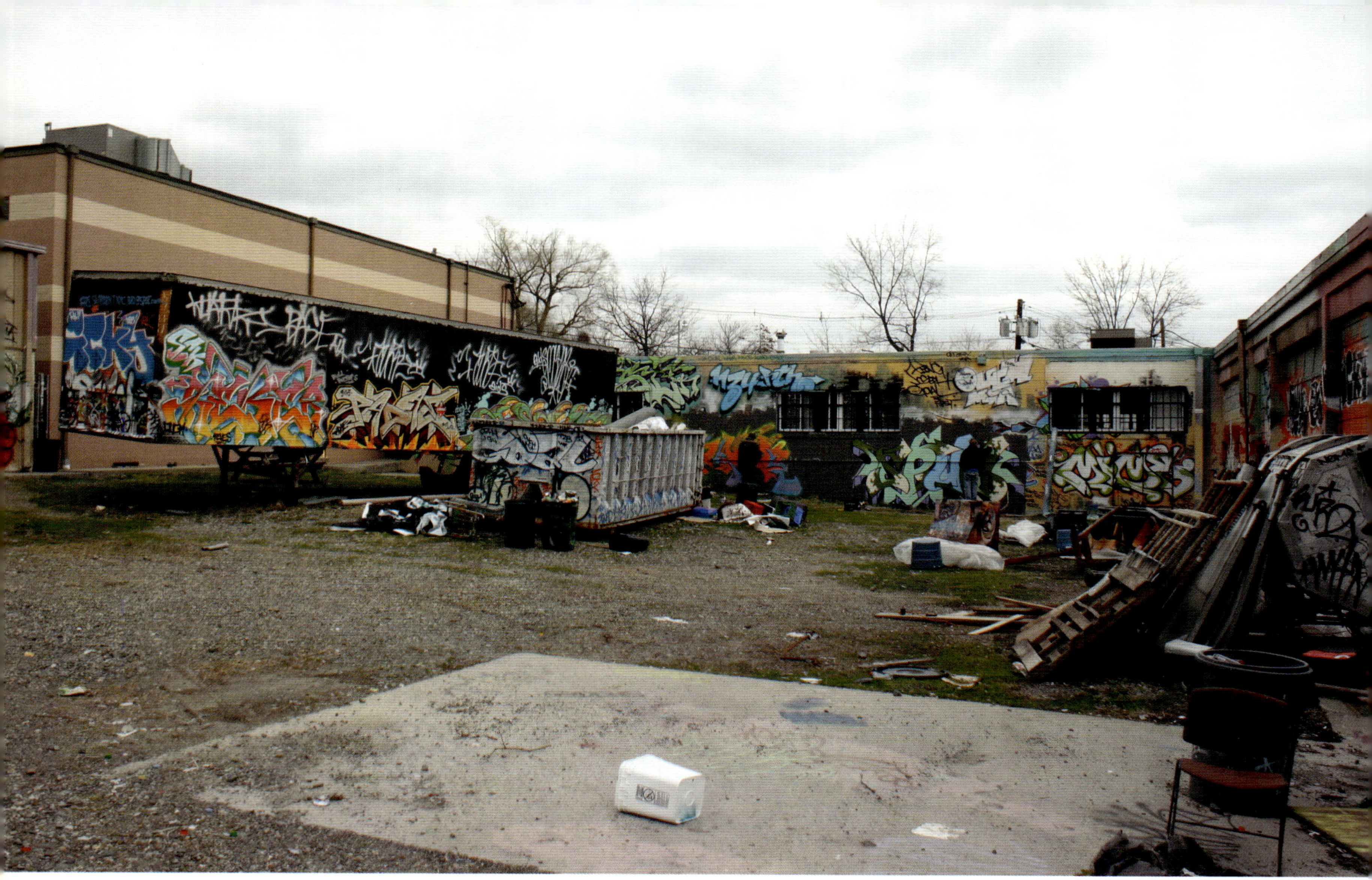

The courtyard at TerraCycles's office, featuring pieces from, among others, Goal, Spun, Icky, Reker, Padae, and Mime, circa March 2011. Photo by Patrick Verel

know, they loved it. I've had the old ladies hold the flashlight for me, or bring me stuff to drink on a hot day, and you know, that type of thing, the police have come, and once they see you have permission, or you tell them you have permission, it's just like, "Oh, OK," and they're like, "Why don't you do the character leaning against the wall?" or whatever.[113]

The work that Rain and Will Kaso do is perhaps the best example of putting art to work in the service of community. Rain embraces legal painting in part because, like Nicer, he has business interests tied up in it (he also does body painting), but also because he does not see it as any less interesting than illegal work.

> When you are doing stuff in the street, you learn how to paint fast and clean, you're in and out, you're learning how to whip the can, your mind is just going, and you're thinking of all the possibilities, and you're hearing all of the sounds, and everything. When you're painting a legal spot, you're thinking, "How dope can I make this? How beautiful can it be?" or just working out the different angles. It just has the aesthetic, you know?[114]

Working in a place like Trenton presents challenges that are different from those in New York City. Rain said he tends to steer clear of buildings that are owned by corporations or chains. He feels the city of Trenton supports them, befitting its status as the state capital, but the city is also the home of county, state, and federal authorities that are not as accommodating. So the collective's work tends to be focused on neighborhoods outside the downtown. Even in neighborhoods where murals are welcome, Rain has found himself negotiating with local residents about what is proper and what is not. For example, in response to an elderly woman's request, he once changed an angel and demon drawing in an alley to a mural that was inspired by the phrase "An idle mind is the devil's playground"—a devil reaching into a person's head, which contained drugs and guns. She hated that, too.

> So I tried to get my friend Ross, and we did this beautiful mural. It had like beehives and mad flowers, but the way I did it was hot. But Ross did this character, and she was black, and it was in a black area, but he painted her blue, just because you, it's his shit, you know what I mean? If he wants to paint her blue, he can paint her blue. But the woman said because she was blue, she looked like a demon! Heh, heh, heh. But you know, but the building owner, he seen us in the paper a couple of times, and he said, "That woman is crazy! That's not graffiti, that's art."[115]

Rain tends to steer clear of politically tinged graffiti, but he is very much in tune with Harvey's notion that murals—being an original, creative, authentic, and unique phenomenon—are an explicit symbol of power. Harvey cautions that monopoly rent derived by symbolic capital is forever in danger of being captured by multinationals and powerful segments of the local bourgeoisie, whereas Rain makes the case that even though no one has exclusive control of the US citizenry, the elite need to feel in control. The existence of graffiti is a direct challenge to that because it is an exertion of control over physical space.

> Other than our name, we're not gonna paint, all the [political] stuff that the government would be afraid of, but just the fact that they don't have the control petrifies them.[116]

He also scoffs at the notion that blank walls might be preferable to murals, making a point that was seldom brought up: It's silly to debate the question of mural versus blank walls when our public spaces are already dominated by commercial advertising.

> What's the point of all these billboards along Route 1? Why is that better than seeing the sky? You know what I mean? So the way that I'm looking at it, is that, if there's places for people to have paid spaces in our society, then there should be places for people to have free spaces in our society. Why should the corporations that have tons of money be able to be the only ones that put what they want out there? Why can't we express ourselves and what our views are? You know,

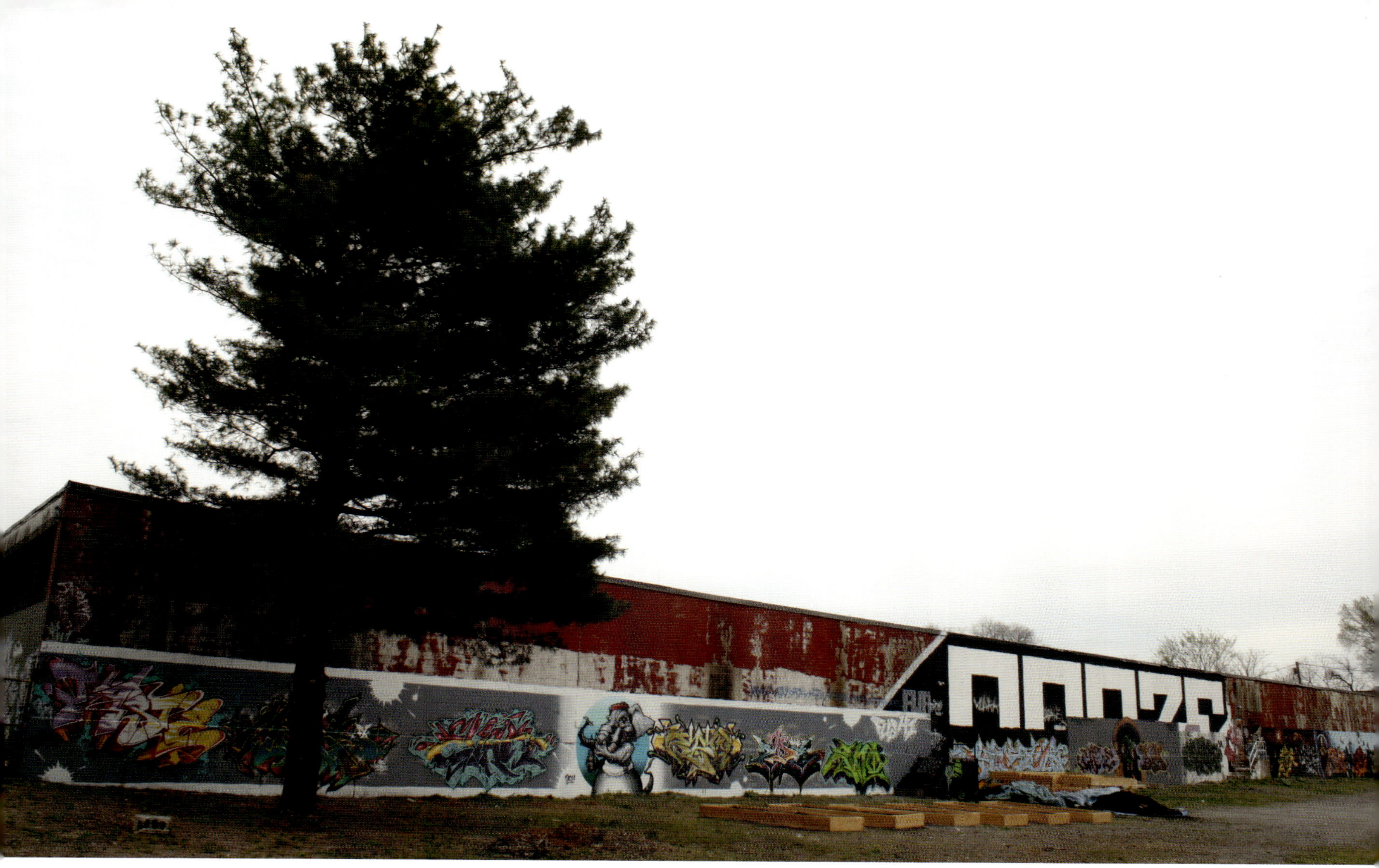

At a warehouse at the end of Roberts Ave., works from left to right: Taste, Mek, Evak, Reo, Zoe, Sno, Sew, Bird, Pro, Ras, Mek, Mek, Zoe, Perv, Reo, Evak, Rage3, circa April 2011. Photo by Patrick Verel

a lot of what we do is just color and style, but in our reality, we should be able to express that freely.[117]

TerraCycle has an obvious connection to graffiti in the sense that it dovetails with the company's self-image as a hip, young company. But in inner-city Trenton, that rationale is not as common. Rain said that unlike New York City, Trenton does not have much illicit tagging, so when he approaches a building owner to ask permission for their space, graffiti prevention is not part of his selling points. But that doesn't mean there isn't a benefit to the owner.

> Basically I'm taking the burden of maintaining that space away from the owner. A lot of the walls might not be tagged, but some of these walls, if they haven't been maintained for fifteen years. They have splotches of where they were tagged ten years ago and someone just put a big mess over it, or just from having shitty paint; the paint's flaking up, or there's something crappy in the wall. We'll paint over it, and the way that I look at it, it looks better than what was there.[118]

And what of those who see the work of artists like Rain? As with Borax Paper in Hunts Point, TerraCycle is in a very desolate part of town, so finding neighbors who were willing to talk about the collective's work was very difficult. Sylvester Street, which runs perpendicular to the building, has several houses with back yards that border the courtyard, but few residents were around during my visit; one declined to speak, and another asked that I call him at another date, only to rebuff me when I did. I was also rebuffed by the business behind TerraCycle on Hillside.

Brian, the owner of the next closest business, Hawkins Towing, did take a few minutes from his job dispatching tow trucks around the region. His two storage yards full of car carcasses were the defining feature of this end of New York Avenue. He'd been there for fifteen years; he said he took over from another auto body shop that had been there previously. He had mixed feelings about the goings on next door. On the one hand, he said the neighborhood was rough, so anything that was "constructive" would make it a better place, and that what was going on was neat. At the same time, he hedged when asked if the murals made the neighborhood a better place.

> Yeah. I mean, either way I guess it doesn't make a difference. To me, it doesn't, you know? But it's pretty neat, because it kind of goes with their you know, it's a Terra Cycle thing.[119]

He echoed Rain's assertion that graffiti is not something that he sees in Trenton as often as in New York City.

> I don't think it should be done on stuff that people don't want it on, obviously. You see a lot of it. I know there's lot more of that in New York than there is here, I think. I see a lot of trucks graffitied on, stuff like that. You do see it here, but not as much as you see it in New York.[120]

Sindy, whose mother has lived on Brunswick Avenue, a block uphill from TerraCycle, since 1995, was much more emphatic in her endorsement of the murals. The house where her mother lives is a little further away from TerraCycle than the houses on Sylvester Street, but I figured the lack of response from the residents there warranted a walk a block further.

> **Q:** Are you familiar with murals that are over there around the corner?
> **A:** Yes, I am.
> **Q:** What do you think of them?
> **A:** Oh, I like them. Every time I go by there, I just like to drive my car really slow so I can admire everything, you know?
> **Q:** Really?
> **A:** It's really nice. I like it.
> **Q:** Is that on your way? I mean [where we are now] is sort of the more main thoroughfare.
> **A:** No, no. But if I'm coming off of work, which, pretty much that's why I'm here, my mom babysits my kids. So I'm getting off of work right now, and I come from Route 1. And I'll come from down the back way here, and up the street. That's how I see it all the time.[121]

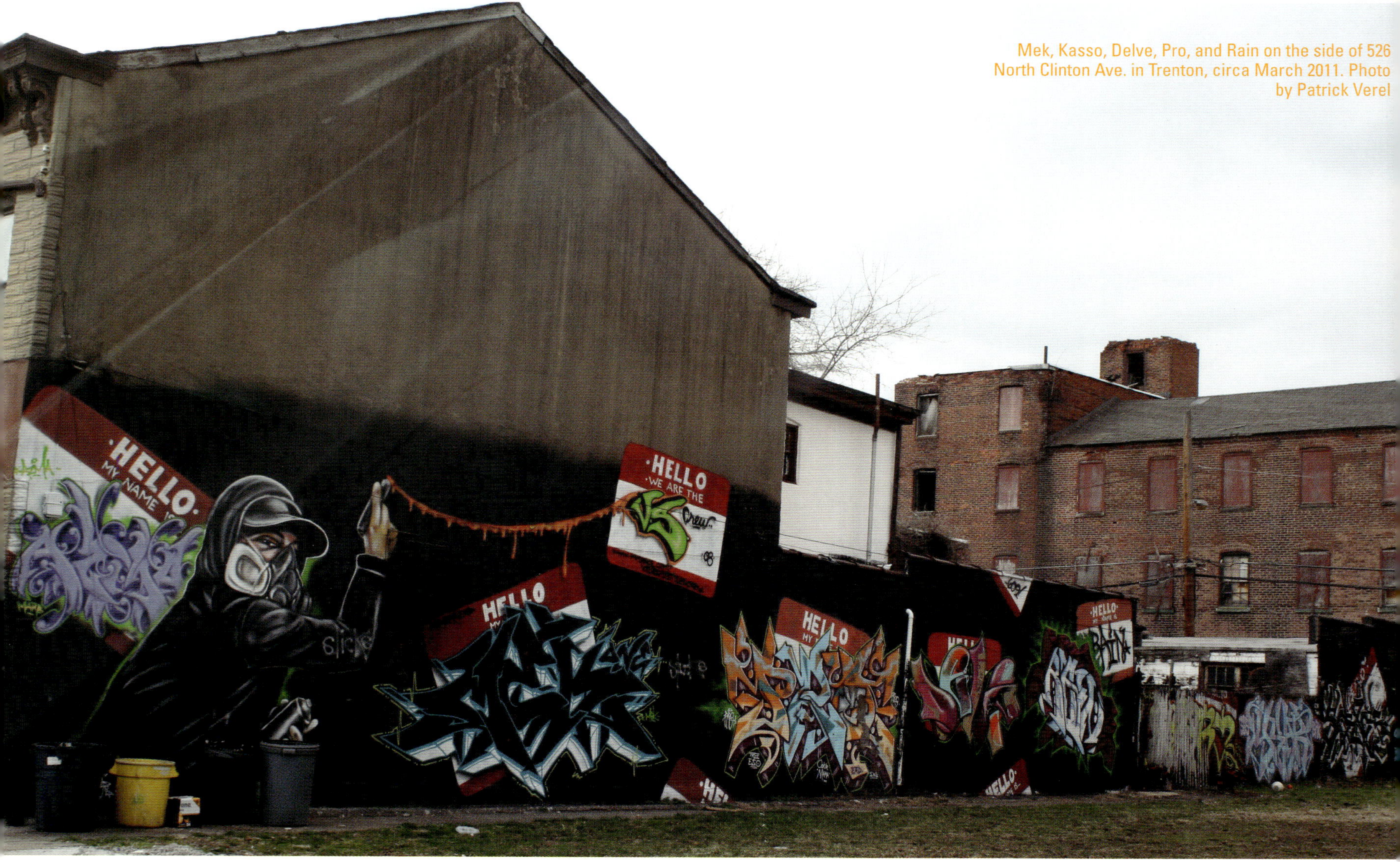

Mek, Kasso, Delve, Pro, and Rain on the side of 526 North Clinton Ave. in Trenton, circa March 2011. Photo by Patrick Verel

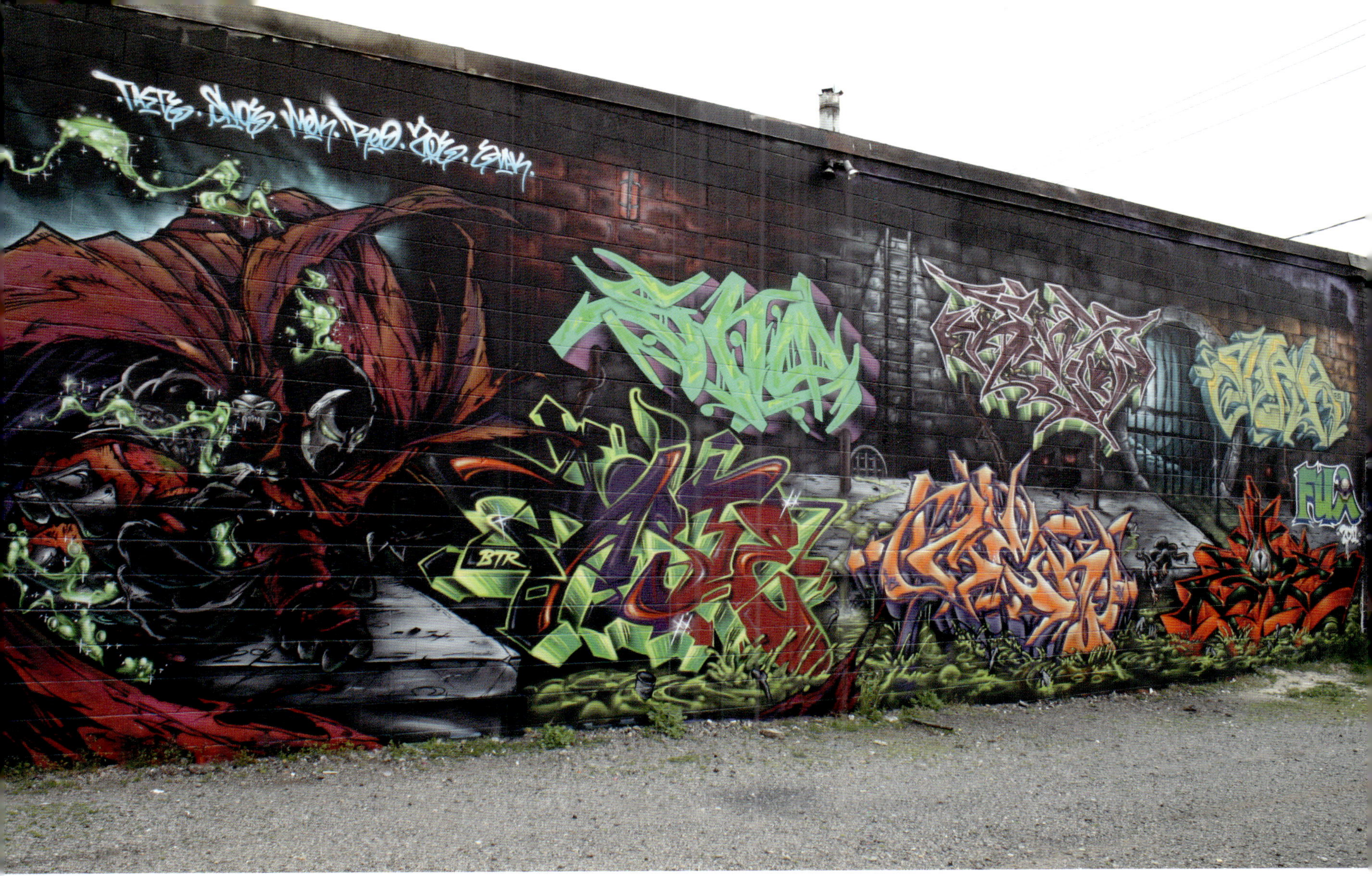

Taste, Mek, Evak, Sno Reo, and Zoe on the wall at TerraCycle, circa April 2011. Photo by Patrick Verel

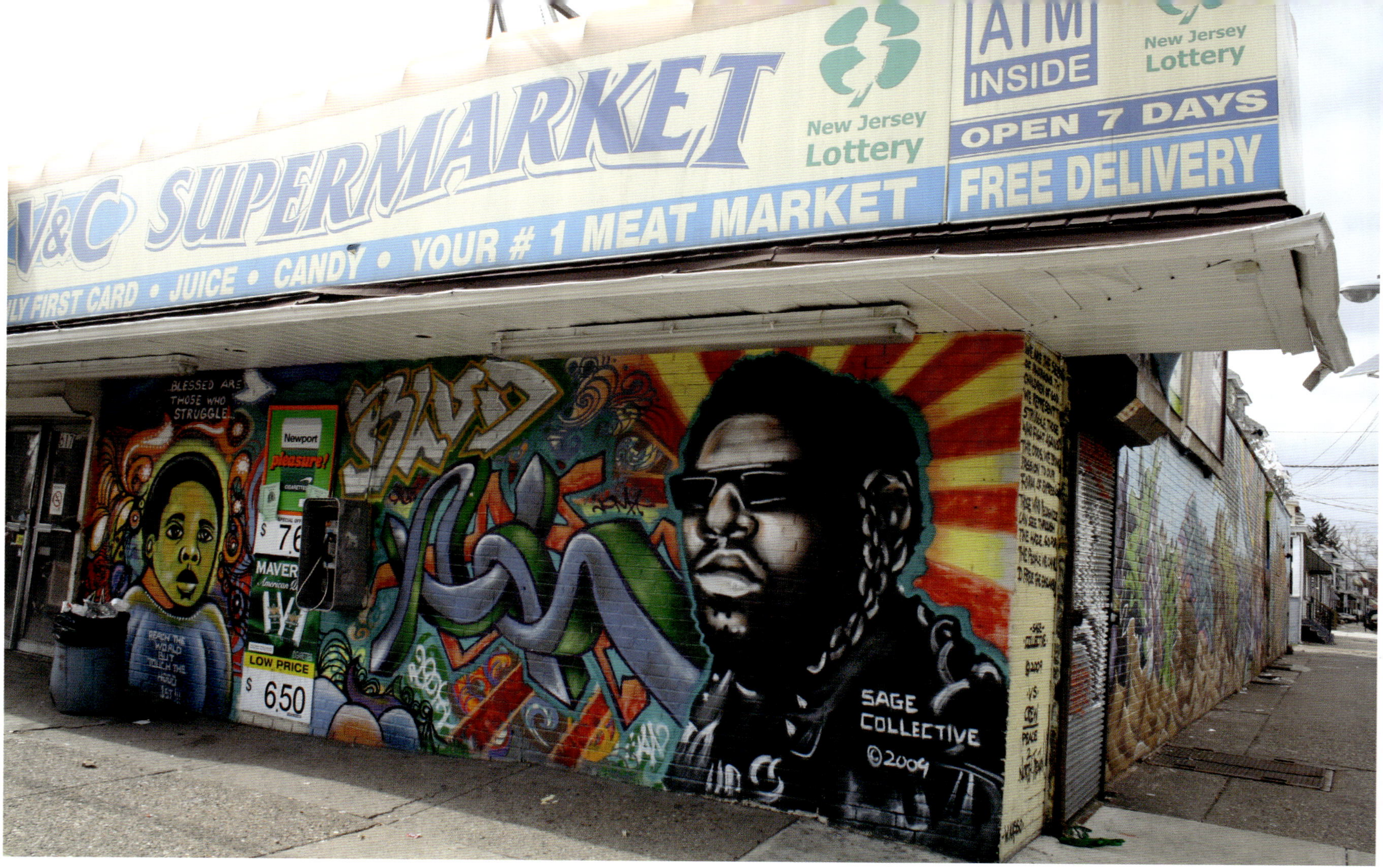

Kasso and Luv 1 on V&C Supermarket on Martin Luther King Jr. Blvd. in Trenton, circa March 2011. Photo by Patrick Verel

{7}

Philadelphia's Mural Arts

Lessons from the City of Brotherly Love

No examination of graffiti and its effects would be complete without a chapter on Philadelphia. Like New York City, the City of Brotherly Love has a rich history of graffiti, with Philly resident Darryl McCray, a.k.a. CORNBREAD, making headlines in March 1971, four months before TAKI 183 did in New York. Perhaps just as important, the city was also the site of the Graffiti Alternatives Workshop (GAW), which was founded in 1972 and "provided alternatives for writers and involved them in art projects around the city."[122]

GAW has been gone for some time, but today the city is home to a plethora of public murals on a scale rivaled by few cities in the United States. Philadelphia's Mural Arts is a huge reason why this is true. Founded in 1984 by former mayor W. Wilson Goode as part of the Philadelphia Anti-Graffiti Network, the organization works with community groups to create murals throughout the city. It has to date produced more than 3,600 murals and works of public art.[123] The Anti-Graffiti Network hired muralist Jane Golden to reach out to graffiti writers and "redirect their energies from destructive graffiti writing to constructive mural painting."

With a history stretching that far back and a collection that large, in a city that is the fifth largest city in the United States and a mere ninety-three miles from New York, it's a natural place to look for ideas. The city's leaders have somehow found a way to embrace public murals, so why can't New York City?

To get a better sense of what the group does, I spoke via phone with spokesperson Amy Johnston. One of my first questions was how they choose where to commission a mural. Some of her answers were similar to those I'd heard from the artists I'd spoken to in New York. She said they look for walls that face traffic, so the finished product might be included in tours of the neighborhood, walls that are in good shape and made of stucco, concrete or brick—though not historic brick—and walls that are ideally near a green space that might lend itself to a garden.

> More than that, is there an anchor in the community to help us communicate information about the project and gain support from the surrounding neighborhood, such as a CDC, or a block captain or a church group? Is there some place that might be able to provide meeting space, and ongoing oversight for the project, so that if there are any problems, in addition to the property owner, there are others that can monitor, and let us know what's going on?[124]

Because the Mural Arts program has been around for so long and is so well known in Philadelphia, Johnston said the group rarely has to "sell" a mural to a property owner; fully half the murals commissioned are done at the request of the owners. The average mural measures thirty by thirty-five feet and takes six months to complete. During that time, the group follows a 144-step process involving meetings and consultations with a sundry of residents, the property owner,

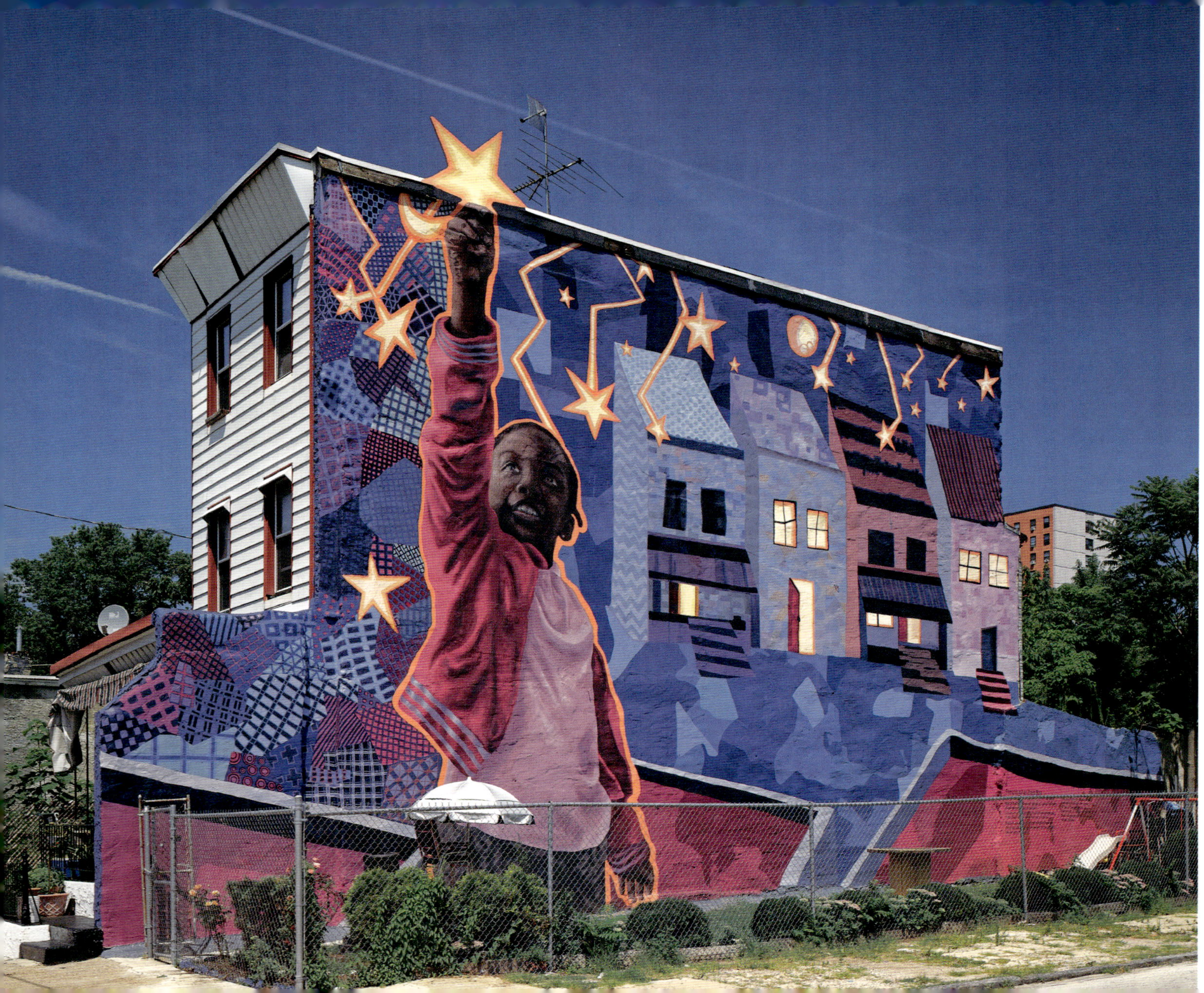

Reaching for Your Star © 2003 City of Philadelphia Mural Arts Program / Donald Gensler. Photo by Jack Ramsdale, circa November 2013. Reprinted by permission.

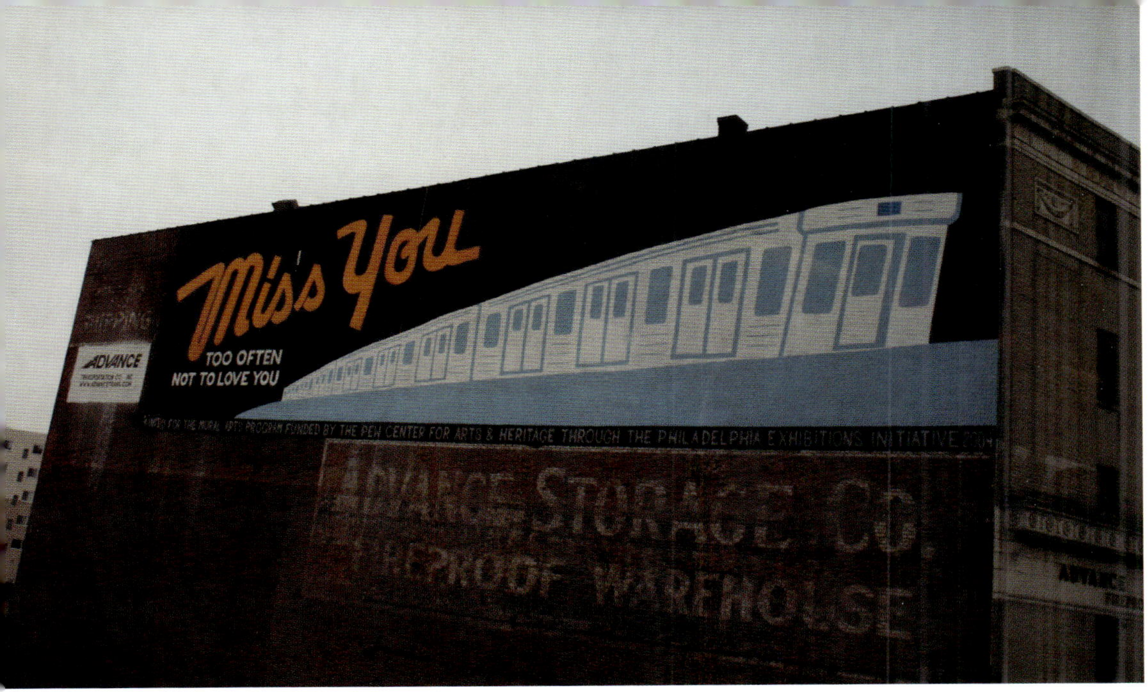

A Love Letter For You © 2009 City of Philadelphia Mural Arts Program / Steve Powers (aka ESPO), circa February 2011. Photo by Patrick Verel. Reprinted by permission.

and the artist. It's an exhaustive gauntlet, but it's one that has been key to the program's success. Perhaps just as important, it ensures that caretakers exist (i.e.: block captain, church group) for murals once they're completed; located as they are outdoors, murals are vulnerable to the elements and require occasional maintenance.

This intense style of formalized, grass-roots level negotiation is in marked contrast to the often haphazard, "gentleman's handshake" agreements that are the hallmark of most of the collaborations that I found in New York City. So too is the variety of murals in the city. Just as there is a gulf between what is acceptable to Stapleton, Staten Island and Hunts Point, so too is there a noticeable difference between HOW and NOSM's mural in City Center and David Guinn's *The Heart of Baltimore Avenue* in West Philadelphia. That's not an accident, as Johnston said they no longer think of themselves as an anti-graffiti program, but rather a pro art program.

> Philadelphia is a city of neighborhoods, with many different stories and cultures, and so the artwork really does reflect those commonalities and those differences. So when you go to North Philadelphia, for example, you'll see more Latin-influenced murals with imagery of Puerto Rico. In South Philadelphia, you may see more murals of Italian American heritage, but also Mexican and Vietnamese, which are incoming cultures. In West Philadelphia, you may see more murals that highlight the traditions of African Americans.[125]

This isn't to say that the murals don't serve as a deterrent to graffiti vandalism. In part because of the sense of ownership of the murals that is instilled in the community, and in part because Mural Arts reaches out to graffiti artists whose work might be covered up and offers them a chance to be involved in the final product, Johnston says they are largely left alone. "It's about a climate of respect, and our community engagement process creates a sense of investment and likability that contributes to the longevity of our work," she says.[126]

Now, Philadelphia has a lot of things in common with New York City, but real estate pressure is not one of them. So although the installation of murals throughout the city is laudable, it is not, as is the case with New York, something that is done in the face of intense pressure to extract monopoly rent from the capital. But it is authentic in the sense that Walter Benjamin advocated something should be. Whether one prefers that an artist work alone to pursue his or her vision of the proper mural, as many of those I spoke to in New York do, or engages in intense collaboration, the way Philadelphia's Mural Arts does, there can be no doubt that the work of the muralists is "embedded in the culture of tradition." It is for this reason that New York would be wise to embrace, if not the entire 144-step process used in Philly, the notion of mural arts as something more than just temporary adornments for spaces awaiting rejuvenation. Johnston notes that the group is not exclusively concerned with supervising murals; it also acts as a resource for property owners who want to commission an artist on their own. They get a request at least once a week.

> Mural Arts can serve as a resource and a clearinghouse for those kinds of requests because we can connect the talent that we know of with folks who have opportunities that, for whatever reason, we're not able to take on directly. It's wonderful to be a kind of conduit for employment.[127]

Johnston agrees that putting a mural on a wall is a more tangible sign of an investment in the community than a buffing might be, because the former necessitates community engagement. The engagement that her organization brings is much more formalized than what is evidenced in the graffiti murals I've featured in my studies, but the result is similar. The biggest difference is Johnston's group has the official support of the city; the artists I have featured do not.

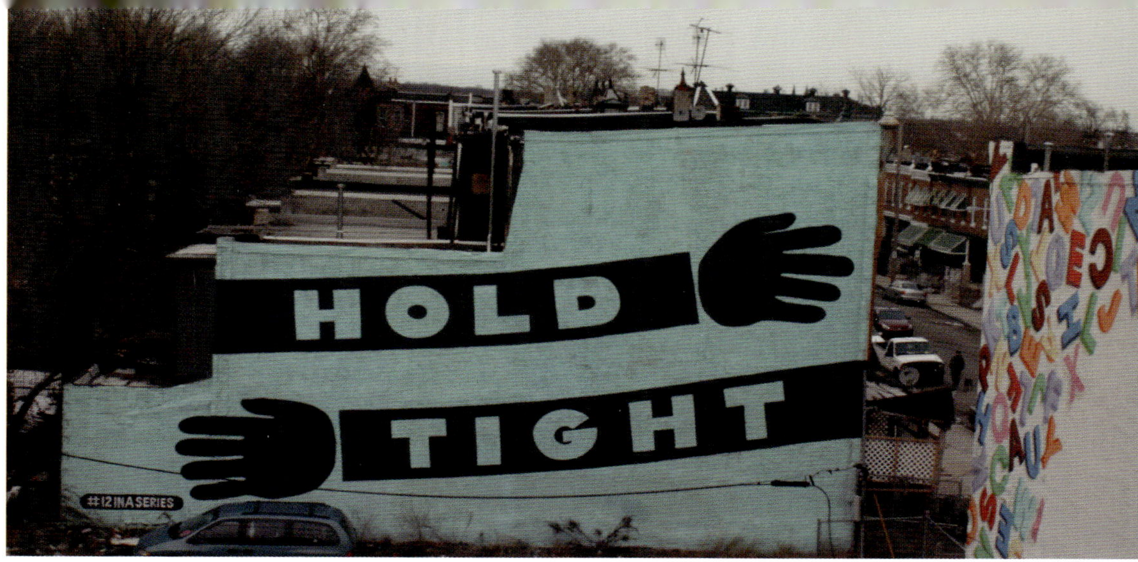

A Love Letter For You © 2009 City of Philadelphia Mural Arts Program / Steve Powers (aka ESPO), circa February 2011. Photo by Patrick Verel. Reprinted by permission.

> Murals have the ability to bring diverse constituents together, people who might not otherwise have had occasion to meet around a common and positive purpose. So connections are formed, and as I said, other positive opportunities can come from that, not necessarily directly but in a catalytic way.[128]

The Mural Arts program in Philadelphia seeks to prove its murals have a tangible effect on their surroundings, beyond vague notions of "community." In the course of my conversations with Johnston, she recommended two studies to help me understand the demonstrable effects of murals on neighborhoods.

One is the work of Susan Siefert, a professor of social welfare and director of the Urban Institute at the University of Pennsylvania and Mark Stein, a city planner who runs the Social Impact of the Arts Project. Focusing on individual neighborhoods, they collected data including census records, child welfare outcomes, and property sales, and layered that with information they gleaned from cultural organizations in the neighborhood. Their definition of a cultural activity was generous, including science museums and libraries. Their *Philadelphia and Camden Cultural Participation Benchmark Project* was published in 2005 by the University of Pennsylvania and was the basis for a report from

The Reinvestment Fund (TRF), which describes itself as a national leader in the financing of neighborhood revitalization.

After reviewing the benchmark data that Siefert and Stein collected, the TRF staff interviewed people involved in community development and cultural activities and examined the arts- and culture-related investments within its portfolio and reflected on how those investments relate to its model of investor-driven change. One of the group's conclusions would find favor with the artists I interviewed.

> In a city like Philadelphia, which has lost half a million residents over a fifty-year period, the recovery of a vacant wall or a vacant lot is akin to fixing the "broken window;" it sends a signal about civic and public norms and neighborhood capacity. It is a relatively low-cost, high-impact form of place-making that creates something authentically public out of a deteriorated piece of real estate.[128]

"Place-making," a multifaceted approach to the planning, design, and management of public spaces, is not a term that I have used in this book, but "authentic" in the sense that Benjamin describes it, certainly is, and "sending a signal" is in line with symbolic interactionism's premise that people act toward things based on the meaning those things have for them.

The other document relevant to this notion of empirically driven evidence of the usefulness of murals in neighborhoods comes from the Econsult Corporation. The group was commissioned by Local Initiatives Support Corporation and the city of Philadelphia to examine commercial corridors in Philadelphia and produce a framework to help funders, the city, and other interested parties better understand the effectiveness of interventions for commercial corridors. Their analysis combined extensive data gathering with econometric analysis to investigate the drivers of commercial success for all 265 of the retail corridors in Philadelphia.

Among the findings of the study were two interventions that demonstrated a "significant relationship to corridor success":

- Business Improvement Districts, which improve the physical environment for businesses
- Pennsylvania Horticultural Society land stabilizations, which convert trash-filled lots into green spaces.

The study also suggested that three additional interventions offered some indication of a positive correlation to corridor success:

- The city of Philadelphia's Business Security Improvements program, which reimburses business owners for security measures;
- Philadelphia Local Initiatives Support Corporation investments, which provide gap financing for housing and other development initiatives; and
- Mural Arts Program project, which bring communities together to convert abandoned lots and blank walls into public works of art.[129]

As result, one of the five policy actions recommended at the conclusion of the report is an endorsement of the mural programs, using language that distinguishes murals quite plainly from empty walls.

> Because appearance matters, there should be more efforts like *PHS land stabilizations* and the *Mural Arts Program*, because they are effective and cost-efficient ways of replacing eyesores with symbols of care.[130]

I asked Johnston to comment on this notion of a mural being a "symbol of care" and pressed her to explain how it might differ from a freshly cleaned wall. She cited one that was completed in her own neighborhood, on a former carriage house turned auto shop that she called a "big gray cube of a building." Like all of Mural Arts's commissions, this mural went through extensive revisions based on community input, which as I noted earlier is not something I feel is necessary

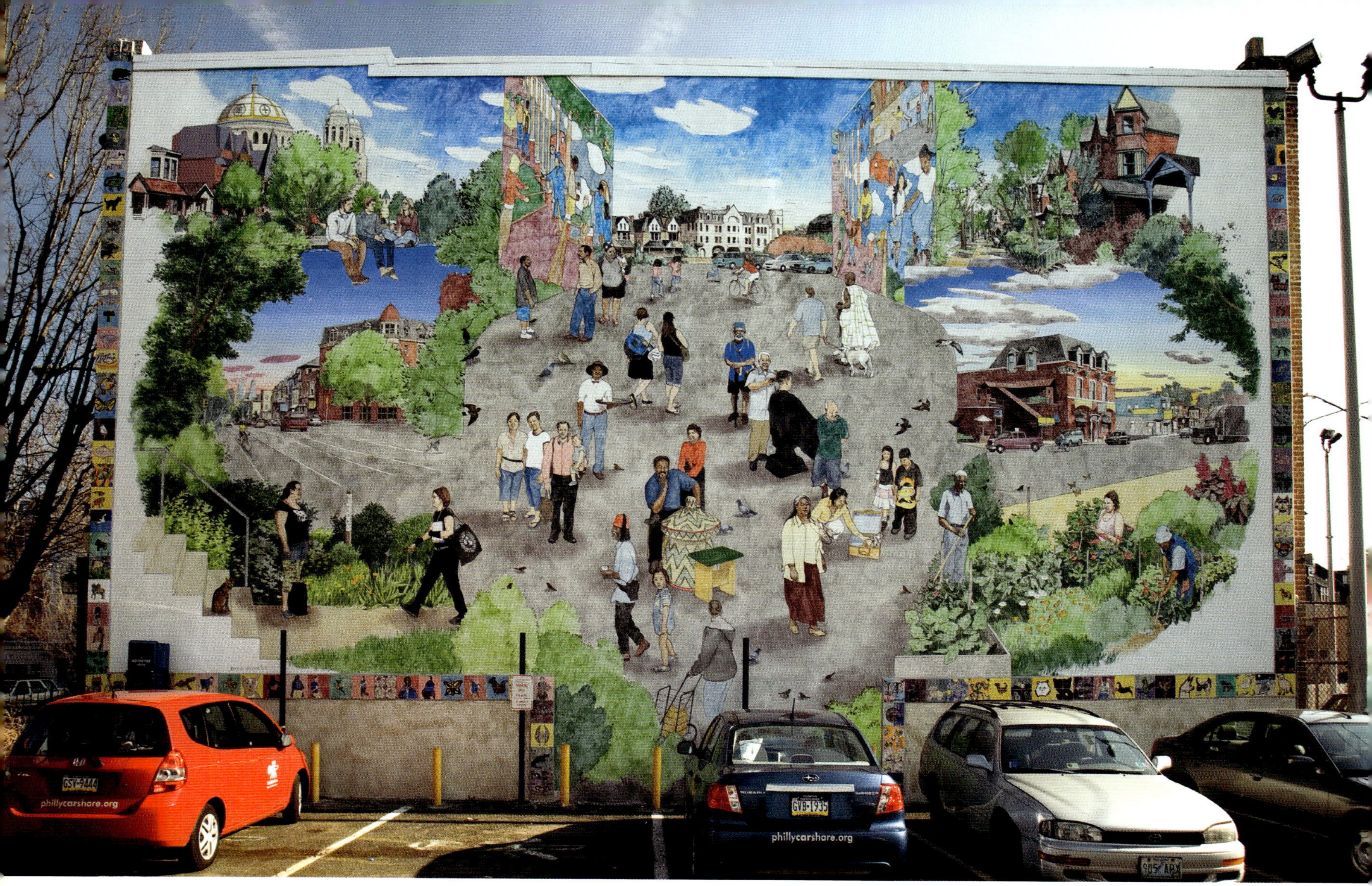

The Heart of Baltimore Avenue part I. David Guinn, circa December 2007. Photo by Jack Ramsdale. Reprinted by permission.

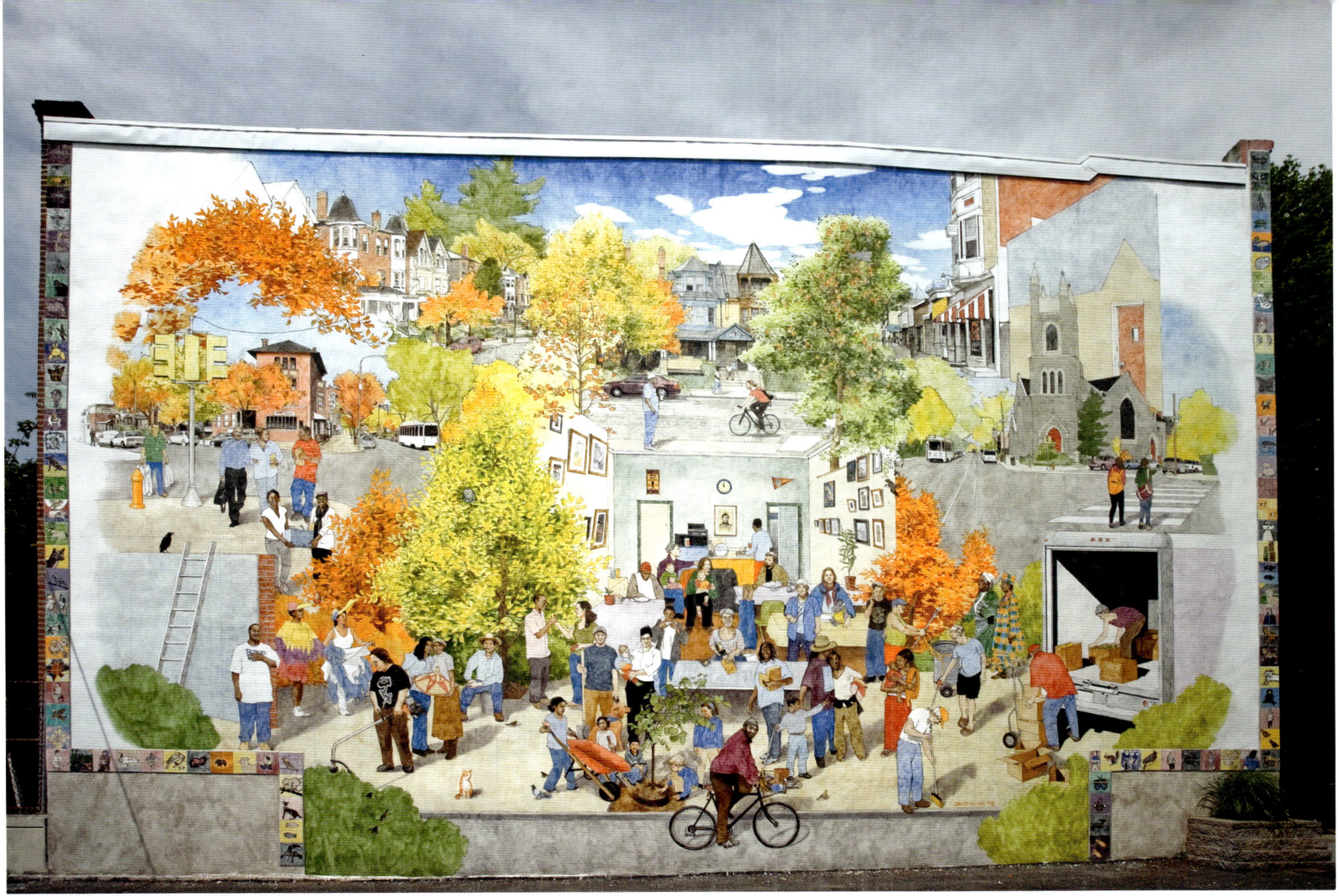

The Heart of Baltimore Avenue, part II. David Guinn, circa July 2008. Photo by Jack Ramsdale. Reprinted by permission.

in all the case studies I've detailed. But her story does speak to the power that public art can have on a community, especially when it's reflective of the neighborhood in which it is located.

> There's a Section 8 (low-income rental) house on the block where the mural was painted. After the mural dedication, it came to light that the neighbors had had some serious trouble with a former tenant and the tenant had to be evicted. That experience caused neighbors to be slow to warm to the new tenant, because they didn't know what to expect and didn't want to take a chance on getting to know the family.
>
> Well, the new tenant made these wonderful shish kabobs for the mural dedication ceremony, which was a potluck barbecue. Everybody loved her dish, and her generous gesture changed neighbors' perceptions. "Oh, this is somebody who's making a contribution and who we want to welcome and get to know," they thought. The neighborhood is demographically and financially diverse, but it's still considered fairly affluent. I had no idea that the mural would help to heal the neighborhood, but that's exactly what it did. So, what that said to me was, really anywhere, in any situation, murals can have positive and unexpected effects.[132]

{8}

NYC Mural Makers

Urban Art Successes

Philadelphia is not alone in its support for public art. In New York City, officially sanctioned art installations are peppered across the city's 468 square miles. The New York City Department of Transportation is just one of the agencies that is responsible for bringing art to the public, but it is an important one because of its size. The agency is responsible for 6,300 miles of streets and highways, more than 12,000 miles of sidewalks, 781 bridge structures, and six tunnels. It also maintains more than 1.3 million street signs and traffic signals at more than 12,000 signalized intersections, more than 300,000 streetlights, and 69 million linear feet of markings.[133]

Since October 2008, art has been part of that equation, via the department's Urban Art Program. In conjunction with community organizations, the agency turns public plazas, fences, barriers, footbridges, and sidewalks into canvases for temporary art. As of this book's publication date, the group had commissioned eighty-five "site responsive" projects. Its mission is stated on its website as such:

> Artists help to transform the landscape from ordinary to extraordinary with temporary, unexpected interventions—colorful murals, dynamic light projections, thought-provoking sculptures.

The department was created at the behest of Jannette Sadik-Khan, who was the department's commissioner from April 2007 to December 2013. Sadik-Khan tasked Wendy Foyer with creating the program from scratch, and Foyer brought Emily Colasacco, the program's manager on board. The program is split into three different areas: "pARTners," "Barrier Beautification," and "Arterventions." Of the three areas, the first bears the closest relation to the collaborations described in my case studies, with the second playing an important role, too. That's because both programs often work through the medium of paint on outdoor surfaces that might otherwise be the target of vandalism.

When it comes to the barrier beautification, the agency collaborates with the volunteer group New York Cares, artists and designers who produce murals on the concrete barriers that separate bicycle lanes from cars, trucks, and other vehicles on the road. Materials for the murals are provided by NYC DOT via a $2,500 stipend, and the department chooses the location. Artists take responsibility for the translation of their design onto the barriers, and the murals are required to remain for eleven months.

The pARTners program is similar in that it pairs artists and community organizations together at sites owned by the department. NYC DOT announces its list of "priority sites" twice a year, and artists and organizations are solicited for their ideas. Proposals for alternate sites are encouraged, and concepts for "site-responsive art" are expected to be completed within six months. Once a project is completed, it is exhibited

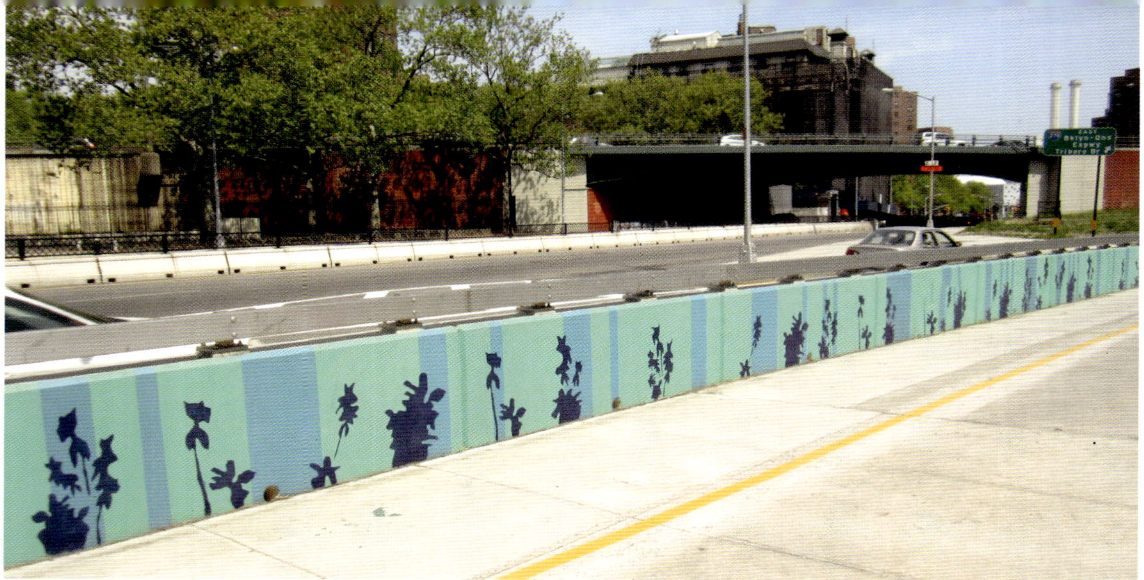

Fictional Landscape, a 500-foot-long painting alongside the Manhattan Bridge Ramp in Brooklyn by Abby Goldstein, circa April 2012. Photo courtesy New York City Department of Transportation. Reprinted with permission.

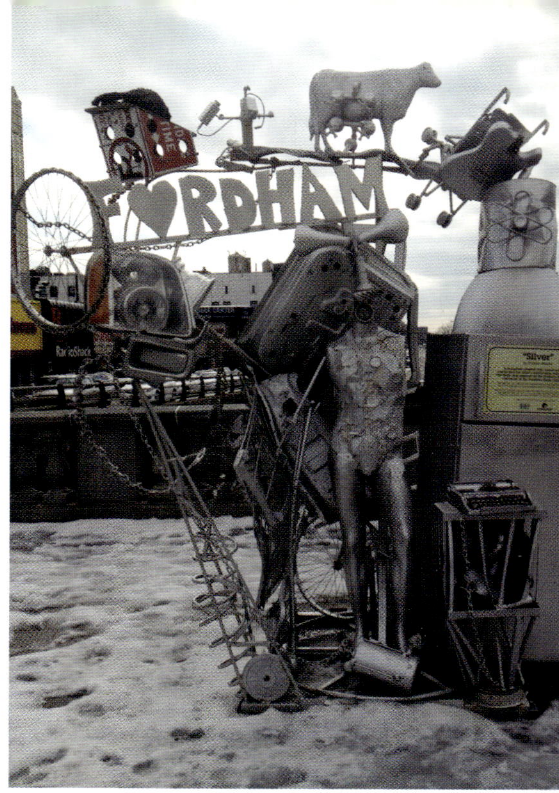

Silver by Christian Marche, in partnership with the Fordham Road Business Improvement District and the NYC Department of Transportation's Art Program (E. Fordham Road and the Grand Concourse, Bronx). Circa February 2013. Photo by Patrick Verel

for eleven months, with responsibility for maintenance and site remediation falling on the creators. DOT reimburses nonprofit organizations up to $5,000 for costs inferred for the project.

pARTner projects run the gamut, from a plot of maize grown between concrete blocks in Boerum Hill, Brooklyn, to an abstract metal sculpture at East Fordham Road and the Grand Concourse in the Bronx. But the program is also responsible for a number of murals, including several on a corrugated metal fence under the Manhattan Bridge in DUMBO. Colasacco says installations make for good vandalism deterrents.

> I find that when we install a temporary art project, whether it's a sculpture or a mural, graffiti tends not to happen on the sites. There's always an issue of tagging in certain areas, but I find if it's a really good, quality work, they tend to stay away from the project. So with a lot of our footbridges around the city, the ones that we've painted tend to remain in better shape than the ones we don't put murals on. So we are trying to do more murals on our footbridges.[134]

Since deterring graffiti vandalism is the kind of thing that graffiti removal crews would be interested in, I asked Colasacco if they'd ever worked with the ones in Graffiti Free New York, a group discussed in the next chapter. Her answer was yes, but only once, at the entrance to the 1 train subway station at 191st Street and Broadway, in Washington Heights.

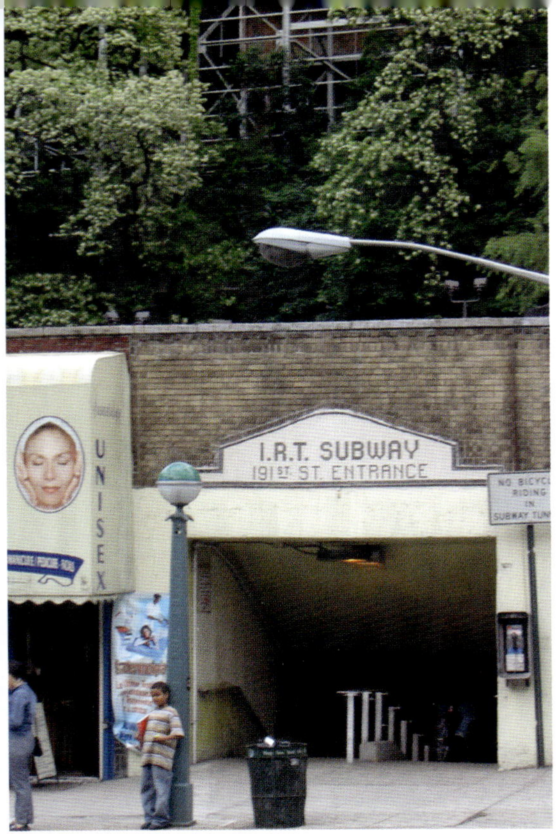

The entrance to the 191st Street subway station, circa 2005. Photo courtesy of WikiCommons.

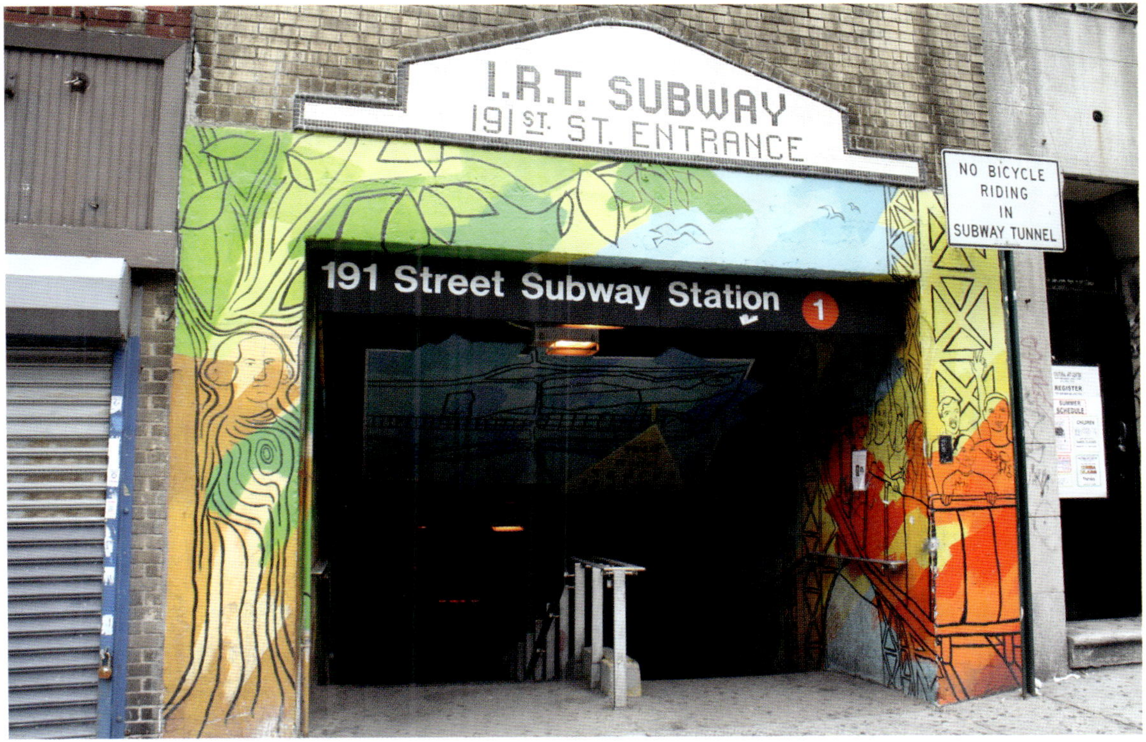

New York is a Rollercoaster by Belle Benfield, in partnership with Groundswell Community Mural Project and the NYC Department of Transportation's Art Program (190th Street and Broadway, Manhattan) circa July 2011. Photo by Patrick Verel

This particular entrance leads to a three-block-long tunnel to the mezzanine of the station, which at track level is 180 feet deep, the deepest in the entire subway system. Colasacco said NYC DOT commissioned a mural at the tunnel entrance as a pilot project in 2008, in collaboration with Brooklyn-based Groundswell Community Mural Project.

> Originally, they were just going to go up to the site and repaint the tunnel that leads to the 1 train. It's a super-long tunnel, and it's a huge graffiti issue, because it's dark and there isn't much patrolling over there. Instead of just painting it solid color, we decided to commission an artist and work with a group of students to paint an actual mural over there, and we found that the mural really did stop the tagging.[135]

Unfortunately, because the tunnel is three blocks long, the mural, *New York is a Roller Coaster* by artist Belle Benfield, only extends a short distance into the tunnel from the entrance. The rest of the tunnel had to settle for less, and Colasacco admitted it has made a difference.

> We focused on a really nice, detailed mural on the entrance, but within the full tunnel, we couldn't use the same style mural. We could only do a very basic leaf design, so the tagging still popped up in the tunnel. But it didn't pop up on the tunnel entrance, so it was a very interesting study on, if you can produce a better mural, a more detailed mural, it really will stop vandalism.[136]

A visit to the station bore out this assertion. Three years after its installation, the entrance showed some minor signs of age—a scrape here, a scuff there, with some fading. The abstract leaf signs inside the tunnel were a disaster in comparison. When I visited the station, it seemed as if every other inch of the walls was either encrusted with dirt, tagged with amateurish drawings and tags, or both. It was very clear that even if real effort had been put into this part of the project, little had been devoted to the maintaining of it. In this instance, it might actually be preferable to whitewash the walls more frequently, light the tunnel differently, or coat the walls with a different surface. I shudder to think of how uninviting a space it must be at night.

Since this project seems to have been most successful in deterring vandalism in the area where most attention was paid, I asked Colasacco why Groundswell, DOT, and the vandalism squad haven't teamed up since.

> The programs just have such different missions. They're just going in and wiping away graffiti and painting it the original color, whereas Groundswell and other programs really try to create a really interesting, exciting experience for pedestrians and bicyclists. So it's taking it to the next step. It's not just painting over, it's developing a site-responsive piece.[137]

Groundswell program manager Jessica Poplawski confirmed this via e-mail correspondence.

> **Q:** When the city sends one of its graffiti removal trucks to a private building to clean it of tags and such, does it ever refer the building owner to your group to do a mural in place of the graffiti there?
> **A:** No, we do not work directly with the NYPD or the vandal squad. When potential community partners approach us about starting new projects, they do often cite deterring graffiti as one of the reasons to pursue a large-scale outdoor mural.[138]

In a follow-up question, Poplawski said she could not say exactly why Groundswell does not work with the NYPD, beyond speculating that the group is "process-oriented toward creating community-driven and community-designed imagery, not solely focusing on beautification."

Groundswell has been, in the group's own words, "bringing together artists, youth, and community organizations to use art as a tool for social change." The group's website explains further:

> In 1996, a group of New York City artists, educators, and activists founded Groundswell based on the belief that there is something unique and powerful about the collaborative art making process. This process combines the sanctity of personal expression with the strength of community activism.
>
> Groundswell's programs are based on principles of individual, group, and community development. Collaborating with communities, we strive to physically and mentally build up the individual, group, and community during the making of the mural or other artwork.[139]

This is very similar to the goals of the Philadelphia Mural Arts Program, and indeed, many of the murals that Groundswell spearheads are as ambitious in scope as those in Philadelphia. The group's emphasis on working with children of low-income and working-class families (up to 800 young people annually, ages fourteen to twenty-one) brings to mind the work that Charlie Balducci is doing with NYC Cypher, but on much larger scale.

And although Groundswell sees its goals as more than simple beautification, Poplawski affirmed both that one of the selling points for their murals is that they act as a deterrent for

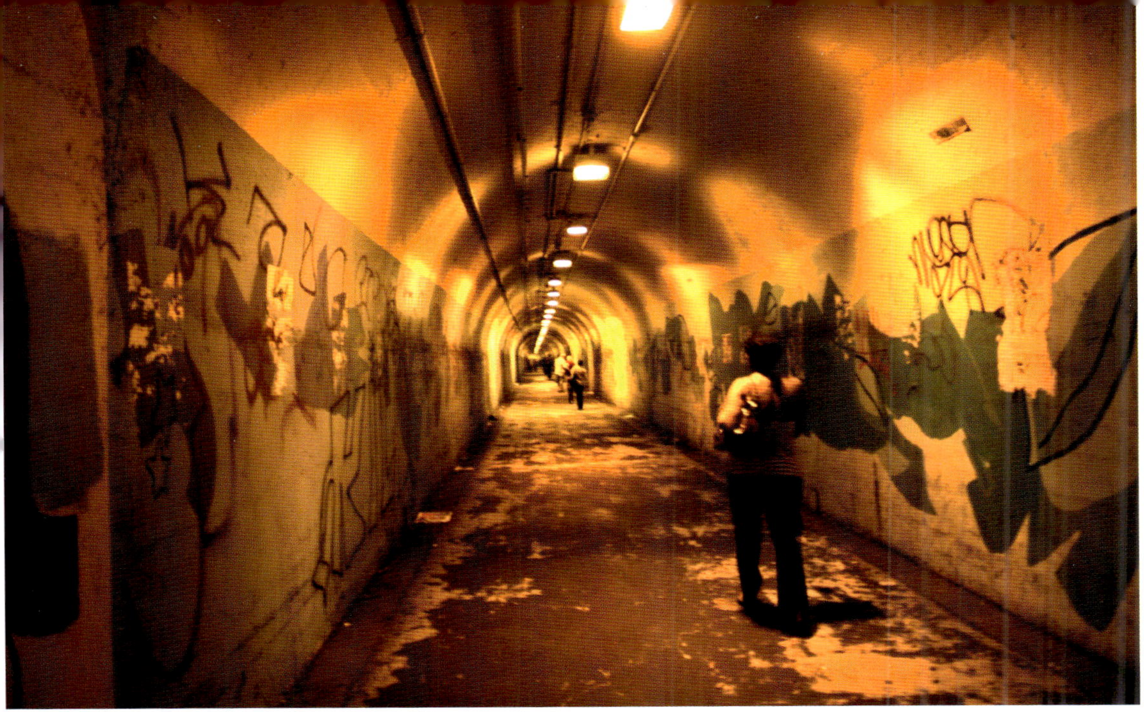

The tunnel leading from Broadway and 191st Street to the station, circa July 2011. Photo by Patrick Verel

vandalism and that the group often refers artists to building owners looking to organize a mural of their own. As the preceding case studies illustrate, even graffiti murals organized between owners and artists require collaboration and attention to neighborhood sensitivities. In fact, when asked to describe how they convince both private and public building owners to let them use their wall for a mural, Poplawski's answer is very similar to the artists in my case studies, but with more formality.

We often go out on foot. We use a press kit for introductions highlighting our history and the sweep and scope of the work. The owner is NOT asked to contribute any funds, and we honor them on the mural and in our press announcements. If the wall owner agrees, they sign a contract specifying that the work will remain on the wall for at least five years.[140]

Could a group like Groundswell work as a clearinghouse of sorts for artists (graffiti-inspired and otherwise) who building owners could turn to in lieu of the blank slate offered by the NYPD's graffiti removal teams? It might be difficult to convince some graffiti artists to go along, as many already have enough work to keep them busy, and many might conclude from visiting a space that it's not high profile enough to warrant their time. Groundswell also currently advertises that all their artists hold either bachelor's and/or master's degrees in fine arts and have experience working with youth; these requirements would need to be waved for referrals if the field were to be truly open.

That said, the group's involvement in such a project would go a long way toward changing attitudes about public art, even art that is inspired by graffiti. The group's explicit goal of promoting the "sanctity of personal expression" lends it an air of authority when it comes to authenticity, and its embrace of low-income residents jibes extremely well with Harvey's exhortation to share symbolic capitol in an equitable fashion. The way Nicer speaks of introducing art in rough and tumble areas of the South Bronx, his Tats Cru would certainly make for a fine partner to the group. As my last chapters will illustrate, there are attitudes about graffiti murals that are very much in need of change.

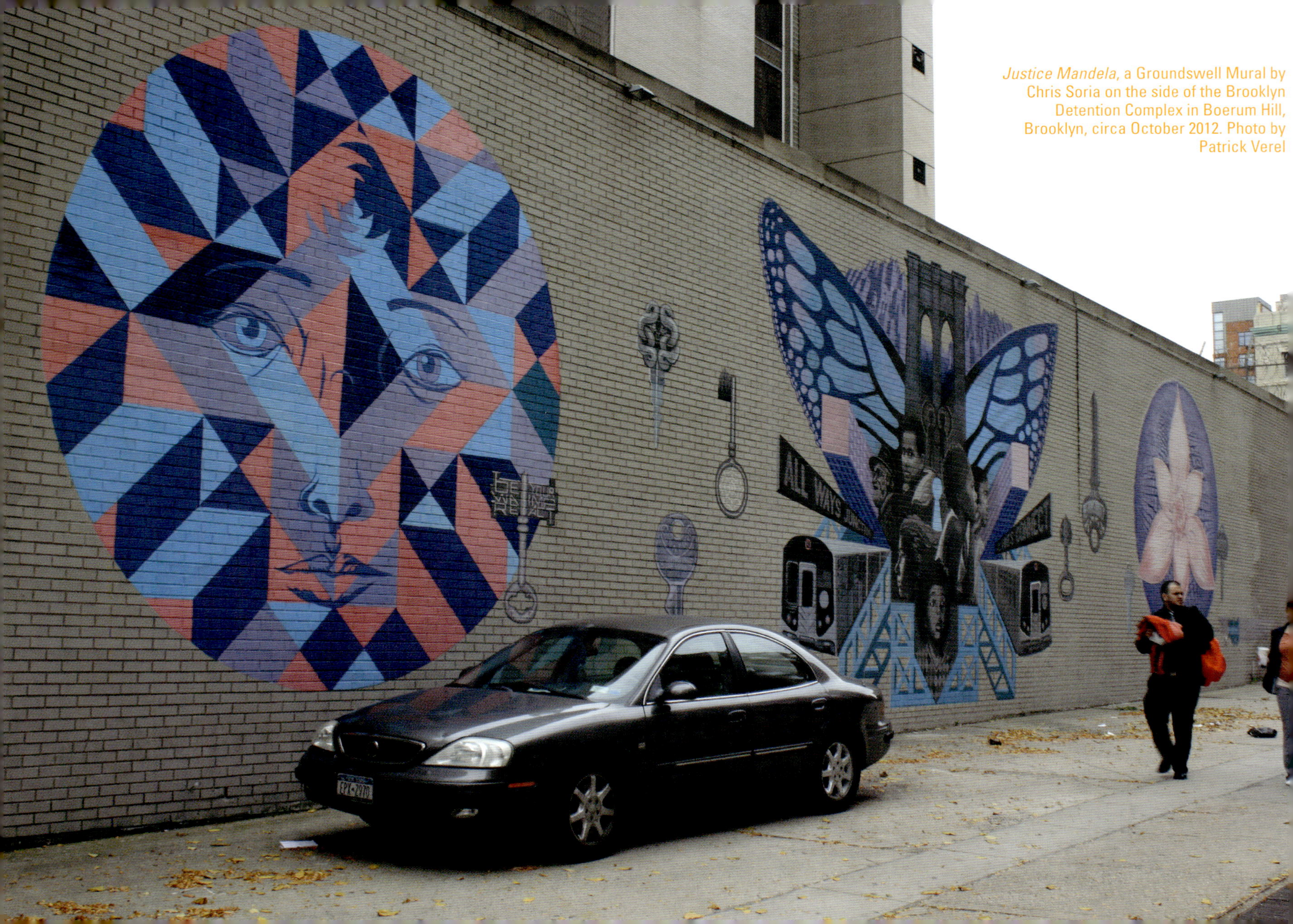

Justice Mandela, a Groundswell Mural by Chris Soria on the side of the Brooklyn Detention Complex in Boerum Hill, Brooklyn, circa October 2012. Photo by Patrick Verel

{9}

Graffiti-Free New York

A Multiagency Effort

New York City's 331-word-long anti-graffiti statute covers a wide spectrum of activities, from the act of creating graffiti to displaying spray paint and markers in store windows (See Appendix I). While the New York City Police Department is responsible for enforcing the laws, the removal of graffiti falls to several different agencies. Graffiti-Free NYC, which is a partnership between the mayor's Community Affairs Unit, the Economic Development Corporation, and the Department of Sanitation, seeks to "allow New Yorkers to take graffiti removal into their own hands by either calling in sites for cleanup or driving their own cleanup efforts."[141]

Befitting its multiagency status, information about Graffiti Free NYC can be found on the websites for the NYPD, the Community Affairs Unit, and most prominently, on the Economic Development Corporation (EDC). It is on the EDC's website that a 1,600-word-long 2009 press release trumpeted the removal of "more than 170 million square feet" of graffiti, as well the recent addition of ten new graffiti power-wash trucks purchased with federal funds, for a total of twenty-seven trucks.[142]

How serious is the city about the conditions on the street? The same release also noted that since 2007, a "Street Conditions Observation Unit," or SCOUT, program has traveled every block in New York City every month, reporting conditions that negatively impact quality of life, thus increasing by sixty percent the amount of graffiti identification. As noted in the last chapter, that's 6,300 miles of roads. The numbers cited are impressive: graffiti removed from 3,891 sites, totaling an estimated 2.5 million square feet. Another 727,800 square feet removed by the Parks Department. Almost 2,759,500 square feet of graffiti buffed from streets, bridges, and highways by the Department of Transportation, bringing the running total to 6 million square feet of graffiti removed by city agencies to date in 2009.

But murals? No mention. Nor is there any mention of murals on the Community Affairs website, which is where one is directed to file a complaint of graffiti with the city for cleanup consideration. The NYPD's webpage contains a downloadable pamphlet, *Combating Graffiti: Reclaiming the Public Spaces of New York*, which breaks down graffiti into categories (Hate, Gang, Satanic, Street, and Generic), and has a list of fourteen agencies under the "Resources" section. Even the aforementioned NYC DOT is referred to only for "cleaning of street signs." Notwithstanding the work that T. K. Singleton was doing in the Bronx, there is little obvious coordination between the creators of legal graffiti and the erasers of illegal graffiti.

But why? According to Ray Carrero, quality of life director for the mayor's Community Affairs Unit, the problem is that many building owners care as little for art that's authorized as they do for art that is illicit.

Q: Have you ever suggested to a building owner as one way to combat the tagging that they commission a mural, whether it's by a graffiti artist or another artist?
A: Well, this conversation has gone back and forth throughout the years, with various owners. Has the issue of commissioning a mural at any specific location come up? Sure it has. But the final decision on that would have been made by the building owner. Obviously the city can't force a building owner to do a mural.
Q: But is it something where, when people call you and say, "Hey, I have this problem," is it something that you say, "Well, this is another tactic, as opposed to just painting over it"?
A: Well, in all honestly, there are several different ways to address this problem, and murals, or having a mural commissioned, is not the only one. So, their options are given depending on the owner, and how he sees it. A lot of times they would see a mural and they would consider that graffiti as well.
Q: So that's definitely not considered an option, huh?
A: No.[143]

Carrero confirmed a couple of important points regarding graffiti removal and murals. In 2009, when city law required that property owners "opt in" to the cleanup process, thus putting the burden of proof on the city, the cities' cleanup crews buffed a total of 8,949 buildings. In 2010, the law was changed to an "opt out" system, making it property owners' responsibility to confirm whether or not they wanted graffiti to remain. That year, the number of buildings visited by Graffiti-Free NYC jumped to 18,481. While the amount of resources dedicated to buffing more than doubled, Carrero confirmed that no city agency took on the task of promoting murals. He was sympathetic to owners who prefer to keep their walls blank.

> Some owners are really old school, and they don't see the difference between a mural and graffiti. And lot of times the murals are pretty impressive. Some people would consider them artists. These people can put things up that you can stop, admire, and enjoy. Sometimes, you know, in all honesty, it's just crap.[144]

It is fair to ask whether the director of quality of life is in the position to pass judgment on the artistic merits of murals, but I don't actually think Carrero is a philistine who can't be bothered to learn about art. Rather, he sees his role as an advocate for a larger process that's more inclusive, where collaboration is paramount. And while he endorses the idea that a graffiti mural created by a locally known artist can deter vandalism, he is extremely wary of the deleterious effects the wrong mural might provoke.

> The problem that we encounter when we do something like this or when something like this is done is content. What are you putting up there? Will it be offensive to the surrounding community? Is it going to be a bunch of guys leaning on a light post smoking a joint, or is it going to be Martin Luther King or Malcolm X or some musical artist, like Jennifer Lopez, coming up from The Bronx or something to that effect. It totally depends on content.
>
> We've had some beautiful murals done in the past. One mural that was commissioned was a picture of a pit bull that was owned by a local drug dealer. The local drug dealer loved the dog, so he had the mural done. And it was well done, but was it appropriate? The people in the community didn't think so.[145]

To some extent, Carrero's suspicions are understandable. When I asked if the cleaning crews had ever buffed a mural that was not supposed to be erased, I was thinking of a mural on the Lower East Side that an owner had buffed after misreading the notice sent to him by the city, only to see it tagged again anyway.[146] Carrero's response was a reminder that for city officials, graffiti is not considered just a nuisance. Images have the power to inspire, but they can also intimidate.

> Back in '95 and '96, when we first started the program, one of the first things that we took on that I led was actively going and looking for these gang murals and so on, getting the owners to agree to have them removed, and then coordinating with the

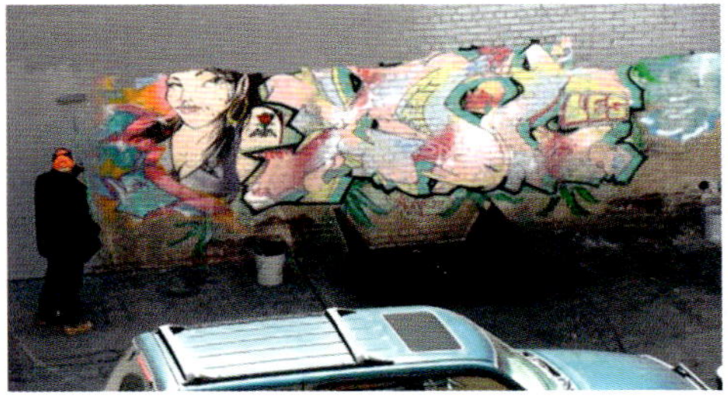

A graffiti mural on the Lower East Side that was mistakenly buffed in 2010. Photo by Bill Morris. Reprinted by permission.

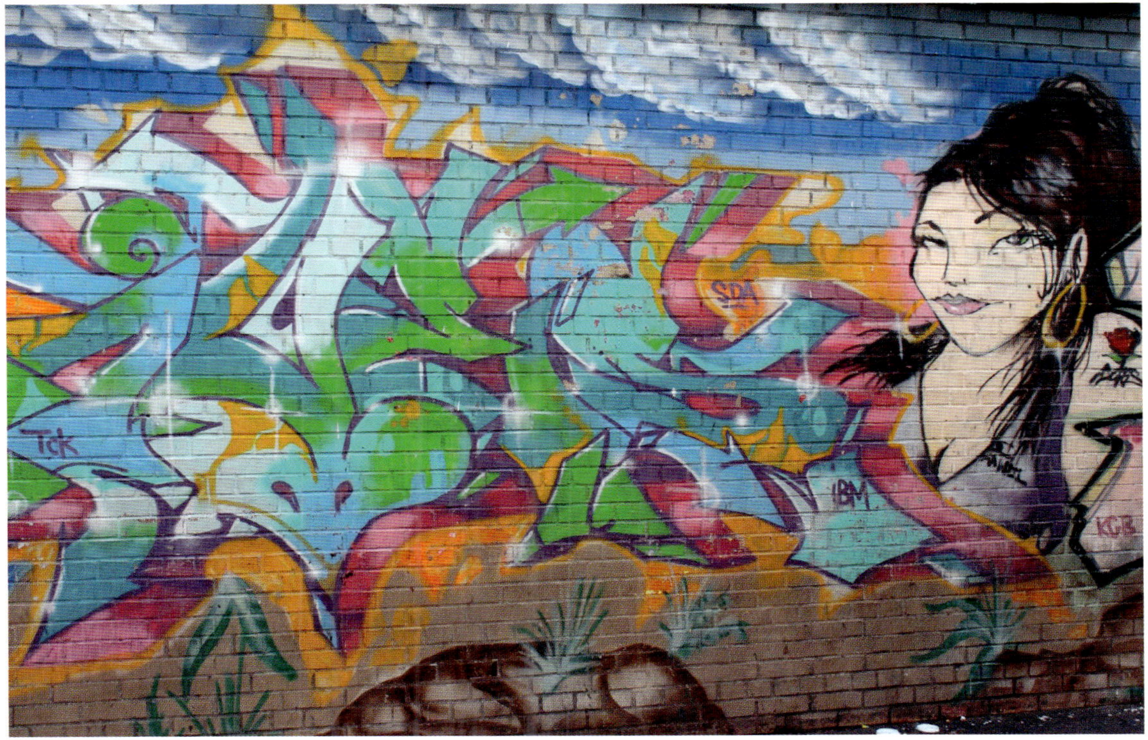

The mural as it looked in 2007. Photo by Stephen Baker. Reprinted by permission.

> local precinct to make sure that the guys doing the removal weren't harassed in the process or worse. So, do we have a history where we do that? Sure. Does it happen now? Sure.[147]

Carrero said gang-related murals aren't as much of an issue as they used to be, and insisted that the city only buffs them if a building owner asks them to. He is familiar with the work that T.K. Singleton did, and agreed that the graffiti murals like those the Tats Cru painted are cheaper than constant buffing. And yet, quotes like that last one illustrate that the "bad old days" are still very much on his mind. At best, he exhibits a neutral attitude when it comes to beautification efforts. Sometimes a building with a graffiti mural on it will be sold, and when the new owner asks the city to buff it, Carrero said the artist will threaten to sue, on the misguided notion that their graffiti mural enjoys some sort of legal protection. While it may technically be true that most graffiti murals enjoy no explicit legal right to protection, it's a depressing example of how authorities in New York City bend so easily to the whims of those wielding capital. From the perspective of officials like Carrero, graffiti murals are more of an incidental benefit than a resource worthy of cultivation.

He neatly encapsulated that indifference when I asked if the city promoted murals as a form of tourism. After all, tourism is such a vital aspect of the city's economy that NYC & Company trumpets not only the number of visitors to the city (50.9 million in 2011, breaking the 50 million mark for the first time), but also the economic impact of each visitor:

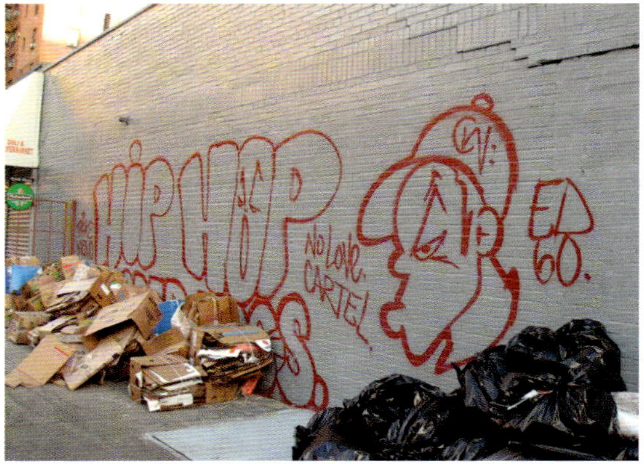

The same wall, tagged less than twenty-four hours later. Photo by Patrick Hedlund. Reprinted by permission.

> Total visitor spending from New York City tourism in 2010: **$31.5 billion**
> Total wages generated by New York City tourism in 2010: **$17.3 billion**
> Total NYC jobs supported by visitor spending in 2010: **310,156**
> Total taxes generated by visitor spending in 2010: **$8.1 billion**
> Each New York City household benefited by an average of $1,350 in tax savings as a result of travel and tourism.[148]

Surely, given the success that Philadelphia has had in making murals such an important part of its identity and the fact that mainstream New York art stores such as Lee's Art Shop in Midtown advertise "manga and graffiti arts" supplies in its fliers, New York City would give a shout out to the form.

> No, we don't. That would lead to other problems. Once we start and we make that as a tourist attraction, then we open ourselves up to opinions. Opinions as to, "I'm an artist, I did this. It wasn't commissioned by the city, but why aren't you including it? It's just as good as Phillipe Renour's wall on 22nd street" or something like that. You can't set the precedent.[149]

Tourism promotion is not the gist of my studies, of course, but I bring it up as a way to illustrate just how powerful the hold graffiti has on officials in New York City. Forget notions of uniqueness or authenticity; even a framework that is tied to money is not embraced. And there is money to be made from graffiti-related tourism, as evidenced by tours offered by Graff Tours[150] and Levy's tours, just to name two examples.[151]

Carrero's excuse for avoiding graffiti mural promotion—that it would be improper to choose which ones to promote—is a cop out. The truth is it wouldn't be difficult to identify someone with the right background to collaborate with a group like Groundswell to identify locations and even encourage their creation. If the city sees buffing as one of its duties, then it should embrace the opposite side of the coin—art creation—too.

{10}

The Clean Slate Club

Why Some Like It Buffed

Up until now, I have focused exclusively on the owners of buildings who have chosen to turn their buildings over to artists for use as a canvas. The reason for this is simple—although they are in the minority, they provide a valuable example for others to follow. I hope that in my interviews, I have given voice to their hopes, concerns, challenges, and the rationales for their actions.

But what about those owners who, when faced with the prospect of graffiti on their buildings, choose not to cover it with a mural, but with a fresh coat of regular paint, courtesy of Graffiti-Free NYC? Might their rationale likewise provide some insight into the situation? I figured it would be worth tracking someone down. At Ray Carrero's direction, I was able to access a vast online public database that the city maintains of every building it has ever visited and buffed. I chose to focus on Red Hook and Gowanus in Brooklyn, since both neighborhoods are industrial and prone to graffiti, as they are mostly deserted at night. When sorting through the records, I took into account the type of building that had been visited and only zeroed in on buildings with large, flat sides, preferably along well-traveled roads. The idea was to only interview someone whose building would be suitable for a mural in the first place.

The exterior walls of 363 Bond Street, circa July 2011. Photo by Patrick Verel

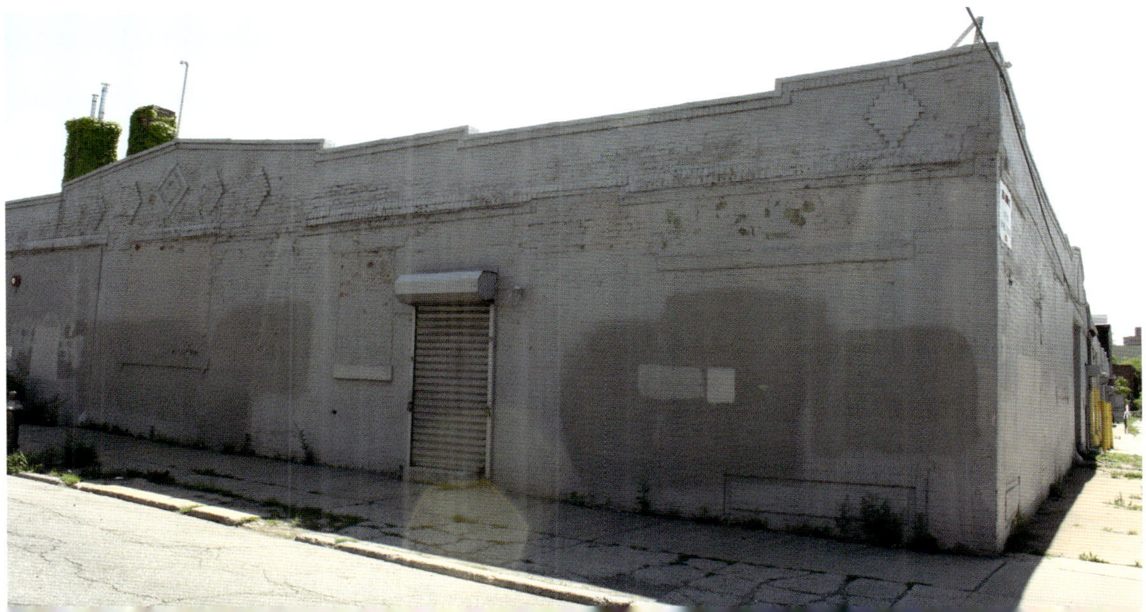

After a couple of false starts, I found my connection at 363 Bond Street, which had been reported for graffiti on July 7, 2010, and according to records, had been visited July 23, 2010, when it was buffed. Asher Lang, the operations manager for Friedknit Creations, welcomed me to his office there, which sits less than half a block away from the Gowanus Canal. He estimated that the company, which imports children's clothing, had been there for twenty-two years. The visit on July 23 was actually Graffiti-Free's second visit, to buff some graffiti that had resurfaced after a more thorough buffing that the city completed in February 2010. Before that, he'd been sending an employee out to buff graffiti on the building, using either a bucket or a spray can of a matching shade of gray. He was pretty sanguine about the process.

> Graffiti comes and goes. It's basically kids in the neighborhood, I guess. If you notice the neighborhood in general, it seems to be a very graffiti-prone area. Maybe it's because it's on a dead-end street. It's also an area where there's not much residential, especially this part of the area near the canal. So kids have been writing, and we've been cleaning. We like a clean building and we try to keep it that way.[152]

The cost is actually pretty minimal; Lang estimated it costs no more than $30 to $60 for a couple gallons of paint. Taggers always seem to paint in areas that have not already been buffed, he noted, which would seem to contradict what I speculated in chapter 3 when I talked about Halsey and Young. Of course, even the casual observer can see that 363 Bond has been coated more times with paint than can be imagined; the result of the never-ending tug of war between taggers and buffers. From a tagger's point of view, no single surface is more desirable, nor is there any spot that is higher visibility. And indeed, the building has served as a veritable jungle gym for the city's clandestine writers.

> They moved to the gates, they've done it on the walls of the side of the building, and then one time they did it off the roof of the building. We couldn't figure out how they did it. But when you walk outside the building, and you look all the way on top there, they get to the places where you don't even think it's possible to get to.[153]

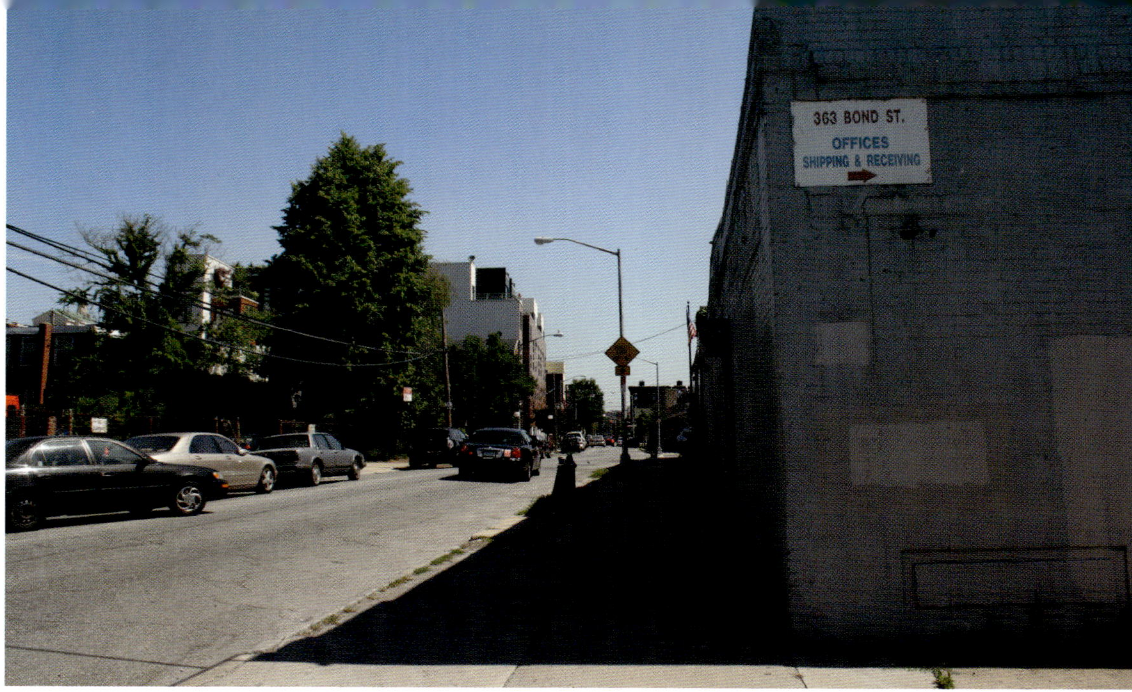

Mismatched buffed walls of 363 Bond Street, circa July 2011. Photo by Patrick Verel

The city's graffiti removal trucks may have made their presence known, but when I visited the site, it was a far cry from clean. Graffiti was not especially prevalent, but blocks of oh-so-close-to-matching paint were evidence of a piece-meal buffing. A crude rendering of Bart

Simpson's head graced one of the security gates. Lang said he'd accepted the city's offer to buff his building because it meant he wouldn't have to do it himself, and while he's never been approached by anyone looking to use either side of his building for a mural, he said that if they did, he'd probably turn them down, because he doesn't want to attract attention to the building.

Q: Would you be open to that if someone like a graffiti artist approached you?
A: Probably not, only because we're not looking for an attraction. It can only cause other graffiti, you understand. I wouldn't want that.

Q: So you think a mural would attract more graffiti?
A: Yes, I think so. That would be my impression. Put graffiti and…it's not graffiti, it's a mural, and people will look to…So I would say graffiti on a building causes other graffiti, even if it's a nice mural. That's what I would think.[154]

The security gate at 363 Bond Street, on 1st Street, circa July 2011. Photo by Patrick Verel

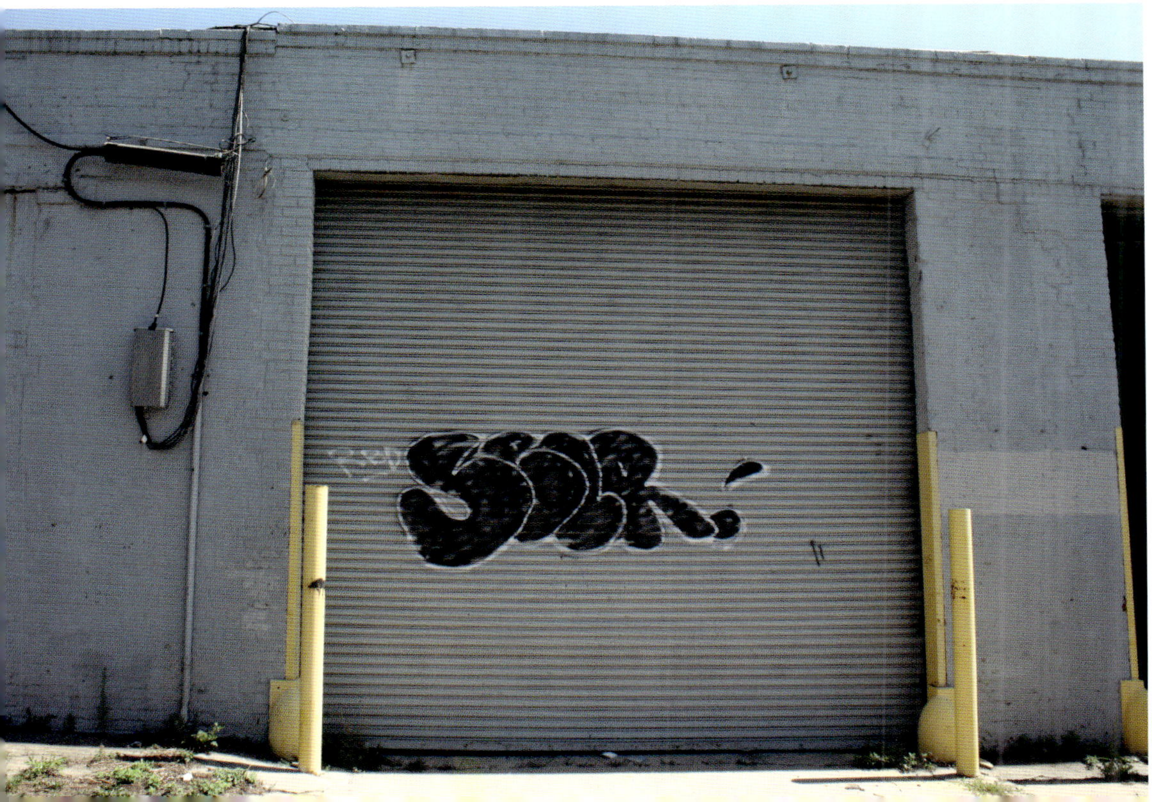

Lang's perspective on graffiti, and on graffiti murals in general, is one less of hostility than of paternalistic dismissal. When asked why a blank wall might be better than a wall with a mural, he noted than one does not graffiti one's own house. The inclination to make a mark on a building is indicative of the "mindset of a child," as he put it, and when I asked him if he could reconcile the fact that he's said that it was "interesting" that graffiti artists had tagged his roof, he assured me that he wasn't a fan.

> No, it wasn't that it was interesting; it was just they were showing their artistic work, because that's their outlet. But they should take that and put it to better use, obviously, either making drawings or…they do try…I mean, some of it is just a boy and a girl, and they're just fooling around with it, and "I love you"… others it's basically stuff that's maybe they're potential artists out there trying to...this is the beginning step of their future.[155]

Earlier in our conversation, he said:

> We've never prosecuted anybody, and I don't think I ever would, because these kids, I don't think they're doing it to really destroy the building, they're doing it because its an activity for them, and that's part of why they do it.[156]

Lang's attitude toward graffiti is somewhat reminiscent of Tom, the gentleman from Clove Place in Staten Island who had no use for even paintings of flowers. On the one hand, he was more forgiving of its creators, as his willingness to consider them "potential artists" indicates. At the same time, his assertion that graffiti murals are a magnet for more graffiti is simply not true. Even if it is true that, in the spirit of Herbert Blumer's "symbolic interactionism," one tagger is attracted to the tag of another, and their collective presence sends a signal that the space is ripe for graffiti, my case studies prove the same cannot be said for graffiti murals.

In fact, Asher need not have traveled far to see how graffiti murals fare. Gowanus has several major murals: alongside the Gowanus canal near Ninth Street (it has since been taken down), in a parking lot on President Street between Third and Fourth Avenue, and a newer one from the Wallnuts Crew on Nevins Street just south of Union Street. Murals that face the street can also be found in nearby Red Hook, where many have been for years, with nary a disturbance to them nor significantly more tags on surroundings.

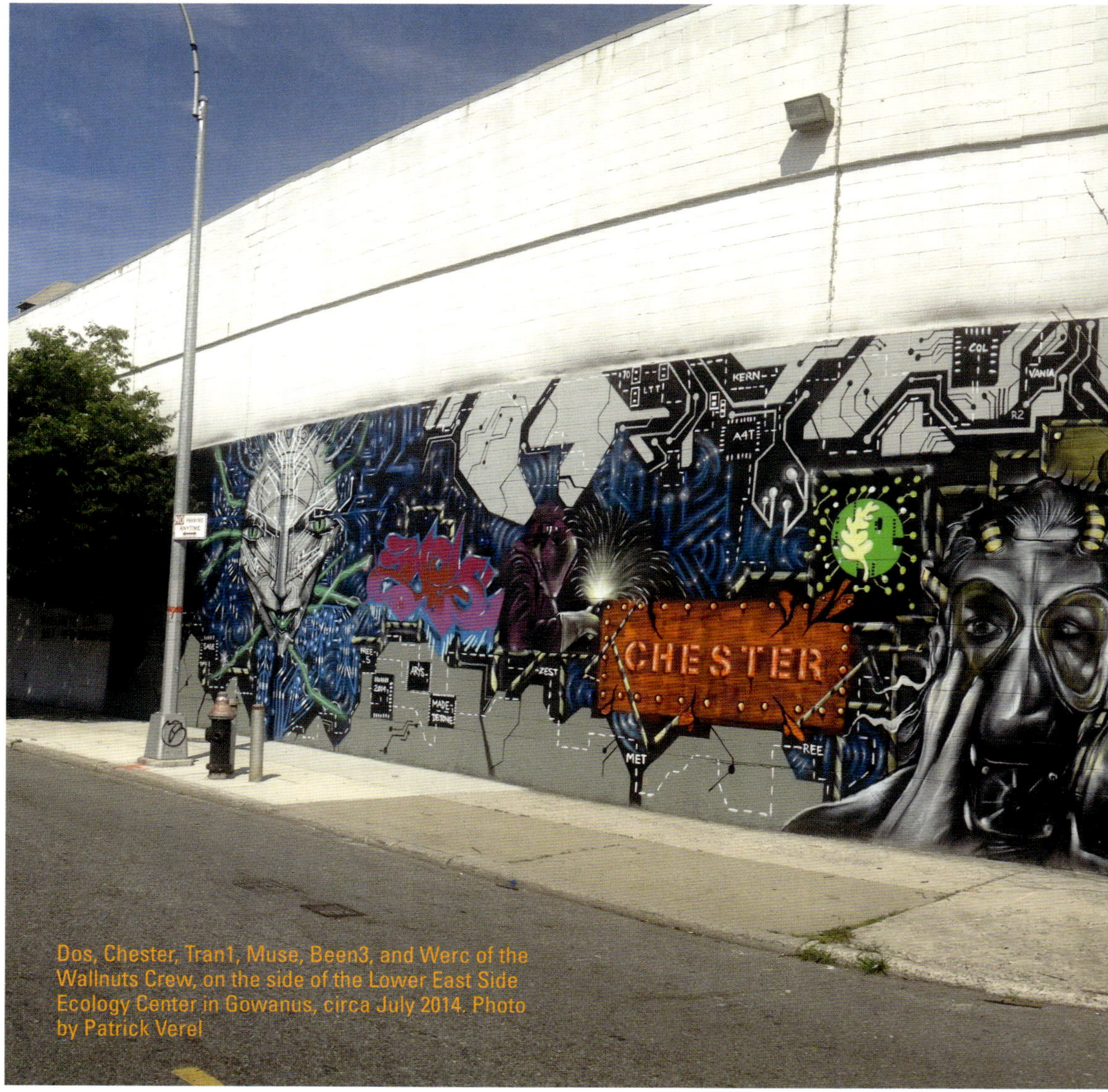

Dos, Chester, Tran1, Muse, Been3, and Werc of the Wallnuts Crew, on the side of the Lower East Side Ecology Center in Gowanus, circa July 2014. Photo by Patrick Verel

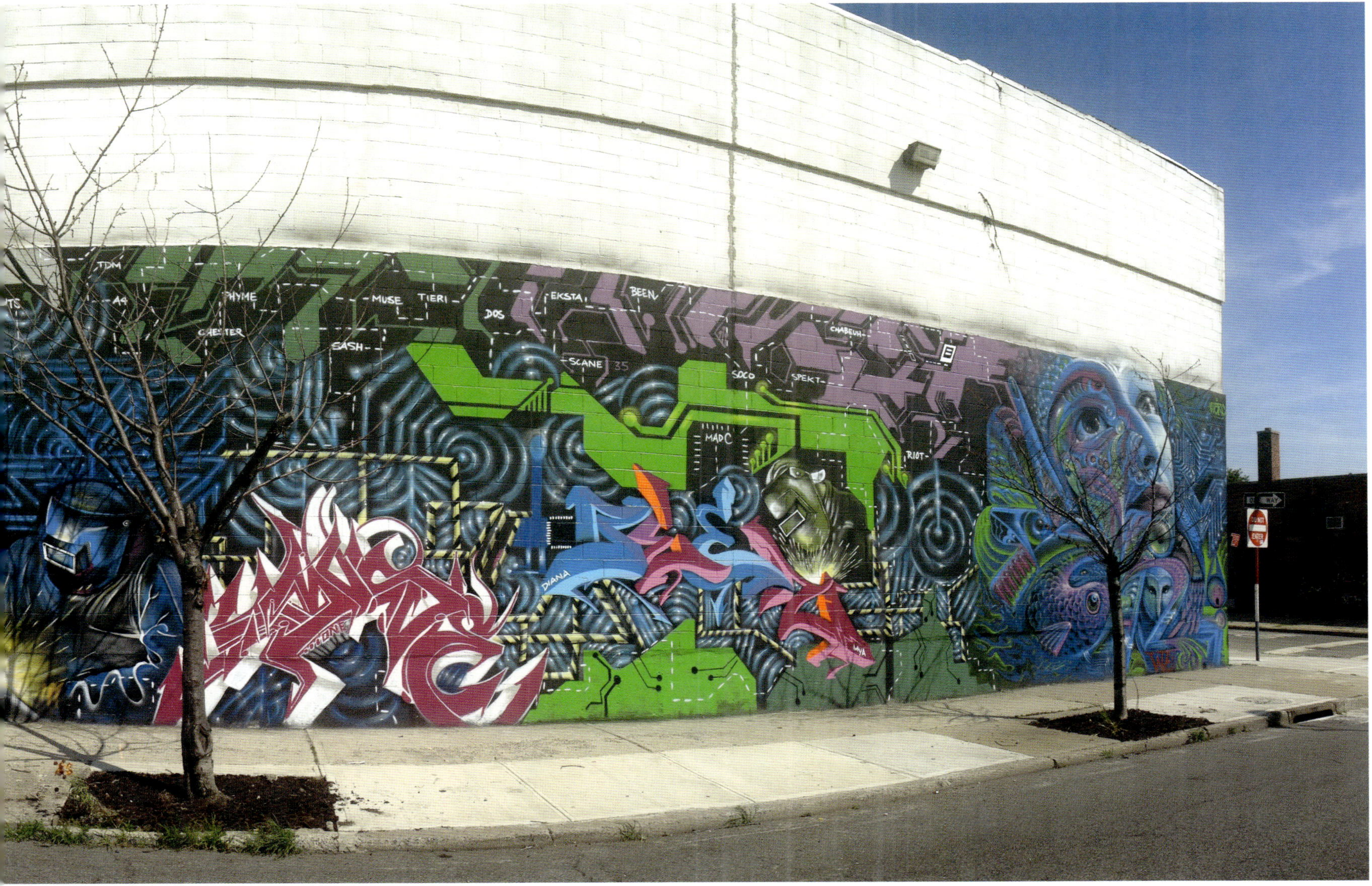
TDM
A4
PHYME
MUSE
TIERI
EKSTA
BEEN
DOS
CHESTER
SASH
CHABEUH
SCANE
SOCO
SPEKT
MADC
RIOT
DIANA

LAOZI, a piece on the side of building overlooking the Gowanus Canal, by the graffiti collective Slavery, circa May 2011. Photo by Patrick Verel

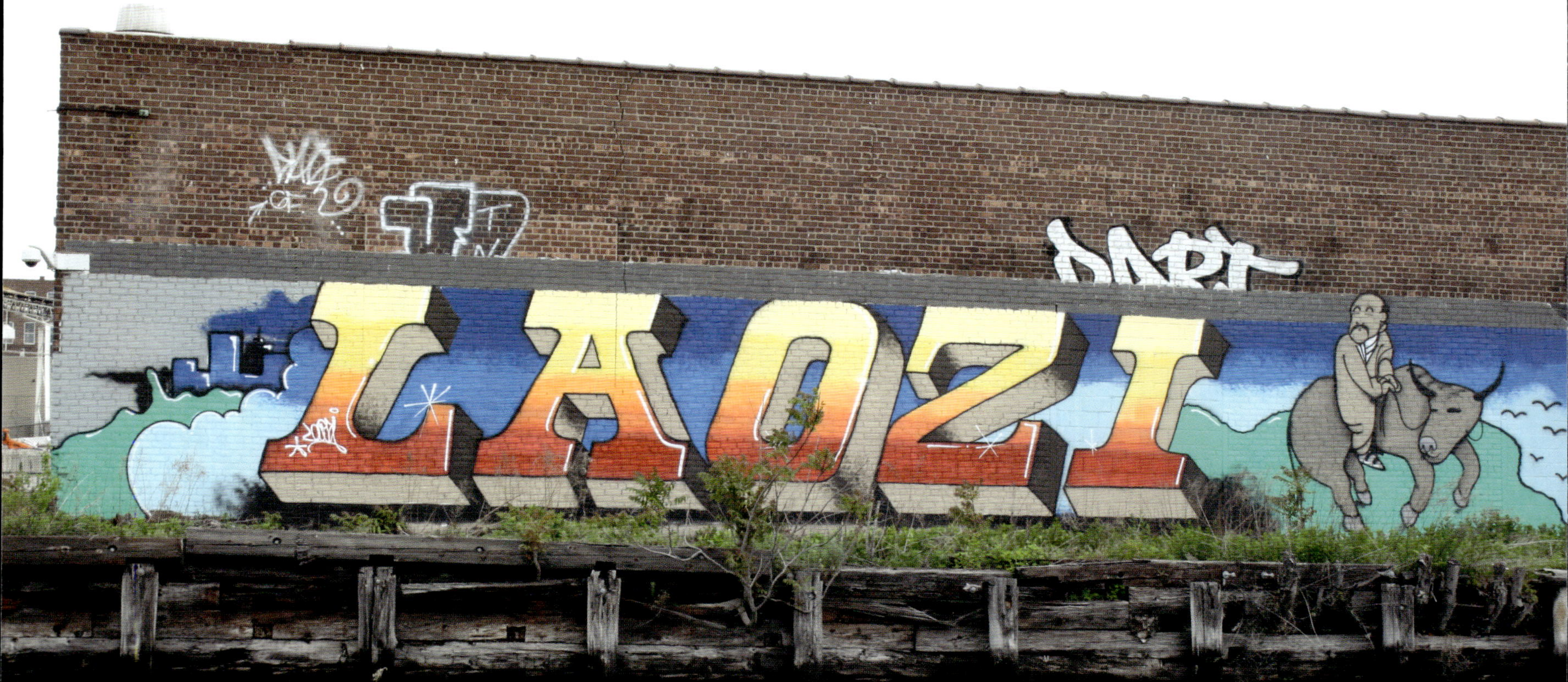

But as noted in chapter 2, there is a notion described by David Harvey as the "supreme rationality of the market versus the silly irrationality of anything else." For Lang and his company, the usefulness of his building ends at its utility for generating profit for his company. Even though his space straddles the border of a residential and industrial section of Brooklyn, he feels no need to visually engage the outside community. There is nothing inherently wrong with this, of course; as a viable business, Friedknit Creations employs New York City residents, pays taxes that are the lifeblood of the city's budget, and fills a demand for children's clothing. But it could also be so much more, if only owners like Lang and officials like Carrero could be shown the value of the symbolic capital such murals impart.

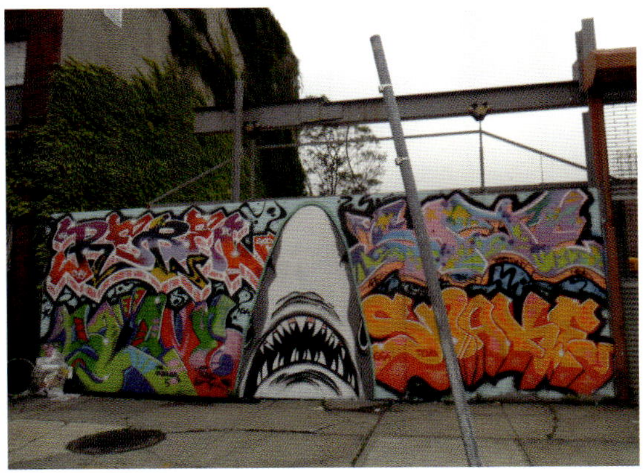

Rebel, Slave, Saju, and Snake, on a fence on Van Brundt Street in Red Hook, circa June 2011. Photo by Patrick Verel

In the end, Lang's take on the subject as it relates to this specific space won't matter too much, as 363 Bond Street and its neighbor at 365 Bond Street are at the heart of a massive planned residential development that has been in the works since 2007 when the developer Toll Brothers unveiled plans to build 447 luxury apartments on the site. The company bailed on the plan when the Gowanus Canal was declared a federal Superfund Site in 2010, but plans were revived by The Lightstone Group for an even larger development that is currently under construction.[157] The building vanished into memory in 2014, but Lang's perspective is a valuable one to take into consideration for future graffiti murals.

{11} 5 POINTZ

Queens

Into the Void

A NOTE: *I first wrote about 5 Pointz long before it was a fait accompli that it would be demolished. Even though rumors were swirling about at the time that the building's future was tenuous, I knew it was worth exploring its genesis, if for no other reason that its high profile and prized location. Because of that outsized profile, it's not the kind of place that can be easily replicated or compared to other sites of legal graffiti. And now that it's gone, it's perhaps best remembered not in nitty-gritty details, but in the larger than life role it once played in a city that has been changing at warp speed for some time now.*

Fifteen minutes. That's the amount of time it took to get from Carnegie Hall, in glitzy Midtown Manhattan, to 5 Pointz, in gritty Long Island City. On a weekday afternoon, the 500,000-square-foot former warehouse colloquially known as the "Institute of Higher Burnin"could have been visited from Carnegie Hall during lunch hour, via the E train, which drops one off all of two blocks away, at the 23 Street/Ely Avenue stop. The M train, which passes through Rockefeller Center, likewise stops at 23 Street/Ely Avenue. Or for those who are closer to Grand Central Terminal or Times Square, there is the elevated 7 train, which slowly creaks around the what used to be the building's southeast corner on a serpentine track and stops at Court Square, also two blocks away.

Fifteen minutes by subway. In the scheme of New York City real estate, and the dreams, visions, and fantastical amounts of capital cycling through regions in such close proximity, 5 Pointz—an industrial building that had been turned into one of the largest galleries of graffiti in the world—never stood a chance. In July 2001, the city government signaled as much, when it included the building in a thirty-seven-block rezoning, adding it to the three-block area that was rezoned in 1986 for the high- density development that facilitated the construction of the 1.25 million-square-foot Citibank tower. At the time, the plan was such:

> In the Long Island City core, the rezoning replaces existing low-density light manufacturing zones with higher density, mixed commercial and residential zones to allow as-of-right developments, including office buildings with large, efficient floor plates.[158]

City planners at the time were not thinking strictly in vague terms that would be sorted out by the forces of the market, as the second page of the aforementioned document contained a graphic that helpfully identifies sites ripe for development. In the bottom right corner is a figurative bull's-eye on 5 Pointz.

And so, for twelve years, 5 Pointz, which was first known as the "Phun Factory" and for a spell housed a vibrant artist colony called Crane Street Studios, had a date with the wrecking ball,

FACING PAGE: The loading dock at Five Pointz, as seen from below the elevated 7 train, circa June 2013. Photo by Patrick Verel

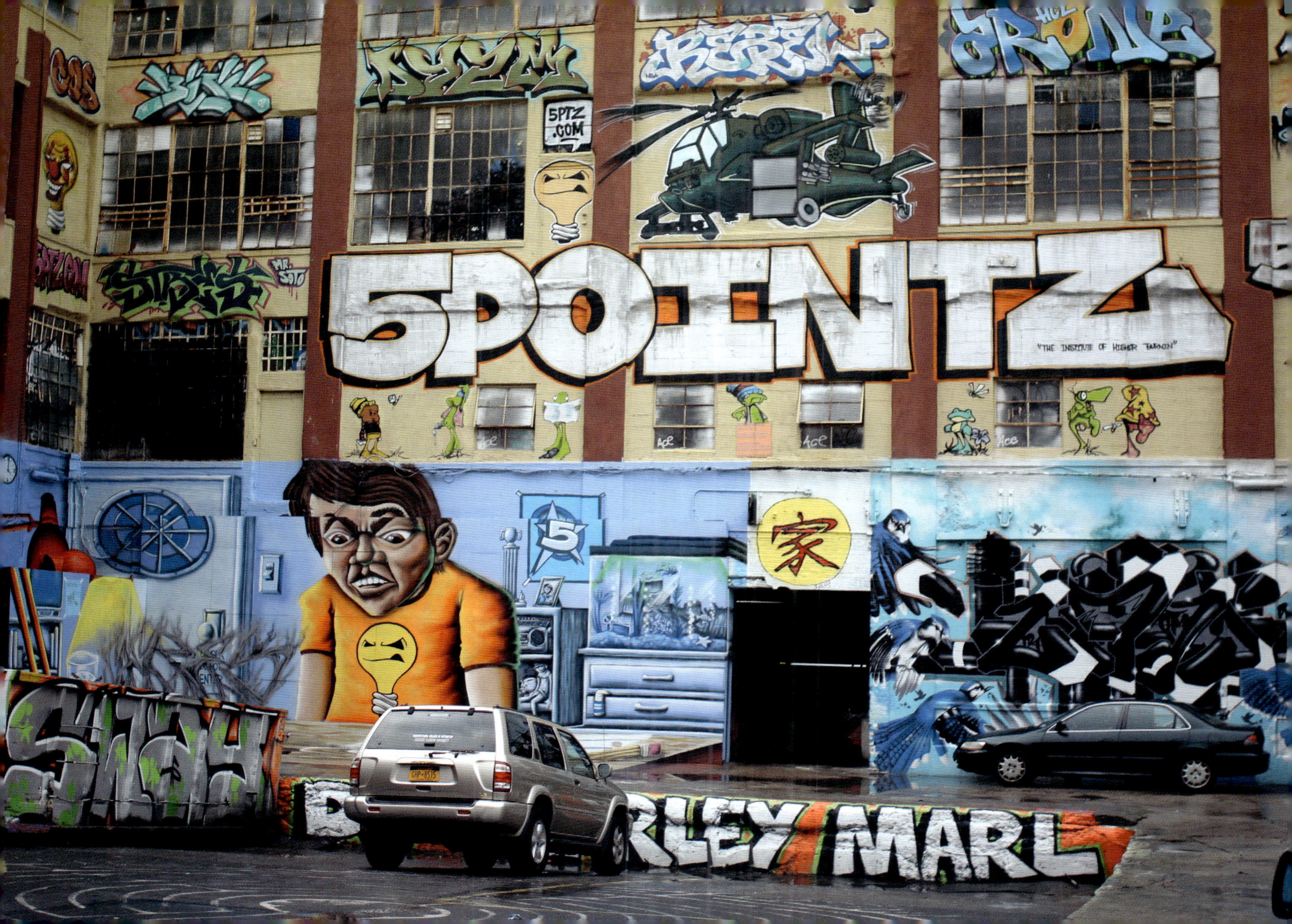
5PTZ
.COM
5POINTZ
MARL

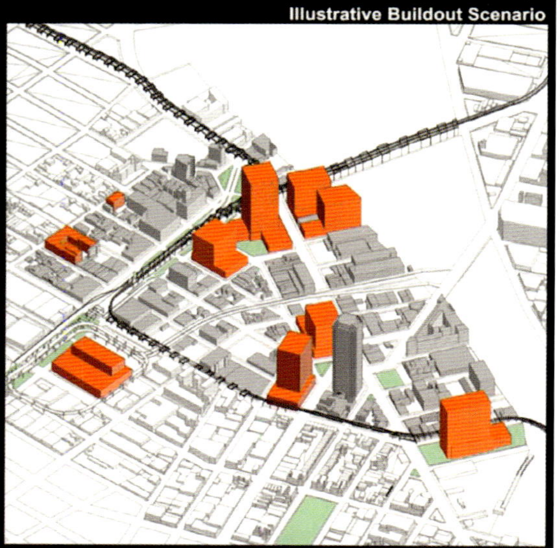

Five Pointz can be seen in the lower right corner. Photo by Patrick Verel

destined to join countless art meccas cleared out in the name of progress.[159]

On November 18, 2013, under cover of darkness, the outside of the building was painted white by crews hired by the building's owner, erasing a myriad of graffiti art. The physical structure was left intact, but its identity as a space connected to art was eradicated. Its demolition a year later was merely a formality.[160]

But I digress. Although 5 Pointz is gone, the space is still worth a critical look, both in terms of its contributions as a node of a global graffiti community that still practices a great deal of its craft in the shadows, and its relation to the city's larger fabric.

The French philosopher Michel Foucault addresses something that is often left unsaid when assessing the merits of public spaces: It is not important that a building or space is constructed in a particular fashion; what matters most is how space is experienced by people. He writes:

> Our life is still dominated by a certain number of oppositions that cannot be tampered with, that institutions and practices have not ventured to change—oppositions that we take for granted, for example, between private space and public space, between family space and social space, between cultural space and useful space, between the space of leisure activities and the space of work. All of these are still controlled by an unspoken sacrilization.[161]

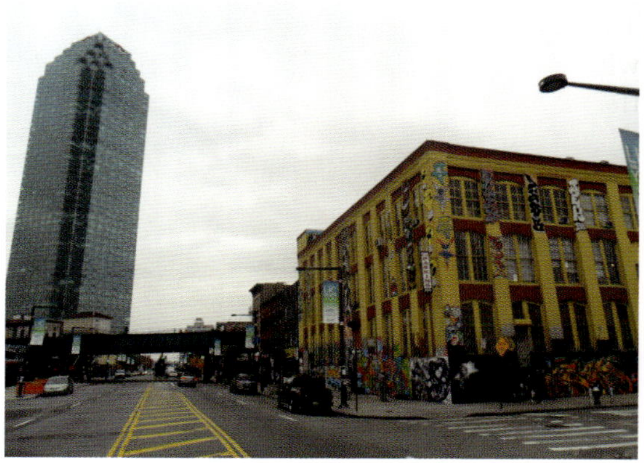

Five Pointz as seen on the corner of Jackson Ave and Crane Street, circa October 2012. Photo by Patrick Verel

Oppositions that separated 5 Pointz from the surrounding neighborhood were numerous and it is helpful to mention them because they locate the building within its context. There is the obvious, in the painted figures, glyphs, and texts that covered well over half the surface of the complex. This was, in fact, what made it unique to New York City—there are spaces dedicated to graffiti scattered all around the five boroughs, but none rose five stories from the ground and wrapped around three-quarters of a city block.

But there were other, less obvious oppositions. There was purpose: This building was constructed for light manufacturing; as noted above, the area was rezoned to exclude this kind of space. The fifty-story Citigroup building is more in line with what the city would prefer there instead.

There was the chaos of the space, particularly when compared to MoMa P S1, the satellite of the museum that is stationed across Jackson Avenue. Whereas PS1 sits in calm repose behind clean concrete and a simple white façade, 5 Pointz was a garish mish-mash of a low-brow, high concept, simplistic and astonishingly complex. It also functioned as a gallery turned inside out—whereas most spaces exhibit art inside, 5 Pointz' exterior *was* the gallery. Additionally, the building was—thanks to its mass, color, outlet, and location—a bone fide landmark that drew visitors from around the globe to see it. Although the art at PS1 is no doubt impressive, and the architecture of the Citigroup building is visually arresting (mostly because it stands so freakishly out of proportion with everything else), neither can compare to the uniqueness of 5 Pointz, which sported an exterior that changed almost as often as the seasons. It was like a chameleon, altering its skin as it saw fit.

Unfortunately, lack of official recognition occupied the final opposition. PS1 has existed since 1971 and has been affiliated with the Museum of Modern Art since 2000. Citigroup is a multinational financial services company with 260,000 employees that was founded in 1812. PS1 is lauded as the type of culture inherently desirable to the city, whereas street art and graffiti get little to no official support from the city. Citigroup's tower, in form if not function, represents the high water mark for the city: maximum capital exerted from the space.

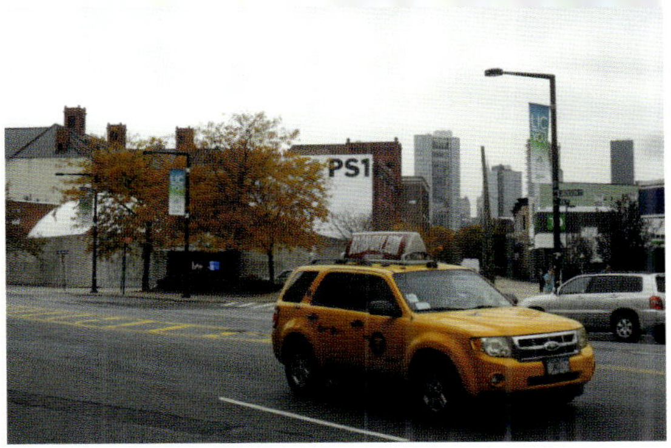

P.S. 1, ensconced behind clean concrete walls across the street from Five Pointz, circa October 2012. Photo by Patrick Verel.

This segues nicely into Rem Koolhaas's discussion of Manhattanism. Koolhaas is known as an architect responsible for unorthodox buildings like the CCTV headquarters in Beijing, but he has also meditated intensely on the zeitgeist of New York City development. In his *Delirious New York* (Monacelli Press, 1997), he discusses how the Waldorf-Astoria hotel's predecessor was demolished to make way for the Empire State Building:

> The model for Manhattan's urbanism is now a form of architectural cannibalism: By swallowing its predecessors, the final building accumulates all the strengths and spirits of the previous occupants of the sight, and in its own way, preserves their memory.[162]

In the case of 5 Pointz, the space was used as a cultural one since 1993, when Pat DiLillo, an artist in the Crane Studios, convinced owner Jerry Wolkoff to let graffiti artists paint the exterior. Wolkoff's son David eventually took over, and gave his blessing to Jonathan Cohen, who goes by the tag MeresOne, to take over and subsequently change the name from DiLillo's Phun Factory to 5 Pointz. In interviews, David Wolkoff expressed sadness that the building would have to come down, but insisted that it would be prohibitively expensive to repair it so that it would be habitable again. While shrugging off complaints from neighbors critical of his decision to turn over his building to artists wielding those spray cans, he was also clear about what he saw as his role:

> We've allowed them to have a safe haven to do their work, and now as a developer I have to be allowed to do the work I do, to create what I consider art, which is building buildings—which is an art form as well as an economic driver.[163]

In the same interview, Wolkoff expressed confidence that the loss of the building wouldn't leave the neighborhood bereft of art, citing PS1's presence. That view, that PS1 is an adequate replacement, was unfortunately echoed by Joe Conley, chairman of New York City Community Board 2, in which the building is situated.

> I can't see that the community would lose anything with that building. It's an outdated building, it's from a bygone era, and it's certainly not the efficient use of space.[164]

To be fair to Wolkoff, he also stated publicly that he'd like to incorporate artists' work into the new development, which would be made up of a forty-seven-story tower and a forty-one-story tower, together encompassing 1,000 rental units and 30,000 square feet of retail space. And this is where the concept of Manhattanism's "architectural cannibalism" comes into play. Given the enormity of the project and the fact that Wolkoff is currently replacing industrial space with residential space, it's almost laughable to think the same sort of artistic freedom can abound in a place that Wolkoff told WNYC radio could have a gym, a pool, a billiards room, and a supermarket.

But just as Koolhaas documented that the majestic Waldorf-Astoria was seen as a fitting site for the Empire State Building, so too does Wolkoff seriously believe that his towers will, in Koolhaas words, "accumulate all the strengths and spirits of the previous occupants of the sight, and in its own way, preserve their memory."

Visitors take turns "tagging" the Ricoh logo, circa December 2009. Photo by Patrick Verel

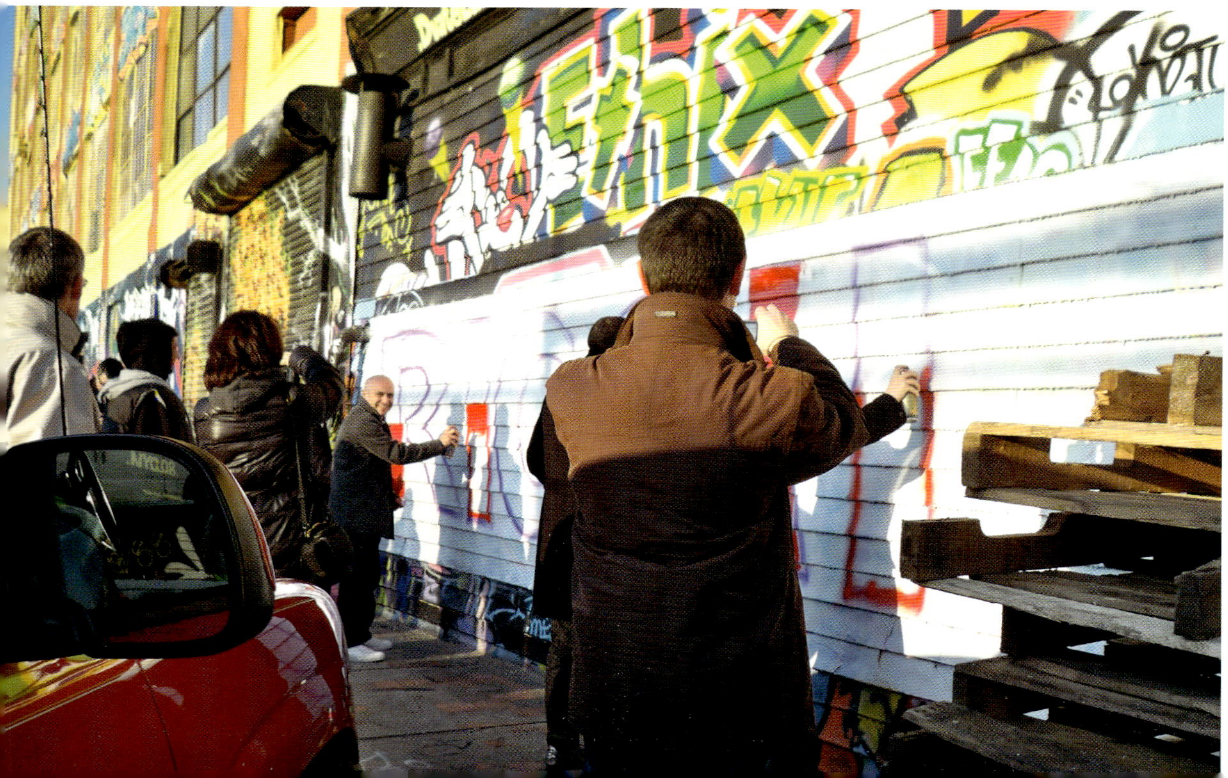

And what of the self-appointed curator of 5 Pointz? When asked why a place like 5 Pointz might be important, with its multitude of pieces presented together on nearly every conceivable space, MeresOne spoke not as someone concerned with the overall look; but as a promoter of a culture near and dear to him.

> It's about people, you know? It's more enjoyable; it's kind of boring to [paint] alone. It's not a gang or anything; when they paint, they just get together and do a wall.[165]

Speaking with a croak that suggested he'd perhaps spent too many days painting without a mask, MeresOne also joked that one of the reasons why graffiti artists crave outdoor spaces like the walls of 5 Pointz and other mural locations over indoor spaces, is it's better on their lungs. But of course, it's really just a simple matter of being seen by an audience that's either large or influential, the latter being other writers and fans of graffiti.

> If you're there, other people will be there, and they may say "Wow, there's a piece where I didn't expect to see it.:[166]

MeresOne estimated that 5 Pointz hosted 1,000 different pieces annually, with many writers returning to the space over and over. He didn't say as much when he cited that number, but I suspect that didn't include installations such as one that I witnessed in person—a red and white blocky "Ricoh," whose outline he painted on the southwest corner of the complex in December 2009. When I visited the site then, a group of about twenty-five visitors who'd piled out of a tour bus were taking turns filling in the outlines of the letters with red spray paint, while posing for pictures. "Tagging," it seems, is something that people will pay for the privilege to do, as MeresOne said they'd compensated him for allowing them to try their hand at the famous 5 Pointz. After they left, he quickly spray painted over it again, creating a space ready for a new, less commercially infected creation.

MeresOne wrestled with the competing interests of art and commerce, on the one hand trumpeting the validity of graffiti and the importance of 5 Pointz, and then accepting money from groups with no interest in creating art. He was not wrong to take money to support the greater cause of 5 Pointz (on November 8, 2012, 5 Pointz was even featured on the TV show *Project Runway*) as he supervised the space for no salary. When he explained the logic behind taking money from the likes of Ricoh, he pinned some blame on Wolkoff's greediness. This might have come across as sour grapes from someone who was getting so much space for free, but it's worth noting that Wolkoff let the building fall into such disrepair that an outdoor stairwell collapsed in April 2009, seriously injuring one of the Crane Street Studio's artists. This lead to the eviction of the studio, and the building sat largely empty from then on.[167]

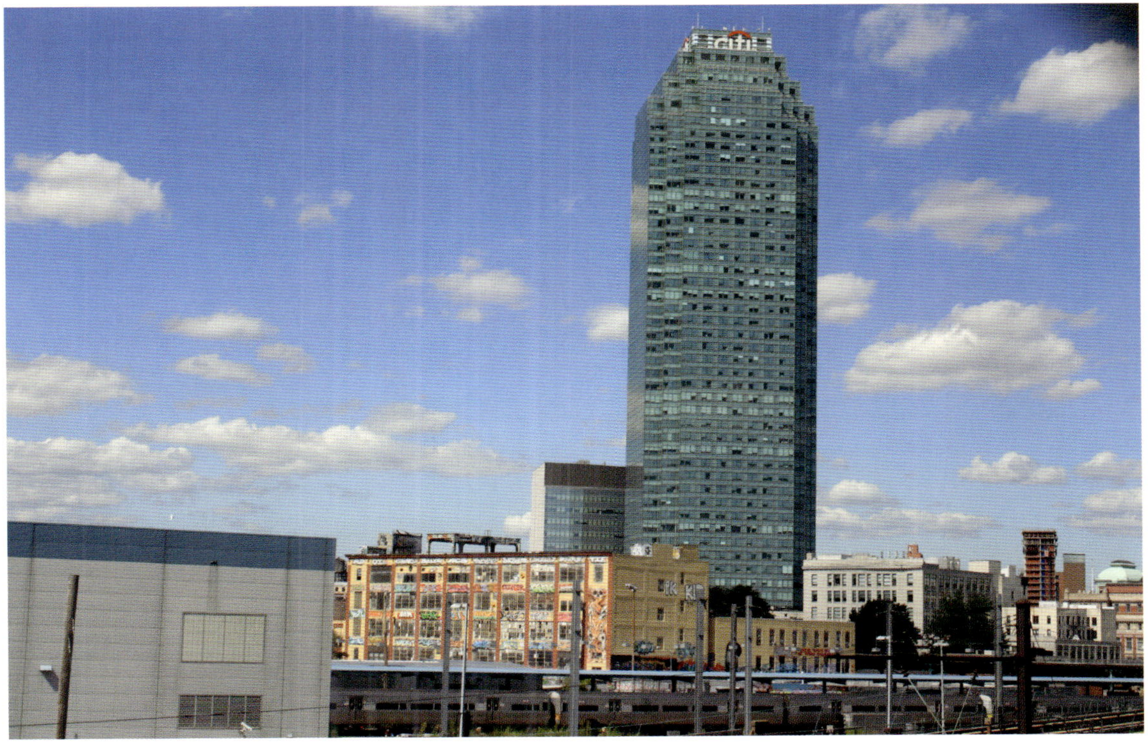

Five Pointz with the Citicorp tower looming behind it, circa August 2011. Photo by Patrick Verel

This raises the possibility that Wolkoff allowed 5 Pointz to fall into disrepair, thus making it easier to justify knocking it down and building something radically different in its place. In a sense, it's an inarguable point, though; the aforementioned rezoning gave an official blessing to the eventual demolition of the building. MeresOne may have been living in a world where he has had to cater to corporate tourists in order to keep his operation going, but Wolkoff is a developer in a town where the demand for housing is astronomical.

When asked about the loss of the tenants of the Crane Street Studios, MeresOne was not terribly moved.

Q: Have things changed much since the closing of the studios inside 5 Pointz?

A: Not really. I don't have to be as conscious if the radios are as loud outside, now we can turn the music on as loud as we want to. Otherwise it's the same. There were some hypocrites who were two-faced, they'd say hello and then talk down on us and label us. So at times that would happen.[168]

If MeresOne was a little too caught up in the importance of his art to the exclusion of others, Wolkoff is much too confident that he can incorporate the past into the present. In a *New York Times* article about the impending demolition, he revealed that the space reserved for the graffiti artists would be a rear wall. This cannot be seen as anything more than a token gesture, akin to a scale model of the original Waldorf-Astoria hotel stored in the lobby of the Empire State Building. [169]

One57, left, dubbed the "Billionaires' Haven," under construction in January 2013. Photo by Patrick Verel

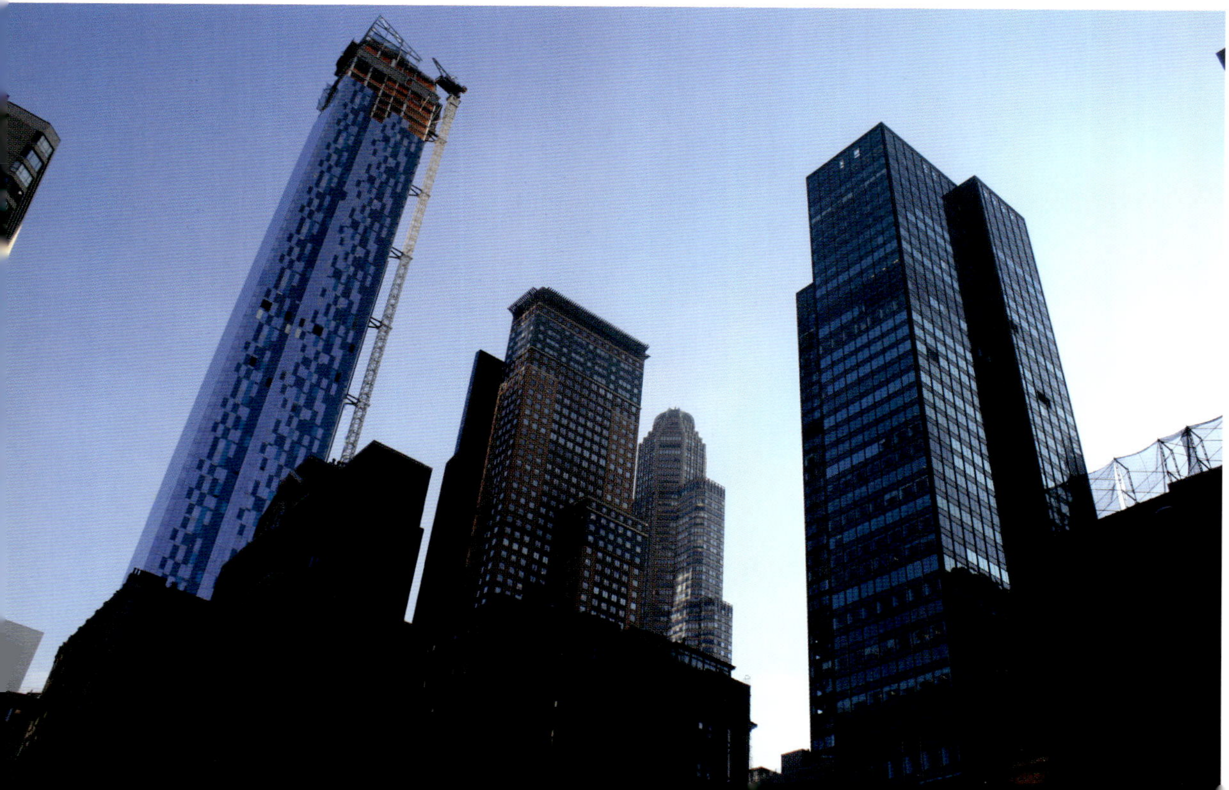

As for the future, renderings of Wolkoff's planned development illustrate that as with the Citicorp Tower, verticality is the key to the future, not spontaneity.[170] Monetary capital will triumph here, as neighborhood cultural capital will be ceded to more trusted keepers at PS1.

For now, the contrast between the squat, crumbling stone building and the cool, shimmering tall glass tower just down the street, can be illustrated neatly by Koolhaas's explanation of the work of architect Hugh Ferriss, who first envisioned New York as the "mega-village."

> Ferriss's most important contribution to the theory of Manhattan is exactly the creation of an illuminated night inside a cosmic container, the murky *Ferrissian Void*: A pitch black architectural womb that gives birth to the consecutive stages of the skyscraper in a sequence of sometimes overlapping pregnancies, and that promises ever new ones.[171]

It is important to note that this is a New York City where a humble building such as 5 Pointz could once be fifteen minutes not only from cultural beacons such as Carnegie Hall, but also from out-of-this-world havens with 11,000-square-foot apartments that are sold to plutocrats for $95 million.[172] So it is depressingly understandable that Ferriss's vision of a void that encompasses all of the Manhattan sky, just waiting to be taken over by successive skyscrapers, extends across the East River into Queens, a borough known more for its parkland and polyglot immigrant population than its skyline. The "Ferrissian void" that will be filled between Crane and Davis streets in Long Island City may not contain the space of business the way its glassy neighbor to the west does, but in the scope of filling the void and adding bulk to fill in the "cosmic container," it is no different.

Now that a wrecking ball has met 5 Pointz, and the name, which is an ode to New York City's five boroughs, is either retired or transferred by MeresOne to some other destination, what replaces it will pale in comparison, if for no other reason than its replacement will sync with the demands of monetary capital, and the void will be overwhelmed with space primarily dedicated to generating profit. One "opposition" that has already disappeared from the scene is change: The morphing "that wasn't there last week" quality of the vast canvas that is the exterior, will be replaced by something static and predictable. To expect anything less from residents within would be unrealistic. Wolkoff might truly believe he's honoring the energy and history of graffiti by providing a space for future artists work, but unless it's a space that is visible from the elevated 7 train and the myriad passersby in the neighborhood, it won't be any more appealing to graffiti artists than the dozen or so spaces around the city that are also open to artists in the know. Just two miles north, for instance, the Welling Court Mural Project, which was started in 2009 by the Ad Hoc Art studio, celebrated its fifth anniversary in 2014 with a full day of painting on a half-dozen blocks in Astoria. A corollary to Wolkoff's plan might be the punk rock club CBGB, which closed in 2006 and was replaced eighteen months later by a high-end John Varvatos men's fashion store, which peddled $250 shirts. Remnants of the original institution remained, but were an echo from the past, useful for reminiscing perhaps, but not much else.

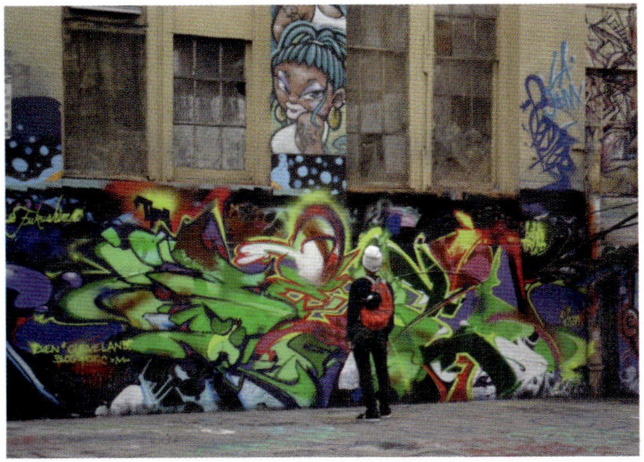

A visitor takes in a piece at Five Pointz in October 2012. Photo by Patrick Verel

{12} Final Thoughts

Graffiti Murals As a City's Best Friend

The official position of the city of New York is that penalties for graffiti must be harsh (the sale of spray paint to minors is illegal, and hefty punishments are handed down when perpetrators are caught, including felony charges for multiple arrests of those over 18), as part of a larger strategy of crime fighting that embraces the "broken windows" theory. But I propose that the city would do well to add another arrow to its quiver in its ongoing campaign against vandalism.

I envision a scenario in which a building owner receives a notice from the city informing the owner that there is graffiti on the building, and that the owner has forty-five days to:

A) Respond with a confirmation that they will buff the graffiti themselves;
B) Respond with a confirmation that they want the graffiti to remain;
C) Ignore the notice, in which case the city buffs the building with or without the owner's permission; or
D) Respond with a request for a referral to a graffiti muralist.

Of these four options, only the first three exist today. But the possibility for this last option is realistic. Groundswell already provides artist referrals, and my case studies show that there are plenty of writers who are experienced at collaborating with owners on a project agreeable to both.

Instead of lumping graffiti together with offenses such as loitering, fare jumping, public urination, public alcoholic consumption, and petty theft—which under the "broken windows" theory are considered an early warning system for larger, more serious crimes—the city should take a cue from the private property owners who currently support graffiti murals. Taking inspiration from the street grid that Simeon deWitt, Gouverneur Morris, and John Rutherford designed, this would stay true the city's history of aiding in the development of the private sector. The difference is that instead of sticking to a bland, unimaginative narrative along the lines of "buffing is better for business," the city can marry the support that exists for traditional public murals to the vibrant, home-grown aerosol art scene that has matured and mutated radically since it first surfaced on subway cars nearly forty years ago.

The need to pursue a program like this has never been greater. New York City is nothing if not blessed with art venues, but at the same time, the pressure to squeeze monopoly rent from every square inch of Manhattan and sections of Brooklyn and Queens has increased drastically. One need only cast an eye to Greenwich Village and Tribeca to see how radically neighborhoods can change in ways that preclude them from being receptive to these home-grown art forms that, as Nicer noted, are in many cases modern-day equivalents to Picassos, Goyas, and Monets.

There's a certain irony currently at work in New York City right now. The cache that the city accumulated from both graffiti and hip-hop cultures was born from the chaos and bankruptcy of the 1970s. Although this book does not address the latter, the former is arguably in danger of becoming fetishized and thoroughly commoditized, like so many key chains and shot glasses available for purchase by tourists. In many instances, that's already happened, as noted in the chapter about 5 Pointz, and in the Ace Hotel in Manhattan, which now sports a lobby with 4,000 reproduced graffiti stickers on the walls.

But while graffiti and all the other variations of street art have become much more accepted in New York City, with a billboard dedicated to a revolving selection of pieces on Houston Street and the Bowery, the role of graffiti murals as a sort of anti "releaser cue," of the sort that Phillip Zimbardo described, is not appreciated. The reason nearly every one I interviewed in my case studies approved of the murals is fairly easy to understand: in a place where money for commercial development is now sloshing around like seawater in a leaky boat, a graffiti mural is a symbol of something not only rooted in local culture, but also rooted in one of the best aspects of the recent past. New York City is not just a draw for visitors who clamber to see spectacles like the Empire State Building or Yankee Stadium. It is also the place where subway-born art maintains, as Walter Benjamin would argue, its aura, in the form of a gritty sidewalk gallery.

This is symbolic capital that's worth its weight in precious metals and shiny baubles. Other cities around the world may have sanctioned sections of town where graffiti is embraced, but New York City has something even better: a select merchant class that has embraced a global art form and done its part to elevate New York City into the upper echelon of global cities. What's especially impressive is that owners such as Jerry Blankman in Jersey City, Jonny Seigel in Bushwick, and Mark Borak in Hunts Point embrace graffiti murals because they see them as good for the neighborhood *and* good for their businesses. This is borne out by studies that mentioned in the Philadelphia chapter, and although there are also doubters, it is the believers and the artists they embrace who deserve all the help we can give them.

It's also important to note that for all the good that has come out of the return of multinational corporations' reinvestment in New York City after the city hit rock bottom in the 1970s, it is still by and large small, locally based business owners who embrace graffiti murals. This is not surprising, given the fact that the artists are small businessmen, too. Some, like the Tats Cru, are more explicit in their embrace of commerce, but all hope to gain something from their work, even if it's just exposure. Exposure is only valuable if it's accompanied by freedom to pursue one's art as one sees fit, and as Rain noted in the Trenton chapter, corporate-owned spaces are not the ideal environment. This is another way the city of New York could support small businesses even as it becomes more connected to the global economy than ever before.

Fortunately, there is awareness in some institutional quarters of the value that graffiti muralists bring to the city. Even as hubs of creativity such as Five Pointz are being zoned out of existence, occasional stories come along that crystalize the tug of war being waged between blank slate obsessives and art boosters. Take, for example, the arrest of artist Kenny Scharf, who was caught spray painting on the side of a building in Williamsburg, Brooklyn on April 19, 2013.[173] Scharf, a thirty-year veteran of the art scene who was a contemporary of Andy Warhol and Keith Haring in the 1980s, is popular enough to be one of four artists, along with Shepard Fairey, Ron English, and Robbie Conal, to be featured in the March 4, 2012, episode of *The Simpsons*, "Exit Through The Quickie Mart." His art has graced murals both legal and illegal, and the piece he was arrested for in Williamsburg bears a resemblance to a character he painted legally on the Bowery and Houston Street. The arresting officers also seemed to know that this was not just a random tagger they'd swept up, because they asked him for his autograph.

It begs the question: If building owners in Manhattan, Queens, Bronx, Brooklyn, Staten Island, Jersey City, Trenton, and Philadelphia, and groups like Groundswell and NYC DOT and even New York City beat cops can appreciate the distinction between an art and vandalism, why can't the city?

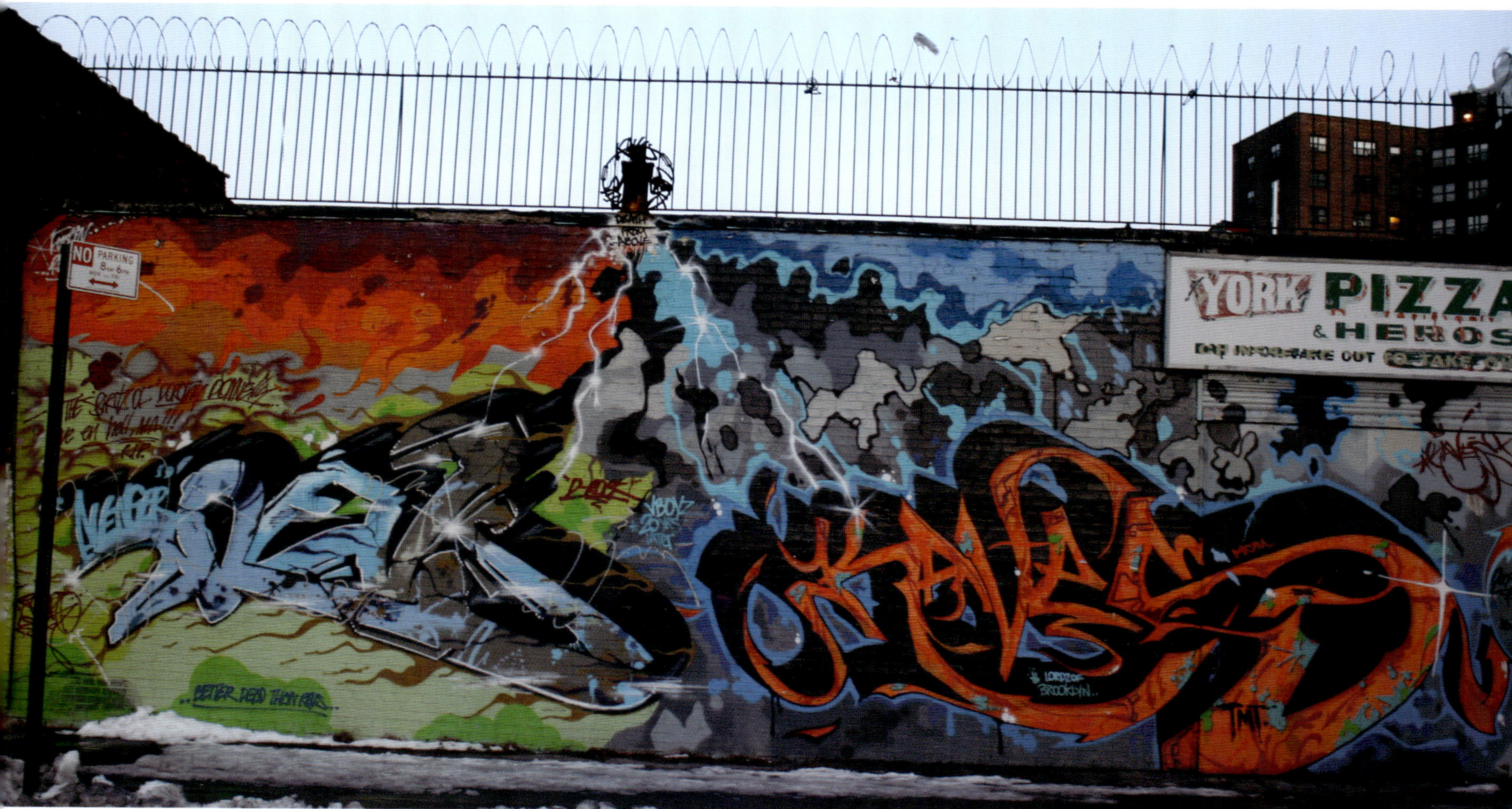

Death From Above by Revs and Kaves in DUMBO, circa February 2010. Photo by Patrick Verel

APPENDIX I

New York City

Anti-Graffiti Laws

New York City, § 10-117. Defacement of property, possession, sale and display of aerosol spray paint cans, [and] broad tipped markers and etching acid prohibited in certain instances.

a. No person shall write, paint or draw any inscription, figure or mark of any type on any public or private building or other structure or any other real or personal property owned, operated or maintained by a public benefit corporation, the city of New York or any agency or instrumentality thereof or by any person, firm, or corporation, or any personal property maintained on a city street or other city-owned property pursuant to a franchise, concession or revocable consent granted by the city, unless the express permission of the owner or operator of the property has been obtained.

b. No person shall carry an aerosol spray paint can, [or] broad tipped indelible marker or etching acid into any public building or other public facility with the intent to violate the provisions of subdivision a of this section.

c. No person shall sell or offer to sell an aerosol spray paint can, [or] broad tipped indelible marker or etching acid to any person under eighteen years of age.

d. All persons who sell or offer for sale aerosol spray paint cans, [or] broad tipped indelible markers or etching acid shall not place such cans, [or] markers or etching acid on display and may display only facsimiles of such cans, [or] markers or etching acid containing no paint, [or] ink or etching acid.

e. For the purpose of this section, the term "broad tipped indelible marker" shall mean any felt tip marker or similar implement containing a fluid that is not water soluble and which has a flat or angled writing surface one-half inch or greater. For the purpose of this section, the term "etching acid" shall mean any liquid, cream, paste or similar chemical substance that can be used to etch, draw, carve, sketch, engrave, or otherwise alter, change or impair the physical integrity of glass or metal.

APPENDIX II
Interview Questions

THE ARTISTS

How long have you been writing graffiti?

Why do you do it?

When did you first do it with permission from the property owner?

How did you learn of this opportunity?

What was here before this mural?

Do you only write with permission now, or do you still do it without permission?

How is it different?

How do you choose a space, and how do you choose a neighborhood?

Is it hard to get permission from a property owner?

Do you get feedback from neighbors?

Do you get feedback from the city?

Do you feel the city is supportive of this sort of thing?

Why do you think your mural is better for the neighborhood than what was there before?

THE OWNERS

How did you first get in touch with this artist?

Why did you allow them to use your property?

What was there before they put their mural there?

How long did it take them?

Did you know what it was going to look like before-hand?

What has the reaction been from your neighbors?

What is your general impression of graffiti?

Have you ever been contacted by the city about graffiti on your property?

Do you feel the city is supportive of this sort of thing?

THE RESIDENTS

How long have you lived here?

Are you familiar with the graffiti mural nearby?

What do you think of it?

Do you think it makes the neighborhood a better place?

Do you think it's better than a blank wall?

What is your general impression of graffiti?

How would you describe this neighborhood?

THE MIDDLEMEN

*These questions were crafted for Jersey City;
a variation of the set was used for Staten Island.*

How did this particular mural come together?

What's your relation to the collective? What's your role?

How did you get into this?

How long have you been doing this?

You're based here in Jersey City?

Where else do you tend to work?

So you're cutting these guys checks here. How does that work?

How did it come to be that it would be a blue whale and look like this? Was this his idea, their idea?

How hard is it to get building owners to let artists use their buildings as canvases?

How much freedom do you guys tend to get when you do these? Are they pretty willing to let them do whatever they want? Do you get a lot of pushback on that?

One of the ways things I've heard from artists is, if you let us do this, that you won't get tags, throw-ups or regular graffiti on it. Do you find that's something that you mention when you talk to them?

Do you feel like the governments you work with are supportive of your efforts?

Notes

Introduction

1. Eric Felisbret, *Graffiti New York* (New York: Abrams, 2009).
2. David Harvey, *Rebel Cities* (Brooklyn: Verso, 2012), 5.
3. Rem Koolhaas, *Delirious New York* (New York: Monacelli Press, 1994): 18.
4. David Harvey, *Rebel Cities*, (Brooklyn: Verso, 2012), 16.
5. Saskia Sassen, *The Global City: New York, London, Tokyo*, (Princeton: Princeton University Press, 1991).
6. "Fetish Fest Organizers Erect Wall to Shield Luxe Condo Neighbors," DNAinfo.com, June 15, 2012.
7. "Times Square Lights Up City's Economy, Study Finds," *The New York Times*, March 19, 2012.
8. David Harvey, *Rebel Cities* (Brooklyn: Verso, 2012), 105.
9. "Citing Finances, Brooklyn Museum Cancels Plans for Graffiti Art Exhibit," *The New York Times,* June 21, 2011.
10. David Harvey, *Rebel Cities* (Brooklyn: Verso, 2012), 110.
11. "Ruling Lets Atlantic Yards Seize Land," *The New York Times*, Nov. 29, 2009.
12. Society for the Study of Symbolic Interaction website, www.symbolicinteraction.org/, accessed Feb. 18, 2012.
13. P. G. Zimbardo, *Making Sense of Senseless Vandalism*, Current Perspectives in Sociology, 4th ed., (Oxford: Oxford University Press, 1976), 129–134.
14. Hugo Martinez, a sociology major at City College of New York, organized the first major exhibition of his group, the United Graffiti Artists, at the Razor Gallery in SoHo, as described by Eric Felisbret DEAL CIA, *Graffiti New York*, (New York: Abrams, 2009), 298.
15. New York City, "Mayor's Anti-Graffiti Task Force," http://www.nyc.gov/html/nograffiti/html/aboutforce.html.
16. Ronald Kramer, *A Social History of Graffiti Writing in New York City, 1990–2005* (New Haven: Yale University Press, 2009), 309.
17. Mark Halsey and Alison Young, "Our desires are ungovernable: Writing graffiti in urban space," *Theoretical Criminology,* Aug. 2006, vol. 10, 3, 275–306..

18. Ronald Kramer, *A Social History of Graffiti Writing in New York City, 1990–2005* (New Haven: Yale University Press, 2009), 199.
19. Gregory Synder, *Graffiti Lives: Beyond the Tag in New York's Urban Underground* (New York, New York University Press, 2009), 97.
20. Cedar Lewisohn, *Street Art: The Graffiti Revolution*, (New York: Abrams, 2008), 48.
21. Walter Benjamin, *The Work of Art in the Age of Its Mechanical Reproduction: Second Version* (Cambridge: Belknap Press of Harvard University Press, 2008).
22. "The Banksy Exhibition We Won't Be Seeing At Art Basel Miami and the Reason Why You Shouldn't Either," Woostercollective.com, Dec. 4, 2012.
23. "TAKI 183 Spawns Pen Pals," *The New York Times*, July 21, 1971.
24. "When TAKI Ruled Magic Kingdom" *New York Daily News*, April 9, 1989.
25. See Appendix I

Case Study 1: Manhattan

26. Eddie Pabellon, graffiti artist, in discussion with the author, July 15, 2011.
27. Ibid.
28. Romeo Marculescu, manager, 5060 Auto Services, in discussion with the author, July 22, 2011.
29. Ibid.
30. Eddie Pabellon, graffiti artist, in discussion with the author, July 15, 2011.
31. Mike Clark, resident, in discussion with the author, July 22, 2011.
32. Marisol Ramirez, resident, in discussion with the author, July 22, 2011.
33. Lillian Rodriguez, resident, in discussion with the author, July 22, 2011.
34. Romeo Marculescu, manager, 5060 Auto Services, in discussion with the author, July 22, 2011.
35. Ibid.

Case Study 2: Brooklyn

36. Herb Smith, graffiti artist, in discussion with the author, April 1, 2010.
37. Ibid.
38. Ibid.
39. Jonny Seigel, owner, SoHo Arts Supply, in discussion with the author, April 5, 2010.
40. Ibid.
41. Max Brennan, owner, Manhattan Molds and Casts, in discussion with the author, April 5, 2010
42. Ibid.
43. Ibid.
44. Loretta Lees, Tom Slater and Elvin Wyly, *Gentrification* (New York: Routledge, 2008).
45. Herb Smith, graffiti artist, in discussion with the author, April 1, 2010.
46. Ibid.
47. Jamar Robinson, resident, in discussion with the author, Aug. 12, 2012.
48. Ibid.
49. Deirdre O'Dwyer, artist, in conversation with the author, Aug. 12, 2012.
50. "Bushwick Gets a Fresh Coat: A Son of Bushwick Turns the Neighborhood Into a Gallery for Street Art," *The New York Times*, May 3, 2013.
51. Jaquay Walker, resident, in conversation with the author, Aug. 12, 2012.

Case Study 3: The Bronx

52. "South Bronx is poorest district in nation, U.S. Census Bureau finds: 38% live below poverty line," *New York Daily News*, Sept. 29, 2010.
53. Hector Nazario, founder, TATS CRU, in conversation with author, Sept. 27, 2010.
54. Ibid.
55. Ibid.
56. Roy Mangione, director of operations, Borax Paper, in conversation with author, Oct. 18, 2010.
57. Ibid.
58. Mark Borak, owner, Borax Paper, in conversation with author, Oct. 18, 2010.
59. Roy Mangione, director of operations, Borax Paper, in conversation with author, Oct. 18, 2010.
60. Frank Ruiz, truck driver, in conversation with with author, Oct. 18, 2010.
61. "In the Bronx, a Collision of Cars, Celebrity and Copyright," *The New York Times*, Nov. 28, 2011.
62. T. K. Singleton, community initiatives coordinator, Bronx Community Solutions in conversation with author, Oct. 10, 2010.
63. Ibid.
64. Ibid.
65. Hector Nazario, founder, TATS CRU, in conversation with author, Sept. 27, 2010.

Case Study 4: Jersey City

66. Dylan Evans, art curator and consultant, in conversation with author, Nov. 7, 2010.
67. Ibid.
68. Ibid.
69. Luv1, graffiti artist, in conversation with author, Nov. 7, 2010.
70. Ibid.
71. Luv1 and Will Kasso, graffiti artists, in conversation with author, Nov. 7, 2010.
72. Will Kasso, graffiti artist, in conversation with author, Nov. 7, 2010.
73. Jerry Blankman, property owner, in conversation with author, Nov. 22, 2010.
74. Ibid.
75. Ibid.
76. Ibid.
77. Ibid.
78. Ibid.
79. Ronnie Houghtalin, resident, in conversation with author, Nov. 23, 2010.
80. Ibid.
81. Rama Parachuru, resident, in conversaton with author, Nov. 23, 2010.
82. Michelle Fuller, resident, in conversaton with author, Nov. 23, 2010.
83. Ibid.
84. Junior Maldonado, resident, in conversation with author, Nov. 23, 2010.
85. Ibid.

Case Study 5: Staten Island

86. New York Arts Cypher website, http://nycartscypher.com, accessed March 3, 2012.
87. Charlie Balducci, founder, NYC Arts Cypher in conversation with author, March 29, 2011.
88. Ibid.
89. Ibid.
90. Ibid.
91. Wayne Miller, vice president of sales and marketing, The Clover Club, in conversation with author, April 25, 2011.
92. Ibid.
93. Ibid.
94. Geoff Rawling, artist, in conversation with author, April 19, 2011.
95. Ibid.
96. Ibid.
97. Ibid.
98. Jeff Li, vice president and project director, Leewood Real Estate, in conversation with author, May 10, 2011.
99. Ibid.
100. Kent Dylan, resident, in conversation with author, April 25, 2011.
101. Ibid.
102. Tom Stone, resident, in conversation with author, April 25, 2011.
103. Louise DiNardo, resident, in conversation with author, April 25, 2011.

Case Study 6: Trenton

104. Terracycle website, http://www.terracycle.net/en-US/graffiti-at-terracycle, accessed April 15, 2011.
105. George W. Chevalier III, spokesman, TerraCycle, in conversation with author, April 22, 2011.
106. "New statistics show nearly 30% of Trenton residents live below the poverty line," *The Times of Trenton*, September 24, 2011.
107. George W. Chevalier III, spokesman, TerraCycle, in conversation with author, April 22, 2011.
108. Ibid.
109. Ibid.
110. Leon Rainbow, graffiti artist, in conversation with author, March 13, 2011.
111. Ibid.
112. Ibid.
113. Ibid.
114. Ibid.
115. Ibid.
116. Ibid.
117. Ibid.
118. Ibid.
119. Brian Hawkins, owner, Hawkins Towing, in conversation with author, April 22, 2011.
120. Ibid.
121. Sindy Estrada, resident, in conversation with author, April 22, 2011.

Philadelphia's Mural Arts

122. Neelon Gastman, *The History of American Graffiti*, (New York: Harper Design), 78.
123. Philadelphia Mural Arts website, http://muralarts.org/about/history, accessed Oct. 11, 2012.
124. Amy Johnston, spokesperson, Philadelphia Mural Arts, in conversation with author, July 21, 2011.
125. Ibid.
126. Ibid.
127. Ibid.
128. Ibid.
129. Jeremy Nowak, *Creativity and Neighborhood Development*, (The Reinvestment Fund, 2007).
130. *Commercial Corridors: A Strategic Investment Framework for Philadelphia*, (EConsult, March 2009).
130. Ibid.
132. Interview with author, July 21, 2011.

NYC Mural Makers

133. New York City Department of Transportation website, "About DOT," http://www.nyc.gov/html/dot/html/about/about.shtml, accessed Oct. 21, 2012.
134. Emily Colasacco, project manager, New York City Department of Transportation Urban Arts Program, in conversation with author, Oct. 25, 2011.
135. Ibid.
136. Ibid.
137. Ibid.
138. Jessica Poplawski, program manager, Groundswell Community Mural Project, e-mail to author, Oct. 12, 2011.
139. Groundswell website,http://www.groundswellmural.org., accessed Nov. 15, 2012.
140. Jessica Poplawski, program manager, Groundswell Community Mural Project, e-mail to author, Oct. 12, 2011.

Graffiti-Free New York

141. Graffiti Free Website, http://www.nyc.gov/html/cau/html/graffiti/graffiti.shtml, accessed Nov. 16, 2012.
142. "Mayor Bloomberg and City Council Announce New Steps to Make Graffiti Removal Faster and Easier in NYC," press release, http://www.nycedc.com/press-release/mayor-bloomberg-and-city-council-announce-new-steps-make-graffiti-removal-faster-and, July 9, 2009.
143. Roy Carrero, Quality of life director, New York City Mayor Community Affairs Unit, in conversation with author, March 5, 2011.
144. Ibid.
145. Ibid.
146. "East Village Mural, Painted Over in Anti-Vandalism Campaign, Replaced by Graffiti," DNAinfo.com, April 20, 2010.
147. Roy Carrero, Quality of life director, New York City Mayor Community Affairs Unit, in conversation with author, March 5, 2011.
148. NYC & Company website, http://www.nycandcompany.org/research/nyc-statistics-page, accessed Nov. 20, 2012.
149. Roy Carrero, Quality of life director, New York City Mayor Community Affairs Unit, in conversation with author, March 5, 2011.
150. Graff Tours, http://grafftours.com/, accessed Dec. 10, 2012.
151. Levy's tours, http://levysuniqueny.com/tours/from-graffiti-to-galleries-brooklyn-represent/.

The Clean Slate Club

152. Asher Long, operations manager Friedknit Creations, in conversation with author, July 28, 2011.
153. Interview with author, July 28, 2011.
154. Interview with author, July 28, 2011.
155. Interview with author, July 28, 2011.
156. Interview with author, July 28, 2011.
157. "Grand Plan for a Toxic Site Is Scorned and Celebrated," *The New York Times*, Oct. 8, 2012.

Five Pointz

158. "Long Island City Rezoning: Executive Summary," http://www.nyc.gov/html/dcp/html/lic/lic1.shtml, accessed Oct. 25, 2012.
159. "5 Pointz to Face Wrecking Ball by Sept. 2013," *Sunnyside Post*, June 25, 2012.
160. "Night Falls, and 5Pointz, a Graffiti Mecca, Is Whited Out in Queens," *The New York Times*, Nov. 19, 2013.
161. Michael Foucault, *Aesthetics, Method and Epistemology (Essential Works of Foucault, 1954-1984)*, Vol. 2, (New York: The New Press, 1999) 177.
162. Rem Koolhass, *Delirious New York*, (New York: The Monacelli Press, 1997), 138.
163. "The Fate of 5 Pointz: Why One Man May Demolish New York's Graffiti Mecca," *The New School Free Press*, Oct. 24, 2012.
164. "5Pointz, a Graffiti Landmark, Faces an Uncertain Future in Queens," WNYC, April 29, 2011.
165. MeresOne, founder 5 Pointz, in conversation with author, Dec. 9, 2009.
166. Ibid.
167. "One Artist is Hurt, and 200 Others Are Feeling the Pain," *The New York Times*, April 19, 2009.
168. MeresOne, founder 5 Pointz, in conversation with author, Dec. 9, 2009.
169. "Writing's on the Wall (Art is, Too, for Now)" *The New York Times*, Aug. 27, 2011.
170. Rem Koolhass, *Delirious New York* (New York: The Monacelli Press, 1997), 117.
171. "New Look: 22–24 Jackson Avenue, 5Pointz Redevelopment," *NY Yimby*, July 31, 2013.
172. "Rising Tower Emerges as a Billionaires' Haven," *The New York Times*, Sept. 18, 2012.

Final Thoughts

173. "Kenny Scharf Arrested & NYPD Asks Him For Autographs," Artsucks.com, accessed, April 22, 2013.

Bibliography

Austin, Joe. *Taking The Train: How Graffiti Art Became an Urban Crisis in New York City*, New York: Columbia University Press, 2001.

Bagli, Charles. "Ruling Lets Atlantic Yards Seize Land," *The New York Times*, November 29, 2009, http://www.nytimes.com/2009/11/25/nyregion/25yards.html.

Barrionuevo, Alexei. "Rising Tower Emerges as a Billionaires' Haven," *The New York Times*, September 18, 2012, http://www.nytimes.com/2012/09/19/realestate/rising-tower-in-manhattan-takes-on-sheen-as-billionaires-haven.html.

Benjamin, Walter. *The Work of Art in the Age of Technological Reproducibility, and other Writings on Media.* Cambridge, Mass: Belknap Press of Harvard University Press, 2008.

Berger, Joseph. "Grand Plan for a Toxic Site Is Scorned and Celebrated," *The New York Times* October 8, 2012, http://www.nytimes.com/2012/10/09/nyregion/development-plan-near-gowanus-superfund-site-is-scorned-and-celebrated.html.

Berry, Michele. "The Fate of 5 Pointz: Why One Man May Demolish New York's Graffiti Mecca," *The New School Free Press,* Oct. 24, 2012, http://www.newschoolfreepress.com/2012/10/24/the-fate-of-5-pointz-why-one-man-may-demolish-new-yorks-graffiti-mecca/.

Buckley, Cara. "One Artist is Hurt, and 200 Others Are Feeling the Pain," *The New York Times*, April 19, 2009, http://www.nytimes.com/2009/04/19/nyregion/19pointz.html.

Castleman, Craig. *Getting Up: Subway Graffiti in New York*, Cambridge, Mass: MIT Press, 1982.

Commercial Corridors: A Strategic Investment Framework for Philadelphia, EConsult, March 2009, http://www.instituteccd.org/resources/5007.

Fair, Matt. "New statistics show nearly 30% of Trenton residents live below the poverty line," *The Times of Trenton,* September 24, 2011, http://www.nj.com/mercer/index.ssf/2011/09/new_statistics_show_nearly_30.html.

Felisbret, Eric. *Graffiti New York*, New York: Abrams, 2009.

Fertoli, Annmarie. "5Pointz, a Graffiti Landmark, Faces an Uncertain Future in Queens," *WNYC, April 29, 2011,* http://www.wnyc.org/articles/wnyc-news/2011/apr/29/5-pointz-article-be-added/.

Ferrell, Jeff. *Crimes of Style: Urban Graffiti and the Politics of Criminality*. Boston: Northeastern University, 1993.

Finn, Robin. "Writing's on the Wall (Art is, Too, for Now)" *The New York Times*, August 27, 2011, http://www.nytimes.com/2011/08/28/nyregion/5pointz-arts-center-and-its-graffiti-is-on-borrowed-time.html.

"5 Pointz to face wrecking ball by Sept. 2013," *Sunnyside Post*, June 25, 2012, http://sunnysidepost.com/2012/06/25/5-pointz-to-face-wrecking-ball-by-sept-2013/.

Foucault, Michael. *Aesthetics, Method and Epistemology (Essential Works of Foucault, 1954-1984), Vol. 2,* New York: The New Press, 1999, 177.

Ganz, Nicholas. *Graffiti World: Street Art from Five Continents.* New York: H.N. Abrams, 2004.

Gastman, Neelon. *The History of American Graffiti*, New York: Harper Design, 2011, 78.

Gonzalez, David. "In the Bronx, a Collision of Cars, Celebrity and Copyright," *The New York Times*, Nov. 28, 2011, http://wheels.blogs.nytimes.com/2011/11/28/in-the-bronx-a-collision-of-cars-celebrity-and-copyright/.

Graffiti Free website, https://www1.nyc.gov/nycbusiness/description/graffitifree-nyc.

Groundswell website, http://www.groundswellmural.org/our-story, accessed November 15, 2012.

Halsey, Mark and Alison Young. "Our Desires Are Ungovernable: Writing Graffiti in Urban Space." *Theoretical Criminology* 10 (3), 2006. 275–306.

Harper, Douglas. "On the Authority of the Image: Visual Methods at the Crossroads," Thousand Oaks, Calif: *Handbook of Qualitative Research*, 1994, 403–412.

Harvey, David. *Rebel Cities*, Brooklyn, Verso, 2012, 5.

Hedlund, Patrick, "East Village Mural, Painted Over in Anti-Vandalism Campaign, Replaced by Graffiti," *DNAinfo.com*, April 20, 2010, http://www.dnainfo.com/new-york/20100420/manhattan/east-village-mural-painted-over-antivandalism-campaign-replaced-by-graffiti.

Katz, Mathew. "Fetish Fest Organizers Erect Wall to Shield Luxe Condo Neighbors," *DNAinfo.com*, June 15, 2012, http://www.dnainfo.com/new-york/20120615/chelsea/fetish-fest-organizers-build-barrier-shield-neighbors-eyes.

Kenny Scharf Arrested & NYPD Asks Him For Autographs, Artsucks.com, April 22, 2013, http://www.artsucks.com/blog/2013/apr13/kenny-scharf-arrested-4-22-13.php.

Koolhaas, Rem, *Delirious New York*, New York: Monacelli Press, 1994, 18.

Kramer, Ronald. *A Social History of Graffiti Writing in New York City, 1990–2005.* New Haven: Yale University Press, 2009.

Lees, Loretta, Tom Slater and Elvin Wyly. *Gentrification.* New York: Routledge, 2007.

Levy's tours, http://levysuniqueny.com/tours/from-graffiti-to-galleries-brooklyn-represent/, accessed November 20, 2012.

Lewisohn, Cedar. *Street Art: The Graffiti Revolution.* New York: Abrams, 2008.

Long Island City Rezoning: Executive Summary, http://www.nyc.gov/html/dcp/html/lic/lic1.shtml, accessed Oct. 25, 2012

"Mayor Bloomberg and City Council Announce New Steps to Make Graffiti Removal Faster and Easier in NYC," July 9, 2009, http://www.nycedc.com/press-release/mayor-bloomberg-and-city-council-announce-new-steps-make-graffiti-removal-faster-and.

McGeehan, Patrick. "Times Square Lights Up City's Economy, Study Finds," *The New York Times*, March 19, 2012, http://cityroom.blogs.nytimes.com/2012/03/19/times-square-lights-up-citys-economy-study-finds/.

Murray, James and Karla Murray. *Broken Windows.* Corte Madera, CA. Jackson: University Press of Mississippi, 2002.

New York Arts Cypher website, http://nycartscypher.com, accessed March 3, 2012

New York City Department of Transportation website, "About DOT," http://www.nyc.gov/html/dot/html/about/about.shtml, accessed October 21, 2012.

New York City, "Mayor's Anti-Graffiti Task Force" http://www.nyc.gov/html/nograffiti/html/aboutforce.html.

Noble, Craig. "A Semiotic and Visual Exploration of Graffiti and Public Space in Vancouver," 2004, http://www.graffiti.org/faq/noble_semiotic_warfare2004.html.

NYC & Company website, http://www.nycandcompany.org/research/nyc-statistics-page, accessed November 20, 2012.

Paynter, Steven. "Subversion of Public Space: A Study into Architecture and Graffiti." 2005, http://www.duncancumming.co.uk/subversion.doc.

Philadelphia Mural Arts Website, https://muralarts.org/about/history-and-overview, accessed October 11, 2012.

Powers, Steven. *The Art of Getting Over: Graffiti at the Millennium*. New York: St. Martin's Press, 1999.

Rahn, Janice. *Painting Without Permission: Hip-Hop Graffiti Subculture*. Connecticut: Bergin and Garvey, 2002.

Reisner, Robert. *Graffiti: Two Thousand Years of Wall Writing*. New York City: Cowles Book Co., Inc., 1971.

Sassen, Saskia. *The Global City: New York, London, Tokyo*, Princeton: Princeton University Press, 1991.

Siegel, Joel. "When TAKI Ruled Magic Kingdom," *New York Daily News*, April 9, 1989.

Sisk, Richard. "South Bronx is poorest district in nation, U.S. Census Bureau finds: 38% live below poverty line," *New York Daily News*, Sept. 29, 2010, http://articles.nydailynews.com/2010-09-29/local/27076750_1poverty-rate-poverty-line-south-bronx.

Smith, Stephen. "New Look: 22–24 Jackson Avenue, 5Pointz Redevelopment," NY Yimby.com, July 31, 2013. http://newyorkyimby.com/2014/07/new-look-22-24-jackson-avenue-5pointz-redevelopment.html.

Snyder, Gregory. *Graffiti Lives: Beyond the Tag in New York's Urban Underground*. New York: New York University Press, 2009.

Society for the Study of Symbolic Interaction website, www.symbolicinteraction.org/, accessed February 18, 2012.

"TAKI 183 Spawns Pen Pals," *The New York Times*, July 21, 1971, graphics8.nytimes.com/packages/pdf/arts/TAKI183.pdf.

Taylor, Kate. "Citing Finances, Brooklyn Museum Cancels Plans for Graffiti Art Exhibit, *New York Times*, June 21, 2011, http://www.nytimes.com/2011/06/22/nyregion/brooklyn-museum-cancels-controversial-graffiti-art-show.html?_r=0.

Terracycle website, http://www.terracycle.net/en-US/graffiti-at-terracycle, accessed April 15, 2011.

Womak, Jeremy. *Creativity and Neighborhood Development*, The Reinvestment Fund, 2007, http://www.trfund.com/resource/creativity.html.

Zimbardo, Philip. *A Situationist Perspective on the Psychology of Evil: Understanding How Good People are Transformed into Perpetrators*, The Social Psychology of Good and Evil, New York: Guilford Press, 2004, 21–50.

Zimbardo, Phillip. *Making Sense of Senseless Vandalism*, Current Perspectives in Sociology fourth edition, Oxford: UK Oxford University Press, 1976, 129–134.

Patrick Verel was born in New York City and grew up in Norwalk, Connecticut. He graduated from Fairfield Preparatory School in 1992 and earned a BS in journalism from St. John's University in Queens, New York, in 1997. He wrote for the *Stamford Advocate* and the *Augusta Chronicle* newspapers, freelanced for publications such as *The New York Times* and *amNewYork*, and most recently, joined the news and media relations team at Fordham University. In 2009, he enrolled in Fordham's urban studies masters program, where he completed a thesis that was the basis for this book. He lives in Brooklyn with his wife, Kelly, and daughter, Eliza. This book combines a few of his favorite things: Taking pictures of street art, telling people's stories, and exploring obscure corners of New York City.

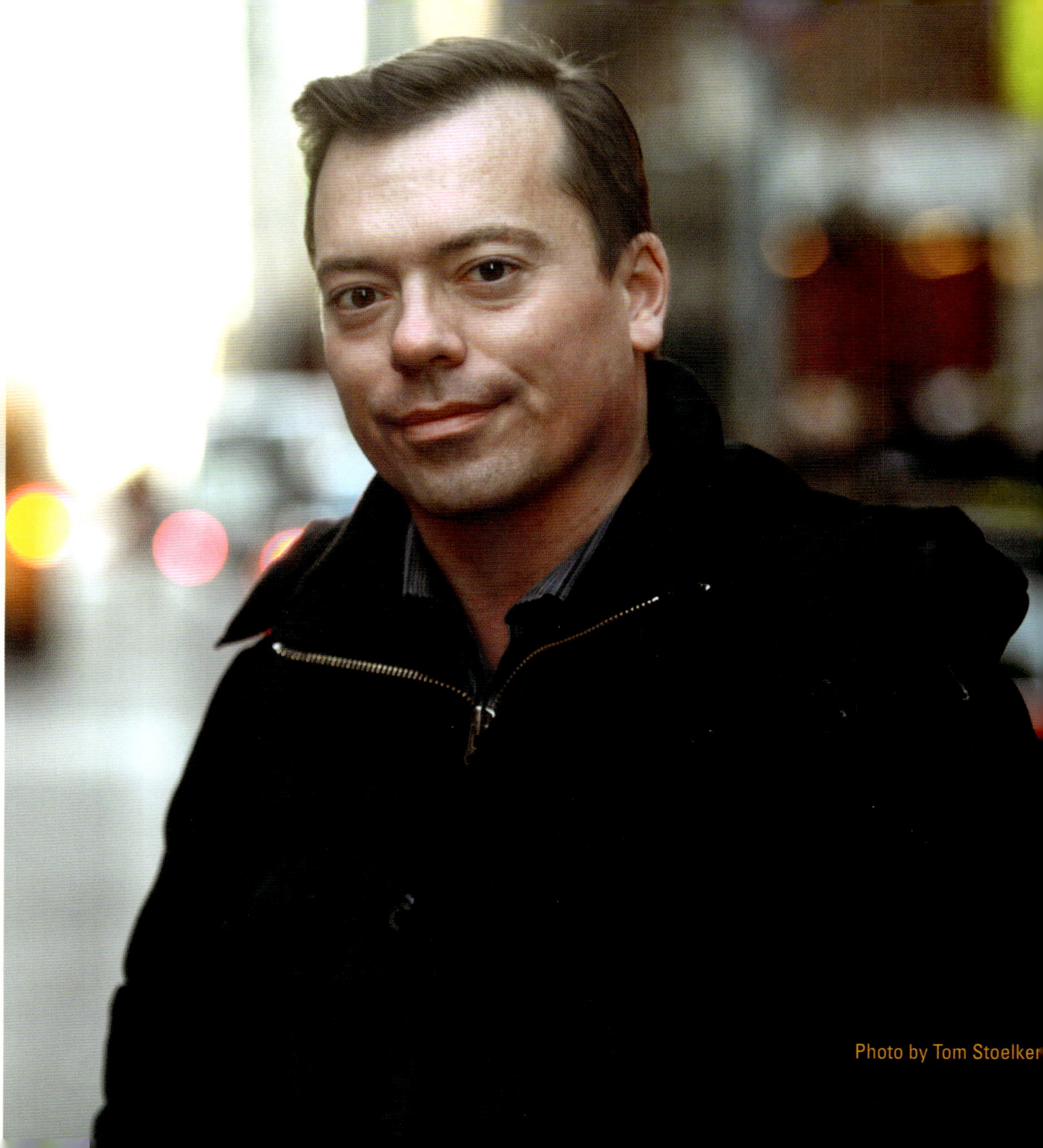

Photo by Tom Stoelker

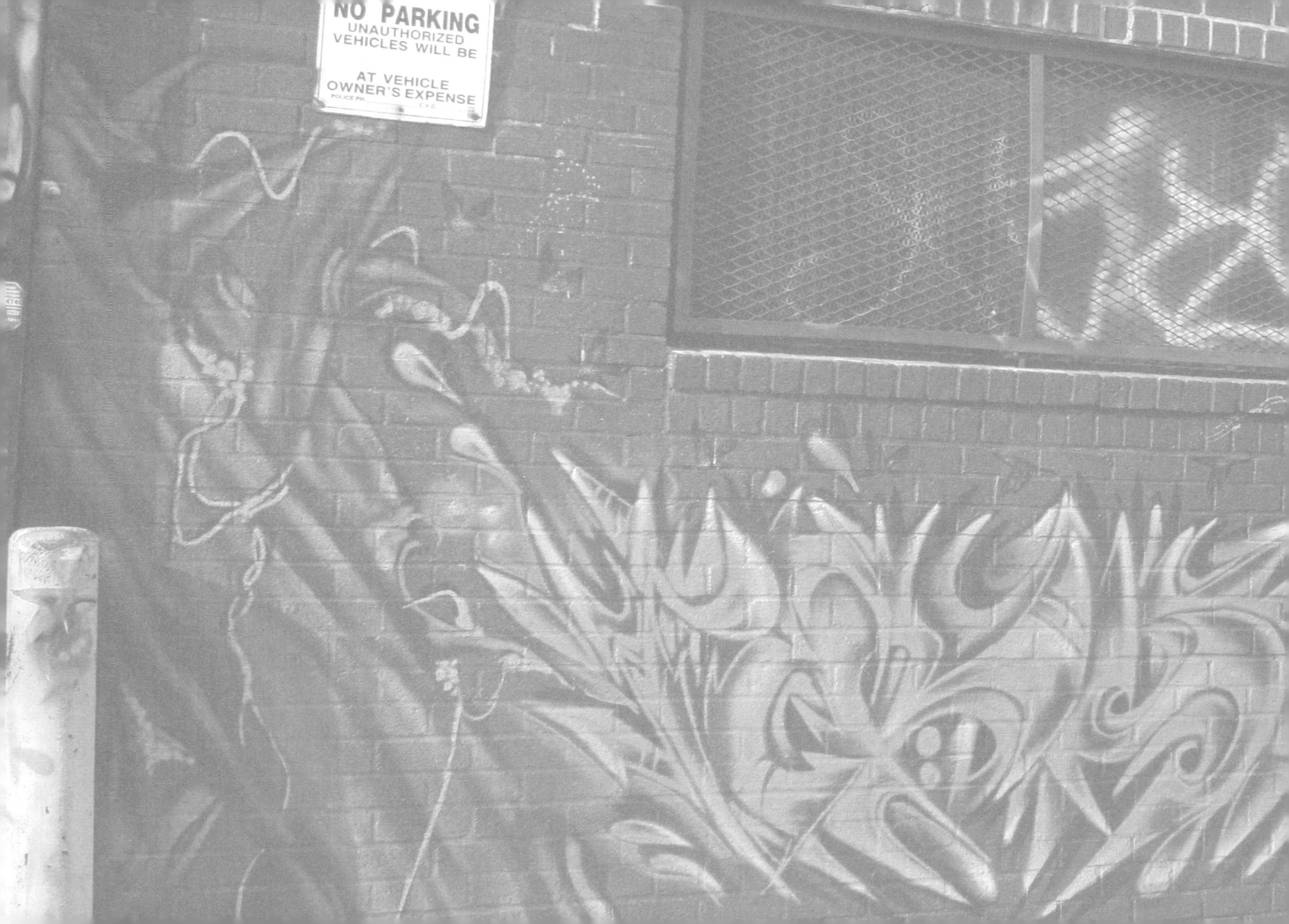
NO PARKING
UNAUTHORIZED
VEHICLES WILL BE
AT VEHICLE
OWNER'S EXPENSE